T0374304

Russ Meyer: Interviews

Conversations with Filmmakers Series

RUSS
MEYER

I N T E R V I E W S

Edited by Ed Symkus

University Press of Mississippi / Jackson

The University Press of Mississippi is the scholarly publishing agency of
the Mississippi Institutions of Higher Learning: Alcorn State University,
Delta State University, Jackson State University, Mississippi State University,
Mississippi University for Women, Mississippi Valley State University,
University of Mississippi, and University of Southern Mississippi.

www.upress.state.ms.us

The University Press of Mississippi is a member
of the Association of University Presses.

Library of Congress Cataloging-in-Publication Data

Names: Symkus, Ed, editor.
Title: Russ Meyer : interviews / Ed Symkus.
Other titles: Conversations with filmmakers series.
Description: Jackson : University Press of Mississippi, 2025. | Series: Conversations with
    filmmakers series | Includes bibliographical references and index.
Identifiers: LCCN 2024047970 (print) | LCCN 2024047971 (ebook) | ISBN 9781496855862
    (hardback) | ISBN 9781496855855 (trade paperback) | ISBN 9781496855879 (epub) |
    ISBN 9781496855886 (epub) | ISBN 9781496855893 (pdf) | ISBN 9781496855909 (pdf)
Subjects: LCSH: Meyer, Russ, 1922–2004—Interviews. | Meyer, Russ, 1922–2004—
    Criticism and interpretation. | Motion picture producers and directors—United States—
    Interviews. | Motion pictures—Production and direction—United States. |
    Independent filmmakers—United States.
Classification: LCC PN1998.3.M49 A5 2025 (print) | LCC PN1998.3.M49 (ebook) |
    DDC 791.4302/33092—dc23/eng/20241214
LC record available at https://lccn.loc.gov/2024047970
LC ebook record available at https://lccn.loc.gov/2024047971

British Library Cataloging-in-Publication Data available

Contents

Introduction   vii

Chronology   xvii

Filmography   xxiii

King Leer: Top "Nudie" Filmmaker Russ Meyer Scrambles to Outshock Big
Studios   3
    Steven M. Lovelady / 1968

The King of the Nudie Movies Is Going Respectable   8
    Marci McDonald / 1971

Sex, Violence and Drugs—All in Good Fun!   12
    Stan Berkowitz / 1972

Pensées of a Porno Prince   22
    Scott Eyman / 1976

Russ Meyer Thinks Big   27
    R. Allen Leider / 1976

Russ Meyer   33
    Nat Segaloff / 1979

Porn King: Russ Meyer Still Upfront with Films and "Fillies"   45
    Karin Winegar / 1979

Russ Meyer   50
    Craig Reid / 1981

The Breast of Russ Meyer   57
  Anton Rush / 1983

Tit for Tat   63
  Tom Teicholz / 1986

Russ Meyer   72
  Jim Morton / 1986

Some of My Brest Kept Secrets   86
  Paul Sherman / 1987

Mondo Russo   103
  Dale Ashmun / 1988

Russ Meyer   112
  David K. Frasier / 1990

Russ Meyer: Between the Valleys of My Ultravixens   123
  Arv Miller / 1990

Russ Meyer: The World's Breast Director   145
  Jim Goad / 1991

Russ Meyer—Hellcats for a Modern World   150
  Beth Accomando / 1995

Russ Meyer   155
  Ed Symkus / 1995

Additional Resources   163

Index   165

Introduction

When I was approached by University Press of Mississippi (UPM) about editing a book in the *Conversations with Filmmakers* series, and immediately said yes, I was asked who I'd choose for a subject.

"Spielberg," I said. "Sorry, he's already been done." "Scorsese." "No, already done." "Altman?" "Nope." "De Palma?" "No." I made a tactful shift. "Werner Herzog?" "No." "Kathryn Bigelow?" "Already done." Eighteen names later, despairing and a bit slaphappy, I blurted out, "Russ Meyer?"

The initial response was a stunned silence, and I thought to myself, "Why would an eminent publisher want anything to do with a book about a maker of softcore pornography films?" But they didn't say "no." Two weeks later, I received an email from UPM: "We would be delighted to add a volume on Meyer to the series."

The silence was understandable; the green light was an unexpected surprise.

Russell Albion Meyer (1922–2004) was a provocative independent filmmaker. Controversy nipped at his heels from the release of the first of his twenty-three theatrical films—*The Immoral Mr. Teas*—in 1959, through his final one—*Beneath the Valley of the Ultra-Vixens*—in 1979. There's no doubt that Meyer and his films were politically incorrect well before that ambiguous phrase became rooted in our culture. Yet throughout those two decades he was to become as celebrated as he was reviled.

Much to his displeasure, Meyer was labeled a pornographer, albeit of the softcore variety. He preferred the title of satirist and insisted that the abundant sex and violence in his films were presented in a manner so outrageous, he expected audiences to laugh, sometimes uncomfortably. He was not a fan of, nor did he ever portray, any hardcore sex in his films.

If there was anything hardcore about Meyer movies, it was that they almost always featured a deep-seated sense of morality. Usually of the eye-for-an-eye sort. If someone did something wrong, if someone harmed someone else, they would get it back in spades. And a lot of people do a lot of wrong things in his films. Among the most heinous acts were rape and murder, and bounteous other displays of physical suffering. Men would attack women; men would attack men;

women would attack men; women would attack women. But there was always some kind of retribution.

With these sorts of ingredients, it's clear why Meyer's work would rankle a great many people. But why did he have so many fans and such enduring success?

Except for a few grim mid-1960s entries, his films were often funny—laugh-out-loud funny—even if some audience members weren't sure if it was appropriate to laugh. Most of the films, once he got into the groove, were also very well made, featuring crisp photography, inventive framing, and clever, rapid-fire editing, all of which he picked up during his stint as an industrial filmmaker in the 1950s. And when Meyer cast strong actors, he found a way to get bigger-than-life, accessible performances out of them as his entertainingly absurd stories were spun.

And yes, getting around to the elephant in the rooms of nearly every Meyer film (*Blacksnake!* was an exception), he populated them with rather busty women, for whom Meyer had a real-life predilection.

I came late to Meyer's films. My knowledge of him was that he made "dirty movies," and that two of them had peculiar titles—*Beyond the Valley of the Dolls* and *Faster, Pussycat! Kill! Kill!*

A longtime film lover, by the mid-1970s, I had been caught up in and spoiled by "Hollywood's Second Golden Age," featuring the daring, innovative work of, among others, Francis Ford Coppola, Robert Altman, Sam Peckinpah, Martin Scorsese, and Brian De Palma. In June 1975 I was knocked out by Steven Spielberg's mainstream entry *Jaws*. A month later I decided to sample Russ Meyer's twenty-first film, *Supervixens*, which opened at the Cinema 57 in Boston on July 30.

I had no idea what I was in for. Here's what I experienced: buxom, lustful, scantily clad (often topless) strong-willed women; clueless as well as dangerous men, the latter personified by Charles Napier's unhinged performance as Harry Sledge; simulated sex galore; bountiful sight gag-induced belly laughs; and moments of cringeworthy, sadistic violence—all of it exaggerated.

I'd never seen anything like this. I was hooked. Alas, I would have to wait a year and a half before *Up!* was released, another three years until *Beneath the Valley of the Ultra-Vixens*, and then two more before a friend sneaked me some pirated videocassettes of Meyer's earlier films so I could play catch-up. I found a few of them to be awful, and a few to be terrific.

The eighteen interviews that appear in the following pages—from magazines, newspapers, and radio—are presented chronologically, beginning with Steven M. Lovelady's piece, which graced the front page of the *Wall Street Journal* in 1968, up through my own chat with Meyer when he was doing press for the theatrical reissue of 1965's *Faster, Pussycat! Kill! Kill!* in 1995.

In order to grasp the spirit of what Meyer was about, you might want to check out some of the sundry nicknames delegated in headlines and articles over the years, starting with the *Wall Street Journal*'s "King Leer." There followed, in other publications, "King of the Nudies," "The Glandscape Artist," "The Chaucer of Sex," "The Rural Fellini," "The King of D-Cup Cinema," and "The Titan of Tits."

If it wasn't yet clear, Meyer's films are raunchy. There are some serious issues and adult themes, but it's also evident that Meyer had some naughty-little-boy sensibilities.

For those viewers who were true Meyer fans, he developed what evolved into his trademarks, beyond the mayhem and mammaries: fancy cars, his own cameos, repeated lines of dialogue.

Faster, Pussycat! Kill! Kill! features drivers at the wheels of a Porsche 356, a Triumph TR3, an MGA, and an MG; *Good Morning . . . and Goodbye!* had a Camaro SS/RS 350; *Beyond the Valley of the Dolls*, a Corvette Stingray; *Supervixens*, a Porsche 911 Targa; and in *Up!*, a police patrol car was a Mercedes.

Meyer shows up on-camera, briefly, in *The Immoral Mr. Teas*; *Cherry, Harry & Raquel!*; *Mudhoney*; *Supervixens*; *Heavenly Bodies*; and *Up!* And he has speaking roles in *Motorpsycho!* and *Beneath the Valley of the Ultra-Vixens* (though in that one, his voice is dubbed by actor John Furlong).

Dialogue repetition became a staple. In *Beyond the Valley of the Dolls* (1970), seductive Ashley says to innocent Harris, "You're a groovy boy; I'd like to strap you on sometime." In *Supervixens* (1975), frisky SuperLorna says on the phone to jealous Angel, "Can't wait to strap on your groovy old man." In *Up!* (1976), unfaithful Paul says to comely Margo, "I'd like to strap you on sometime." Shifting over to Meyer's Shakespearean side of things, in *Beyond the Valley of the Dolls*, Z-Man says to Lance, "I vow it, ere this night does wane, you will drink the black sperm of my vengeance." And in *Up!*, Alice yells to Margo, while both women are running, naked, "Prepare to taste the black sperm of my vengeance!"

When it came down to the task of making films, Meyer was referred to—rightly so—as an auteur. The opening credits of *Supervixens* memorably concluded with the impressive "Written, Photographed, Edited, Produced, and Directed by Russ Meyer." Though variations of this busy credit appeared often, Meyer wasn't always a one-man band, and a few of his films were photographed, edited, or written by others—most notably the cinematographer Walter Schenk (*Faster, Pussycat! Kill! Kill!* and *Mudhoney*) and the critic Roger Ebert, who scripted *Beyond the Valley of the Dolls* and later, under the pseudonyms Reinhold Timme and R. Hyde, cowrote *Up!* and *Beneath the Valley of the Ultra-Vixens*. But Meyer reigned over and, in almost every case, had final word on everything (*Fanny Hill*, produced by Albert Zugsmith, not, as usual, by Meyer, was an exception).

Although he later developed into a self-promotion machine, tirelessly touring the country as his films were released in different territories, Meyer didn't do a lot of interviews early on. It was the interest created by the *Wall Street Journal* piece that opened those floodgates for him. Interviews in this book originally appeared in cinema-related magazines such as *Take One* and *Film Comment*, pop culture publications including *Interview* and *Hypno Magazine* and, no surprise, the so-called "gentlemen's magazines" *Fling* and *Adam*.

The lion's share of these interviews was done well before search engines—such as Google—existed as a research tool for journalists gathering background information to turn into questions. Meyer was an outsider in Hollywood. Not many people writing about cinema knew much about him. Very few had seen many of his films, but those with enough gumption would have known that they were being reviewed, that critical opinions were all over the place, and that those thoughts and observations could provide fodder for stimulating conversation with the director.

A microfilm search at any major public library could have revealed the following.

Bosley Crowther, in the *New York Times*, on *Fanny Hill*: "[Viewers] will . . . have a hard time recognizing anything that resembles wit or even good, solid belly-laugh humor in the spirit of low comedy."

Judith Crist, in *New York Magazine*, on *Vixen!*: "There's a wild enthusiasm to the heroine's activities and a deadpan stupidity to the dialogue that provide a redeeming entertainment value for non-up-tight adults."

Vincent Canby, in the *New York Times*, on *Finders Keepers, Lovers Weepers!*: "Although I find his fantasies basically unpleasant—they are almost exclusively concerned with insatiable ladies and the men they wear out—they are made with some cinematic complexity (lots of different camera setups in any one scene) and a minimum of mock piety."

Roger Ebert, in the *Chicago Sun-Times* (a year before he worked with Meyer), on *Vixen!*: "In a field filled with cheap, dreary productions, Meyer is the best craftsman and the only artist. He has developed a directing style so open, direct and good-humored that it dominates his material; what a relief to hear laughter during a skin-flick, instead of the dead silence that usually envelops their cheerless audiences."

Gene Siskel, in the *Chicago Tribune* (five years before he teamed up with Ebert), on *Beyond the Valley of the Dolls*: "Boredom aplenty is provided by a screenplay which for some reason has been turned over to a screenwriting neophyte."

Alexander Walker, in the *London Evening Standard*, on *Beyond the Valley of the Dolls*: "[It's] a film whose total idiotic, monstrous badness raises it to the pitch of near-irresistible entertainment."

Richard Corliss, in the *Village Voice*, on *Cherry, Harry & Raquel!*: "Meyer's heroines are invariably Silicone freaks with breasts large enough to halt both traffic on Wall Street and arousal on 42nd Street."

Of course, sharing one's thoughts on Meyer's films in reviews and sitting down with him to discuss them are two different animals. Meyer made precious few television talk show appearances, but as he approached the second decade of his career, he was more open to print and radio interviews, and he was inherently good at and happy to talk about himself and his films—erudite, well read, a movie buff, proud of his accomplishments, and offering both serious explanations of his work and a lively sense of humor.

Interviewed by Ellen Adelstein on her Tucson-based TV show *Talk It Over* in 1979, he was asked, "Did your mother breastfeed you?" He smiled and said, "I believe so, yes. But then there are a lot of other people that have been breastfed and are not nearly as into this thing as strongly as I am. I don't think there's a basis there. But I don't object to your asking me. In fact, I practice breastfeeding all the time now." In 1993 Conan O'Brien said, "There's a certain theme in your movies. You have an obsession with women's breasts. Is that fair?" Meyer countered with, "Well, I wouldn't say it's an obsession. But I care for them a great deal." The following year, Jon Stewart declared, "Watching your movies, whether men like to admit it or not, you've lived out a great fantasy life, for all men. I want to thank you." Meyer quipped, "The pleasure was all mine."

When Meyer took part in print interviews, where no one was worried about commercial interruptions, and there was a good chance that the Q&A sessions might turn into meaningful conversations, he could relax and give more thoughtful answers. Sometimes he was relaxed enough to casually let a few vulgarities seep into the discussion. Very few questions—be they about the seeds of his creative ideas, his business acumen, or his family life—were off limits, though in at least one instance, when an interviewer asked if any of his female stars had breast enhancement, he politely changed the subject, hinting that the question was too personal.

There was also the challenge of a journalist being up to the task of interviewing such a unique subject. Among those represented in this volume, Arv Miller, writing for *Fling*, ventured into contentious territory when he badgered Meyer to explain why he didn't like hardcore pornography; Craig Reid, in *Adam*, mentioned that all of Meyer's movies are softcore, "featuring very few actual insertion scenes," when in fact, there are no insertion scenes in any Meyer film; Karin Winegar in the *Minneapolis Star* had a hard time hiding her contempt for Meyer and his films, writing that *Beneath the Valley of the Ultra-Vixens* is "racist, sacrilegious, and scatological, as well as sexist," then added, flippantly, "So, what's new?" Yet her questions were asked in a professional manner. Marci McDonald, writing for *The Gazette*, stated that in Meyer's middle period his films "became better, slicker, each one a roaring box office success," even though one on her list—*Faster, Pussycat! Kill! Kill!*—was a resounding box office flop upon its release (though it did quite well three decades later during its rerelease).

Thankfully, among other journalists here, Beth Accomando, writing for *Hypno Magazine*, noted that, while Meyer's production values are high and his films contain more plot and character development "than the average porn audience would ever be able to tolerate," he's still condemned by some "as a pornographer and exploiter of women. Yet anyone who talks with Meyer will quickly recognize the shortsightedness of these critics." But kudos go to Scott Eyman for his *Take One* piece, in which he removes himself and any questions and structures it with only Meyer's responses.

Some of these interviews are straightforward and serious, some are funny, some are a bit naughty—with interviewers hoping to get a rise out of Meyer. And sometimes he obliges. He comes across as open, honest, and not concerned about making obviously chauvinistic statements, and he projects the impression that he's having a great time. Because there was no Google yet, he had to deal with a lot of generic questions, many of them being asked over and over. But a good filmmaker must be a good storyteller, and Meyer was a natural born one. He would have to give the same answers to different people, but as displayed in many of the interviews, he would find a way to add details for one person and omit other details for another, just to change things up, maybe to stay interested in talking about himself.

And there were so many topics to be broached! Some that he loved talking about: his films were his visions, his creations, and only *he* could make them. More and more women started coming to his films, thereby increasing box office numbers. The women in his films were far stronger—emotionally—than the men. His films were to be taken as comedies or, at the very least, satires. His thoughts about feminists. His thoughts about censorship.

Because these interviews were done so long ago, no mention is made of how Meyer's films have since then made their mark on contemporary pop culture.

For instance, in the season four episode of *Seinfeld*, titled "The Pilot," Jerry and Elaine are in Monk's Café, which has changed management. Jerry notices that all the new waitresses are overly buxom, and says to Elaine, "I haven't seen four women together like this outside of a Russ Meyer film!" The season twenty-five episode of *The Simpsons*—"Yellow Subterfuge"—features a Jamaican version of *The Itchy & Scratchy Show*, renamed *The Itchem & Scratchem Blow*, in a segment called *Rasta, Pussycat! Kill! Kill!* Meyer fan John Waters has regularly included Meyer posters in the backgrounds of his own films—*Vixen!* in *Multiple Maniacs*,

Lorna in *Pink Flamingos*, and *Faster, Pussycat! Kill! Kill!* in *Polyester*. The iconic bit of dialogue—"This is my happening, and it freaks me out"—from *Beyond the Valley of the Dolls*, is slightly modified to "It's my happening, baby, and it freaks me out" in *Austin Powers: International Man of Mystery*. The line is accompanied, in both films, by Strawberry Alarm Clock singing "Incense and Peppermints."

Numerous pieces other than interviews have been published about Meyer over the years, with a variety of writers freely opining on his pluses and minuses. As this book sticks with just interviews, the narrative pieces don't appear here, but snippets of them help bring a picture of him a little more into focus.

Richard Schickel, in a 1970 *Harper's Magazine* article, says Meyer's first feature *The Immoral Mr. Teas* has "a charm, even an innocence, lacking in the films that followed it," including *Faster, Pussycat! Kill! Kill!*, *Mudhoney*, and *Lorna*, which are "heavy-breathing dramas of rural rape and revenge," and that in late Meyer films, the "humor is conscious, the editing snappier, concern with character and motivation less careful."

A David Ansen overview of Meyer in a 1975 *Real Paper* calls *Beyond the Valley of the Dolls* "trashy, but deliriously so. Hilariously so. And what came as the biggest surprise, deliberately so. . . . It was at once gaudy, cartoon-style parody and far more outrageous than the genres it mocked."

Owen Gleiberman, in a 2011 appreciation in *Entertainment Weekly*, claims that while *Supervixens* marked a return to form for Meyer, it was "followed by what, for me, may be the most arresting (and underrated) phase of his career, kicked off by the jaw-droppingly perverse erotic fairy tale *Up!*, which was like *Smokey and the Bandit*, *Li'l Abner*, Sam Peckinpah, and the postwar legend of Adolf Hitler all thrown together into a raunchy redneck stew, topped off by dialogue and narration as florid as anything from the zaniest Coen brothers outing."

I've seen all but three of Meyer's twenty-three theatrical features. I haven't been able to find *Eve and the Handyman* or *Erotica*, and I lost interest in the too-wordy *The Seven Minutes* at the thirty-minute mark. For the record, my two favorites are *Faster, Pussycat! Kill! Kill!* (Stuart Lancaster's crippled, angry, woman-hating old man asserts, "They let 'em vote, smoke, and drive. So, what do you get? A Democrat for president.") and *Supervixens* (a whacked-out updating of Voltaire's *Candide*). I think his most underrated film is *Blacksnake!* (A brutal white plantation man constantly whips the slaves he manages, each of whom carries a machete. What could possibly go wrong?)

The arc of the interviews presented here covers Meyer's memories of his early days in the business, his feelings on censorship, off-set sex among his actors, sex and violence in his films, high hopes for films that failed, and dealing with feminists.

The early days (Dale Ashmun in *Film Threat*): "I was put in touch with a man named Gene Walker. He gave me a great shot, shooting industrial movies. It was a great opportunity for me to learn the trade."

Censorship (Anton Rush in *Blitz*): "*Supervixens* had 137 cuts [in England], and in Ireland they had over 300. I think you have really shitty censorship here in England. If you cut that many scenes out of a picture in order to protect the average adult filmgoer, it's insane. It's offensive."

Forbidding sex among actors when the cameras are off (Arv Miller in *Fling*): "I've always been really on that thing very strong. No exchanging of vital juices. Wondrous bodily fluids—oh, no! Everybody's got to be horny and hard-pressed. Maybe a little irascible, sort of. Works better."

Sex and violence in his films (Jim Goad in *Answer Me!*): "Both of them, the sex and the violence, are jokey. And they're outrageous and exaggerated. The violence, by and large, is overdone. Like in *Supervixens*—the [bathtub] murder, the dynamite up the ass—it's all not to be believed."

High hopes for films that failed (Marci McDonald in *The Gazette*): "After *Seven Minutes*, I think a lot of people will start to take us seriously. I mean, it won't win any Academy Awards, but that's not the important thing. Because I will be exonerated—I shall be ripped from the cross."

Feminists (Scott Eyman in *Take One*): "I don't get anywhere near as much flack from the women's lib thing as I'd like. They always expect some shambling slob in a pool of drool. Whenever I do get involved with any feminist groups, they're always very surprised that I can cope with anything they can throw at me. The trouble with those confrontations is that they're so contrived and the people are so angry. Easy pickings."

Many other topics are addressed, but there could have been even more. For instance, the curiously short running time of his films. Fifteen of them were eighty minutes or under. The only "long" one—at 115 minutes—was *The Seven Minutes*, which was also his biggest flop. Another matter that wasn't brought up was why he kept moving on to different genres under the softcore umbrella. Meyer's biographer Jimmy McDonough, in his 2005 book *Big Bosoms and Square Jaws*, brings up Meyer's six phases: the nudies, the roughies, the harder sex films, the soap operas, the studio films, and the sex comedies. Alas, the eighteen interviewers in this book—myself included—didn't get Meyer to talk about that. Nor did anyone ask why there were exclamation points in so many of his films' titles.

What he did passionately talk about in many of these interviews, often without being asked, was a project he intended to put together as his swan song, *The Breast of Russ Meyer*, an overview of his entire career, that he had been working on since the early 1980s, and which would run somewhere between twelve and seventeen hours. Alas, the film remained unfinished when, after a long battle with Alzheimer's disease, he succumbed to pneumonia in 2004.

Looking back on Meyer's cinematic legacy, it's safe to say that he was one of a kind, and that, due to an enlightened society, there will—rightfully so—never be another filmmaker like him. He created something at a time when something like that was still OK to be created.

Still, when his name is mentioned, the first thing that comes to mind is the women who starred in his films, and the fact that, to paraphrase the comedy group the Firesign Theatre, most of them had "balconies you could do Shakespeare from." But his films featured so much more. They were sexual—without being erotic—and violent and funny; they were superbly photographed and inventively edited; and they offered entertaining stories about good clashing with evil. The big-breasted women were just one part of the package, sort of a living, breathing sight gag.

However you look at it, Russ Meyer left his mark on cinema. While some people are always going to consider it a stain, others will celebrate him for making films his own way, without becoming part of the Hollywood system, and even after being invited in briefly, bucking that system, then continuing on his own path. At the end of his career he was a multi-millionaire, and he had secured the reputation of being—in the scheme of things—a minor yet legendary filmmaker.

The interviews in this book are presented in four styles: narrative articles, question-and-answer pieces, one featuring only Meyer's voice and, in three cases, unedited transcriptions of the interview sessions.

Wait! Before you read on, a moment to express my gratitude to: Gerald Peary for getting me involved in this project; Emily Snyder Bandy for guiding me through the ropes; Peter Chaggaris for introducing me to the early Meyer films; David K. Frasier for his generous sharing of research materials; Paul Sherman and Betsy Sherman for, all those years ago, inviting me along to their dinner with Russ Meyer (about which I remember very little because Russ kept ordering bottle after bottle of Corvo Grillo wine); the staff of the Boston Public Library for helping me peruse numerous reels of microfilm; the Moving Image Research Center of the National Audio-Visual Conservation Center at the Library of Congress for, in 1984, granting me access to a moviola and headphones in order to view *Motorpsycho!*, *Fanny Hill*, and *Europe in the Raw*—yes, right in the Library of Congress; and to my wife, Lisa, for saying it was OK to watch so many Russ Meyer films in our living room (and even joined me for *Mudhoney*). Thank you, all!

ES

Chronology

1922   Russell Albion Meyer is born on March 21 in San Leandro, California, to Lydia Lucinda Hauck and William Arthur Meyer. They are divorced a few weeks later.

1936   Lydia pawns her engagement ring to buy Russ a Univex 8mm movie camera.

1938   Russ shoots a short film on Catalina Island, enters it in a Kodak filmmaking contest, and wins.

1940   Only interested in film as a hobby, he enrolls at a junior college to get a degree in chemistry but drops out after six months due to lack of funds.

1941   Russ is hired by the Corps of Engineers, initially as a messenger boy, then working his way up to becoming an accounting clerk.

1943   A subscriber to *Popular Photography*, he sees an ad in the magazine placed by the Academy of Motion Picture Arts and Sciences, asking for volunteers to be trained by Hollywood directors and cinematographers as combat photographers in WWII.

1944   Upon completion of the course, he goes to Missouri for army training, is given some time off, then in November, becomes an army staff sergeant with the 166th Signal Photographic Company and is sent to the frontlines of the war in Europe where, as a member of Newsreel Unit 1, he shoots combat photographs and motion pictures for newspapers and newsreels.

1945   Russ receives an honorable discharge in December.

1946   After failing to find any film work in Hollywood, he lands a job as a cinematographer at Gene K. Walker Productions in San Francisco, shooting industrial and promotional films for Southern Pacific Railroad, Standard Oil, and others. *This Is My Railroad* can be found on YouTube.

1948   Russ marries Betty Valdovinos.

1949   Army pal Don Ornitz suggests that he should try making a living in glamour photography, shooting photos for "gentlemen's" magazines. He buys a Speed Graphic camera, begins photographing the stripper

Evelyn "Treasure Chest" West at a club in Oakland, and meets and photographs other strippers.

1950   Russ sees Tempest Storm dancing at a club in Los Angeles, and when she moves to the El Rey Burlesk Theater in Oakland, he photographs her there and becomes friendly with the owner Pete DeCenzie. Russ and Pete set up a business deal, selling professional photos of strippers. Russ begins working for Globe Photos, and his pictures are purchased by numerous magazines, including *Gent*, *Fling*, and *Frolic*. He has an affair with Tempest Storm, and he and Betty are divorced.

1952   Russ films *The French Peep Show*, one of the stage presentations at the El Rey. Pete brings it on the road and screens it at art houses. Rumor has it that after Pete's death, his wife destroys any remaining copies of it. Russ meets and marries Eve Turner, and they move to Hollywood.

1954   He is hired as cinematographer for the lurid exploitation film about abortion: *The Desperate Women*.

1955   He gets his first centerfold assignment for *Playboy*; his subject is his wife, Eve.

1956   He lands the job of still photographer on the set of the James Dean film *Giant*.

1957   He begins a string of assignments as still photographer on many TV shows including *Perry Mason*, *The Twilight Zone*, and *The Fugitive*.

1958   Whitestone Books publishes *The Glamour Camera of Russ Meyer*. Russel Albion Meyer and Peter A. DeCenzie form Pad-Ram Enterprises (the company name comes from their initials), with the idea of making a commercial nudie film.

1959   The film *The Immoral Mr. Teas*, with a "script" scrawled on a laundry ticket, starring Russ's army pal Bill Teas, and produced by Pad-Ram, opens as part of a twin bill with the Gary Cooper film *The Hanging Tree* on May 27 at the Balboa Theater in San Diego. At one point in the film, the title character walks by a movie theater that has *The French Peep Show* on the marquee. The San Diego screening is raided by the police twenty minutes in, and the print is confiscated. It doesn't play again in California until January 1960, reopening at the Monica Theatre in Los Angeles. The film, made for $24,000, will eventually bring in a box office take of approximately $1.2 million. It's the first film in Russ's nudie-cutie phase.

1961   Russ and Eve form the company Eve Productions. The inaugural release, *Eve and the Handyman*, with Eve in her only starring role, premieres on May 5 at the Paris Theatre in Los Angeles. It's a hit. *Erotica,*

another Pad-Ram production—an anthology of six short films—
released on July 14, is not a hit.

1962   The raucous and silly comedy *Wild Gals of the Naked West* premieres
on May 9. It's a hit and it marks the first appearance of Russ regular
Princess Livingston. It's also the last release under the Pad-Ram banner, as Russ and Pete part ways, apparently over creative and mon-
etary disagreements.

1963   Neither of the Eve Productions—the travelogue-style *Europe in the
Raw* (opens March 28) nor the glamour photography documentary
Heavenly Bodies (opens June 28)—cause much interest for ticket buy-
ers, and their failures result in Russ embarking on his second dis-
tinctive phase of offerings: the grim, mostly humorless and noir-like
black-and-white roughies.

1964   *Lorna*, his first film with an actual story—a sordid and violent tale of
infidelity—and the first to be shot in 35mm (all previous ones were
blown up from 16mm), premieres on September 11, and is a hit. The
first of his three adaptations—*Fanny Hill: Memoirs of a Woman of
Pleasure*, based on the John Cleland novel—is produced by Albert
Zugsmith in Germany. Zugsmith wants Russ to "codirect" with him.
Russ is not happy with the circumstances, and his name is taken off
the film, but later added back on. It opens in West Germany on September 25.

1965   *Fanny Hill*—a sort of stand-alone film, not fitting into any of the Russ
phases—opens in the States on March 25 and is a resounding flop.
A second adaptation, taken from the Raymond Friday Locke novel
Streets Paved with Gold, is initially called *Rope of Flesh*, but the title
is changed to *Mudhoney*, and is released on May 25. It introduces
future Meyer stalwarts John Furlong and Stuart Lancaster, but flops.
The extremely violent *Motorpsycho!*, about three bikers who go on
a murderous rampage, stars Russ regular Haji in her first role, and
upon its release on August 12, becomes a much-needed hit.

1966   His best-known title, *Faster, Pussycat! Kill! Kill!*, has been tagged with
"original" release dates in 1965, 1966, and 1967. The *Variety* review ran
in early 1966, so we'll go with that year. The last of the roughies, it
features remarkable performances from Stuart Lancaster and, in her
first time in any film, the imposing Tura Satana as one of the three
tough women in the lead roles. It's an obvious companion piece to
Motorpsycho!, and an early example of gender reversal in cinema. But
the film, which doesn't have one frame of the nudity that was driving

his earlier films, does no business. It closes almost immediately, but years later, via the video cassette market, becomes a cult classic. Another stand-alone film, *Mondo Topless*, has bare breasts galore, is released on October 1, and does quite well on the drive-in circuit.

1967 The first of his three color soap opera films, the backwoods *Common-Law Cabin* (originally titled *How Much Loving Does a Normal Couple Need?*), is a flop. The follow-up, *Good Morning . . . and Goodbye!*, as sordid as anything he's done, makes money.

1968 Spring is an interesting and important time for Russ. A front-page story runs in the *Wall Street Journal* on April 24. It throws accolades his way, and introduces him to a large chunk of American moviegoers. On May 8, the paper runs a reaction letter from an up-and-coming *Chicago Sun-Times* film critic—Roger Ebert—and his praises for Russ are even stronger. *Finders Keepers, Lovers Weepers!* is released on the same day Ebert's letter runs, and is a hit. But it's in the fall that Russ enters the echelons of spectacular success. *Vixen!*, the first of his two harder—but certainly not hardcore—sex films, is made on a budget of $70,000 and brings in north of $6 million at the box office. It opens on October 15, and the ensuing profit numbers catch the eye of Twentieth Century Fox honcho Darryl Zanuck, who assigns his son Richard to have Russ, who has never worked with a studio, make a film for them.

1969 It's going to be a down and up year for him. His marriage to Eve is in ruins, and they divorce. *Cherry, Harry & Raquel!* opens on November 6, and welcomes both Uschi Digard and Charles Napier into the Russ stable. There's plenty of violence and sex, and it's a hit. Richard Zanuck and his producing partner David Brown make contact, and a deal is made to do a "sequel" to Fox's 1967 hit *Valley of the Dolls*. Russ, who has become friendly with Ebert after seeing his letter, asks him to write the script, but not make it anything resembling a sequel.

1970 Fox announces a three-picture deal with Russ. The first in his studio phase will be *Beyond the Valley of the Dolls*, the next *The Seven Minutes*, and the third *Everything in the Garden*, to be based on the Edward Albee play. Russ meets the actress Edy Williams on the set of *Dolls*. The outrageously over-the-top film, overflowing with nudity, comedy, and violence, opens on June 17 to bad reviews and a strong box office. Russ and Edy are married ten days later. Some of his World War II combat footage appears in the film *Patton*.

1971 *The Seven Minutes*, the third and final adaptation by him, based on the Irving Wallace novel of the same name, opens on June 28. It's a courtroom drama about an obscenity trial. The script is far too wordy, the pacing is snail-like compared to Russ's earlier films, and there's hardly any sex. It quietly closes. The Albee adaptation is never made.

1973   Russ is through with studios and is back financing his own films. *Blacksnake!*, a period piece shot in Barbados and featuring women with normal rather than exaggerated measurements, is another stand-alone, not fitting into any of his phases. It opens on March 28. But it's not what his audiences are expecting or want. The film flops. He decides to get back to more of what he was doing earlier in his career.

1975   *Supervixens*, the first of his three sex comedies, and the first film under the RM Films International banner, isn't exactly an adaptation. But its hapless central character Clint Ramsey goes through travails that are similar in spirit to what happens to the title character in Voltaire's *Candide*. Of course, in this telling, his adventures are comically sexual, and they're right alongside some shocking violence. The film opens on April 2, features a vicious, frightening performance by Charles Napier and a lusty, funny one by Uschi Digard, and is a hit. Alas, Russ's marriage to Edy hits hot rock bottom, and they divorce.

1976   He decides to stick with boisterous comedy while increasing the amount of nudity and the level of violence—committed upon both men and women—in *Up!*, which opens in October. The violence is of the axe-to-the-chest variety. One of the comedy-with-violence bits involves the death of Adolf Hitler—here called Adolph Schwartz—in his bathtub, devoured by a piranha. The violence is too much for some viewers and word of mouth causes it to be only a minor hit.

1977   Russ learns his lesson, reducing the violence to some fist fights, and upping the ante on big-breasted nudity and slapstick sex in his final theatrical feature *Beneath the Valley of the Ultra-Vixens*. But before the film is finished, he gets an opportunity to make *Who Killed Bambi?*, which is to star the Sex Pistols, and is being financed once again by Fox. Ebert writes the script, and Russ and his crew head to England to shoot it. But there are immediately personality conflicts between Russ and a couple of band members, the group's hardheaded manager Malcom McLaren has no concept of film financing, and after a few days of shooting, the production closes down and everyone goes home.

1979   Postproduction work resumes on *Beneath the Valley of the Ultra-Vixens*. The film is released in April and does well but not great at the box office.

1980s   Russ starts releasing his films on videocassettes, later moving on to DVDs. They make him a lot of money.

1987   He directs the music video *Don't Change That Song* by the group Faster Pussycat. He has a cameo role as a video store clerk in the comedy *Amazon Women on the Moon*.

1989   He is one of three camera operators on the documentary *The Story of John Phillips and the Mamas & The Papas: Straight Shooter*.

1991   He directs the music video *Soultwister* by the pop singer Jean Park.

1995   *Faster, Pussycat! Kill! Kill!* is rereleased theatrically in Europe and the States and is a big hit.

2000   He releases his self-published, ten-years-in-the-making autobiography *A Clean Breast: The Life and Loves of Russ Meyer*. It's 1,213 pages long, costs $350, and is "cowritten" by Adolph Schwartz.

2002   Russ, suffering from dementia, directs the documentary *Pandora Peaks*. On December 4, it's released direct-to-DVD.

2004   Russ Meyer, afflicted with pneumonia, dies at his home in Los Angeles on September 18. He was eighty-two.

Filmography

THE IMMORAL MR. TEAS (1959)
Production Companies: PAD Productions, Pad-Ram Enterprises
Producer: Peter A. DeCenzie, **Russ Meyer**
Director: **Russ Meyer**
Screenplay: Russ Meyer
Cinematography: **Russ Meyer**
Editing: **Russ Meyer,** John F. Link Sr. (uncredited)
Music: Edward J. Lakso
Cast: Bill Teas (Mr. Teas), Ann Peters (Coffeeshop Waitress), Marilyn Wesley (Dental Assistant), Michele Roberts (Secretary), Dawn Danielle (Beach Beauty), Don Cochran (Burlesque Stage Manager—uncredited), Don Couch (Dentist—uncredited), Althea Currier (Girl uncredited), Peter A. DeCenzie (Burlesque Announcer—uncredited), G. Ferrus (Narrator—uncredited), Mikki France (Dr. C. P. Floodback, Psychiatrist—uncredited), Earl Leaf (Strawboat Man—uncredited), Brandy Long (Burlesque Dancer—uncredited), Donna Long (Barfly—uncredited), **Russ Meyer** (Burlesque Audience Member–uncredited), E. M. Nathanson (Loverboy/Burlesque Audience Member–uncredited), Paula Parker (Hula Hoop Girl—uncredited), Alicyn Sanborn (Burlesque Dancer—uncredited), Doris Sanders (Final Nude Girl—uncredited), Paul Morton Smith (Photographer—uncredited), June Wilkinson (Nude Torso in Window—uncredited), and Enrico Banducci

EVE AND THE HANDYMAN (1961)
Production Company: Eve Productions
Producer: **Russ Meyer**
Director: **Russ Meyer**
Screenplay: **Russ Meyer**
Cinematography: **Russ Meyer**
Editing: **Russ Meyer**
Art Director: Mel Fowler

Cast: Eve Meyer (Eve/Other Roles), Anthony-James Ryan (the Handyman), Frank Bolger (Street Sweeper), Iris Bristol (Girl in the Laundromat), Rita Day (Girl), James A. Evanoff (Artist), Gigi Frost (Girl), Mildred Knezevich (Girl), Francesca Leslie (Francesca), Lee Merrin (Narrator), Florence E. Moore (Restroom Girl), Ken Parker (Artist), Jacqueline Stevens (Nude Model), Lyle D. Tolefson (Artist), Charles H. Vaughn (Artist), Joseph Carroll, Sam Meyer, B. Granger Moore, Barbara Murphy, George D. Murphy, and Joseph M. Reyes

EROTICA (1961)
Production Company: Pad-Ram Enterprises
Producers: Peter A. DeCenzie, **Russ Meyer**
Director: **Russ Meyer**
Screenplay: **Russ Meyer**
Narration: Jack Moran
Cinematography: **Russ Meyer**
Editing: **Russ Meyer**
Music: David Chudnow, Tommy Morgan
Cast: Sherry Knight (Self), Werner Otto Kirsch (Self), Charles G. Schelling (Strongforte), Peter A. DeCenzie (Caveman), **Russ Meyer** (Cameraman), Denise Daniels (Cavegirl), Althea Currier (Girl at Pool), Joe Cranston (Narrator), Lana Young, and Donna Townsend (uncredited)

WILD GALS OF THE NAKED WEST (1962)
Production Companies: Pacifica Films, Pad-Ram Enterprises
Producers: Peter A. DeCenzie, **Russ Meyer**
Director: **Russ Meyer**
Screenplay: Jack Moran, **Russ Meyer**
Cinematography: **Russ Meyer**
Editing: **Russ Meyer**
Music: Marlin Skiles (uncredited)
Art Director: Mel Fowler
Cast: Sammy Gilbert (the Stranger), Anthony-James Ryan (Crazy Redskin), Teri Taylor (Goldie Nuggets), Franklin Bolger (Snake Wolf), Julie Williams (the Bosom), Princess Livingston (Scary Woman in Saloon), Paul Fox (Redskin), Jack Moran, Ken Parker, Charles G. Schelling, Donna Scott, Peter A DeCenzie, and **Russ Meyer**

EUROPE IN THE RAW (1963)
Production Company: Eve Productions

Producer: **Russ Meyer**
Director: **Russ Meyer**
Screenplay: **Russ Meyer**
Cinematography: **Russ Meyer**
Editing: **Russ Meyer**
Cast: Veronique Gabriel (Self), Gigi La Touche (Self), Abundavita (Self), Denise Du Vall (Self), Heidi Richter (Self), Yvette Le Grand (Self), Greta Thorwald (Self), Shawn Devereaux (Rome's Baby Doll in Pool), Franklin Lamont Thistle (Narrator), Lynn Held (Narrator), Vic Perrin (Narrator), and Fred Owens

HEAVENLY BODIES (1963)
Production Company: Eve Productions
Producers: **Russ Meyer**
Director: **Russ Meyer**
Screenplay: **Russ Meyer**
Cinematography: **Russ Meyer**
Editing: **Russ Meyer**
Music: Igo Kantor
Cast: Althea Currier (Girl with Beachball), Monica Liljistrand (Girl with Beachball), Paulette Firestone (Self), Maria Andre (Girl at Bra-Maker), Ken Parker, Gaby Martine, Marian Milford, Don Cochran, Werner Otto Kirsch, Fred Owens, Billy A. Newhouse, Orville Hallberg, Bill Cummings, Princess Livingstone, F. E. Falconer, Robert J. Ewald, William Knowles, Rochelle Kennedy, Charles Shelling, Nancy Andre, Don Goodwin, Ivana Nolte, Amber Morgan, Binkie Stewart, and **Russ Meyer**

LORNA (1964)
Production Company: Eve Productions
Producer: **Russ Meyer**
Associate Producer: Eve Meyer
Director: **Russ Meyer**
Screenplay: James Griffith
Story: **Russ Meyer**
Cinematography: **Russ Meyer**
Editing: **Russ Meyer**
Cast: Lorna Maitland (Lorna), Mark Bradley (the Convict), James Rucker (Jim), Hal Hopper (Luther), Doc Scortt (Jonah), Althea Currier (Ruthie), F. Rufus Owens (Ezra), Frank Bolger (Silas), Kenneth H. Parker (the Fisherman), and James Griffith (the Man of God)

FANNY HILL: MEMOIRS OF A WOMAN OF PLEASURE (1964)
Production Companies: Central Cinema Company Film, Famous Players, Favorite Films
Producers: Artur Brauner, Albert Zugsmith
Associate Producer: Billy Frick
Directors: **Russ Meyer,** Albert Zugsmith (uncredited)
Screenplay: Robert Hill
Cinematography: Heinz Hölscher
Editing: Alfred Srp
Music: Erwin Halletz
Art Director: Paul Markwitz
Cast: Miriam Hopkins (Mrs. Maude Brown), Alex D'Arcy (Admiral), Walter Giller (Hemingway), Chris Howland (Mr. Norbert), Ulli Lommel (Charles), Helmut Weiss (Mr. Dinklespieler), Letítia Román (Fanny Hill), Cara Garnett (Phoebe), Marshall Raynor (Johnny), Syra Marty (Hortense), Karin Evans (Martha), Christiane Schmidtmer (Fiona), Hilde Sessak (Mrs. Snow), Albert Zugsmith (Grand Duke), Billy Frick (Percival), Erica Ericson (Emily), Heidi Hansen (Fenella), Renate Hutte (One of the Girls), Susanne Hsiao (Lotus Blossom), Patricia Houston (Amanda), Ellen Velero (One of the Girls), Burr Jerger (uncredited), Herbert Knippenberg (uncredited), and Jurgen Nesbach (uncredited)

MUDHONEY . . . LEAVES A TASTE OF EVIL! (1965)
Production Company: Delta Films
Producers: George Costello, **Russ Meyer**
Associate Producer: Eve Meyer
Director: **Russ Meyer**
Screenplay: Raymond Friday Locke, William E. Sprague
Cinematography: Walter Schenk
Editing: Charles Schelling, **Russ Meyer** (uncredited)
Music: Henri Price
Cast: Hal Hopper (Sidney Brenshaw), Antoinette Cristiani (Hannah Brenshaw), John Furlong (Calif McKinney), Rena Horten (Eula), Princess Livingstone (Maggie Marie), Lorna Maitland (Clara Belle), Sam Hanna (Injoys), Stu Lancaster (Lute Wade), Nick Wolcuff (Sheriff Abel), Frank Bolger (Brother Hansen), Lee Ballard (Sister Hansen), Mickey Foxx (Thurmond Pate), F. Rufus Owens (Milton), Wilfred Kues (Lynch Mob Member), Peter Cunningham (Lynch Mob Member), Bill Gunter (Lynch Mob Member), Gilbert Haimson (Mourner—uncredited), William Maley (Townspeople—uncredited), **Russ Meyer** (Townspeople—uncredited), Charles Felix, Milard Ferla, and Clarence Lowe

MOTORPSYCHO! (1965)
Production Company: Eve Productions
Producer: **Russ Meyer**
Associate Producer: Eve Meyer
Director: **Russ Meyer**
Screenplay: **Russ Meyer,** W. E. Sprague
Story: James Griffith, Hal Hopper, **Russ Meyer**
Cinematography: **Russ Meyer**
Editing: Charles G. Schelling, **Russ Meyer** (uncredited)
Music: Igo Kantor
Special Effects: Orville Hallberg
Cast: Haji (Ruby Bonner), Alex Rocco (Cory Maddox), Stephen Oliver (Brahmin), Holle K. Winters (Gail Maddox), Joseph Cellini (Dante), Thomas Scott (Slick), Coleman Francis (Harry Bonner), Sharon Lee (Jessica Fannin), Steve Masters (Frank), Arshalouis Aivazian (Frank's Wife), **E. E. Meyer (Russ Meyer)** (Sheriff), George Costello (Ambulance doctor), F. Rufus Owens (Rufus), and Richard Serly Brummer (Ambulance Driver)

FASTER, PUSSYCAT! KILL! KILL! (1966)
Production Company: Eve Productions
Producers: Eve Meyer, **Russ Meyer**
Associate Producers: George Costello, Fred Owens
Director: **Russ Meyer**
Screenplay: Jack Moran
Original Story: **Russ Meyer**
Cinematography: Walter Schenk
Editing: **Russ Meyer**
Music Director: Igo Kantor
Music Themes: Paul Sawtell, Bert Shefter
Cast: Tura Satana (Varla), Haji (Rosie), Lori Williams (Billie), Ray Barlow (Tommy), Susan Bernard (Linda), Mickey Foxx (Gas station attendant), Dennis Busch (the Vegetable), Stuart Lancaster (the Old Man), Paul Trinka (Kirk), and John Furlong (Narrator—uncredited)

MONDO TOPLESS (1966)
Production Company: Eve Productions
Producer: **Russ Meyer**
Associate Producer: Eve Meyer
Director: **Russ Meyer**

Cinematography: **Russ Meyer**
Editing: **Russ Meyer**
Music: The Aladdins
Cast: Babette Bardot (Self), Darlene Grey (Self), Pat Barringer (Self), Diane Young (Self), Sin Lenee (Self), Darla Paris (Self), Trina Lamar (Self), Mickey Frantz (Pool Cinematography Model—uncredited), John Furlong (Narrator—uncredited), **Russ Meyer** (Minor Role—uncredited), Lorna Maitland, and Donna X

COMMON-LAW CABIN (1967)
Production Company: Eve Productions
Producers: Eve Meyer, **Russ Meyer**
Director: **Russ Meyer**
Screenplay: John E. Moran, **Russ Meyer** (uncredited)
Cinematography: Jack Lucas, Wady C. Medawar, **Russ Meyer** (uncredited)
Editing: **Russ Meyer**
Music: Igo Kantor
Cast: Jack Moran (Dewey Hoople), Babette Bardot (Babette), Adele Rein (Coral Hoople), Franklin Bolger (Cracker), Alaina Capri (Sheila Ross), John Furlong (Dr. Martin Ross), Ken Swofford (Barney Rickert), Andrew Hagara (Laurence Talbot III), and George Costello (Bartender—uncredited)

GOOD MORNING . . . AND GOODBYE! (1967)
Production Company: Eve Productions
Producer: **Russ Meyer**
Associate Producer: Eve Meyer
Director: **Russ Meyer**
Screenplay: John E. Moran
Cinematography: **Russ Meyer**
Editing: Richard Serly Brummer, **Russ Meyer**
Music: Igo Kantor
Cast: Alaina Capri (Angel Boland), Stuart Lancaster (Burt Boland), Patrick Wright (Stone), Haji (Sorceress), Karen Ciral (Lana Boland), Don Johnson (Ray), Tom Howland (Herb), Megan Timothy (Lottie), Toby Adler (Betty), Sylvia Tedemar (Go-Go Dancer), Joe Perrin (Narrator), and Carol Peters (Nude)

FINDERS KEEPERS, LOVERS WEEPERS! (1968)
Production Company: Eve Productions
Producer: **Russ Meyer**
Associate Producer: Anthony-James Ryan
Executive Producer: Eve Meyer

Director: **Russ Meyer**
Screenplay: Richard Zachary
Original Story: **Russ Meyer**
Cinematography: **Russ Meyer**
Editing: Richard Serly Brummer, **Russ Meyer**
Music: Igo Kantor
Cast: Anne Chapman (Kelly), Paul Lockwood (Paul), Gordon Wescourt (Ray), Duncan McLeod (Cal), Robert Rudelson (Feeny), Lavelle Roby (Claire), Jan Sinclair (Christiana), Joey DuPrez (Joy), Pam Collins (First Dancer), John Furlong (Customer), Nick Wolcuff (Nick), Vickie Roberts (Girl), Michael Roberts (Boy), George C. Carll, Barney Caliendo, Louis Innerarity, Robert Pergament, Walter Cummings, George Cole, Robert Massaroli, Harvey Pergament, Robert Mumm, Orville Hallberg (uncredited), **Russ Meyer** (uncredited), and Anthony-James Ryan (uncredited)

VIXEN! (1968)
Production Companies: Coldstream Films, Eve Productions
Producer: **Russ Meyer**
Associate Producers: Richard Brummer, George Costello, Eve Meyer, Anthony-James Ryan
Director: **Russ Meyer**
Screenplay: Robert Rudelson
Original Story: **Russ Meyer**, Anthony-James Ryan
Cinematography: **Russ Meyer**
Editing: Richard Serly Brummer, **Russ Meyer**
Music: Igo Kantor
Cast: Erica Gavin (Vixen Palmer), Garth Pillsbury (Tom Palmer), Harrison Page (Niles), Jon Evans (Judd), Vincene Wallace (Janet King), Robert Aiken (Dave King), Michael Donovan O'Donnell (O'Bannion), Peter Carpenter (Mountie), John Furlong (Sam), Jackie Illman (Tourist), **Russ Meyer** (Tourist—uncredited), and Vic Perrin (Narrator—uncredited)

CHERRY, HARRY & RAQUEL! (1969)
Production Companies: Eve Productions, Panamint Film
Producer: **Russ Meyer**
Associate Producers: Thomas J. McGowan, Eve Meyer, Anthony-James Ryan
Director: **Russ Meyer**
Screenplay: Tom Wolfe (a.k.a. Tom McGowan), **Russ Meyer**
Story: **Russ Meyer**
Cinematography: **Russ Meyer**

Editing: Richard Serly Brummer, **Russ Meyer**
Music: William Loose
Cast: Larissa Ely (Raquel), Linda Ashton (Cherry), Charles Napier (Harry), Bert
Santos (Enrique), Franklin H. Bolger (Mr. Franklin), Astrid Lillimor (Soul),
Michelle Grand (Millie), John Milo (Apache), Michaelani (Doctor Lee), Robert
Aiken (Tom), John Koester (Gas Station Attendant), Daniel Roberts (Delivery
Boy), and **Russ Meyer** (Man in Pool—uncredited)

BEYOND THE VALLEY OF THE DOLLS (1970)
Production Company: Twentieth Century Fox
Producer: **Russ Meyer**
Associate Producers: Red Hershon, Eve Meyer
Director: **Russ Meyer**
Screenplay: Roger Ebert, Manny Diez (uncredited)
Story: Roger Ebert, **Russ Meyer**
Cinematography: Fred J. Koenekamp
Editing: Dann Cahn, Dick Wormell
Music: Stu Phillips
Additional Music: William Loose
Art Directors: Arthur Lonergan, Jack Martin Smith
Special Photographic Effects: Jack Harmon
Cast: Dolly Read (Kelly MacNamara), Cynthia Meyers (Casey Anderson), Marcia
McBroom (Petronella Danforth), John LaZar (Ronnie "Z-Man" Barzell), Michael
Blodgett (Lance Rocke), David Gurian (Harris Allsworth), Edy Williams (Ash-
ley St. Ives), Erica Gavin (Roxanne), Phyllis Davis (Susan Lake), Harrison Page
(Emerson Thorne), Duncan McLeod (Porter Hall), Jim Iglehart (Randy Black),
Charles Napier (Baxter Wolfe), Henry Rowland (Otto), Princess Livingston
(Matron), Stan Ross (Disciple), Lavelle Roby (Vanessa), Angel Ray (Girl in Tub),
Veronica Erickson (Blonde Date), Haji (Cat Woman), Karen Smith (Red Head),
Sebastian Brook (Art Director), Bruce V. McBroom (Photographer), Ian Sander
(Boy in Tub), Koko Tani (Assistant), Samantha Scott (Cynthia), Tea Crawford
(Kathy Page), Heath Jobes (Makeup Man), John Logan (Escort), Susan Reed
(Fashion Model), Robin Bach (Gay Boy), Ceil Cabot (Mother), Mary Carroll
(Middle-Aged Woman), Joseph Cellini (Man), Jackie Cole (First Woman), Frank
Corsentino (Hippie Boy), Mibb Curry (White-Haired Gentleman), Coleman
Francis (Rotund Drunk), Pam Grier (Fourth Woman), T. J. Halligan (Science
Teacher), Rick Holmes (Man with Glasses), Marshall Kent (Dr. Downs), Mi-
chael Kriss (Young Actor), Tim Laurie (Second Gay Man), Bebe Louie (Hippie
Girl), Lillian Martin (Nurse), Ashley Phillips (Fashion Model), "Big Jack" Provan

(Father), Joyce Rees (Marion Harrisburg), Chris Riordan (Gay Boy), Bert Santos (Taxi Driver), George Stratton (Third Gay Man), the Strawberry Alarm Clock (the Strawberry Alarm Clock), **Russ Meyer** (TV Cameraman—uncredited), Charles Fox, and Cissy Colpitts

THE SEVEN MINUTES (1971)
Production Company: Twentieth Century Fox
Producer: **Russ Meyer**
Associate Producers: Red Hershon, Eve Meyer
Director: **Russ Meyer**
Screenplay: Richard Warren Lewis
Cinematography: Fred Mandl
Editing: Dick Wormell
Music: Stu Phillips
Art Director: Rodger Maus
Cast: Wayne Maunder (Mike Barrett), Marianne McAndrew (Maggie Russell), Philip Carey (Elmo Duncan), Jay C. Flippen (Luther Yerkes), Edy Williams (Faye Osborn), Lyle Bettger (Frank Griffith), Jackie Gayle (Norman Quandt), Ron Randell (Merle Reid), Charles Drake (Sgt. Kellogg), John Carradine (Sean O'Flanagan), Harold J. Stone (Judge Upshaw), Tom Selleck (Phil Sanford), James Iglehart (Clay Rutherford), John Sarno (Jerry Griffith), Stanley Adams (Irwin Blair), Billy Durkin (George Perkins), Yvonne D'Angers (Sheri Moore), Robert Moloney (Ben Fremont), Olan Soule (Harvey Underwood), Jan Shutan (Anna Lou White), Alexander D'Arcy (Christian Leroux), David Brian (Cardinal McManus), Berry Kroeger (Paul Van Fleet), Ralph Story (TV Commentator), Charles Napier (Officer Iverson), Kay Peters (Olivia St. Clair), Richard Angarola (Father Sarfatti), Shawn "Baby Doll" Devereaux (Yerkes' girlfriend), Regis J. Cordic (Louis Polk), John Lawrence (Howard Moore), Mora Gray (Donna Novick), Wolfman Jack (Wolfman Jack), Calvin Bartlett (Olin Adams), Ken Jones (Charles Wynter), Bill Baldwin (Commentator), Vince Williams (Reporter), Jim Bacon (Reporter), John Gruber (Dr. Quigley), Chris Marks (Dr. Eberhart), Stuart Lancaster (Dr. Roger Trimble), Peter Shrayder (Merle Reid's cameraman), Lynn Hamilton (Avis), Patrick Wright (Detective), Lillian Lehman (Librarian), Judith Baldwin (Fremont's girlfriend), Paul Stader (Thug), Henry Rowland (Yerkes's Butler), Yvonne De Carlo (Constance Cumberland), Barry Coe (Court Clerk—uncredited), George De Normand (Juror—uncredited), Uschi Digard (Very Big Brunette with Gorilla—uncredited), Robin Hughes (Ashcroft—uncredited), Sally Marr (Juror—uncredited), **Russ Meyer** (Minor Role—uncredited), and Jeffrey Sayre (Juror—uncredited)

BLACKSNAKE! (1973)
Production Company: Trident Films Ltd.
Producer: **Russ Meyer**
Associate Producer: Anthony-James Ryan
Director: **Russ Meyer**
Screenplay: **Russ Meyer,** Leonard Neubauer
Original story: Anthony-James Ryan
Cinematography: Arthur Ornitz
Editing: Fred Baratta
Music: William Loose
Art Director: Rick Heatherly
Cast: Anouska Hempel (Lady Susan Walker), David Warbeck (Sir Charles Walker/ Ronald Sopwith), Percy Herbert (Joxer Tierney), Thomas Baptiste (Isaiah), Milton McCollin (Joshua), Bernard Boston (Capt. Raymond Daladier), Vikki Richards (Cleone), Dave Prowse (Jonathan Walker), Bloke Modisane (Bottoms), Anthony Sharpe (Lord Clive), Robert Lee (Informer), Carl Corbin (Stalwart), Eggie Clark (Cart Driver), Sydney A. Harris (Village Elder), Donna Young (First Running Girl), Lawanda Moore (Second Running Girl), Wendell Williams (Ton-Ton Soldier), Don Dandridge (Second Running Boy), Bruce Richard (First Running Boy), and Bob Minor

SUPERVIXENS (1975)
Production Companies: RM Films International, September 19
Producer: **Russ Meyer**
Associate Producers: Wilfred Kues, Charles Napier, Fred Owens, James Parsons
Executive Producer: Anthony-James Ryan
Director: **Russ Meyer**
Written by: **Russ Meyer**
Cinematography: **Russ Meyer**
Editing: **Russ Meyer**
Music: William Loose
Art Director: Michael Levesque
Cast: Shari Eubank (SuperAngel/SuperVixen/Wife), Charles Napier (Harry Sledge), Uschi Digard (SuperSoul/Telephone Operator), Charles Pitts (Clint Ramsey), Henry Rowland (Martin Bormann), Christy Hartburg (SuperLorna), Sharon Kelly (SuperCherry), John LaZar (Cal MacKinney), Stuart Lancaster (Lute), Deborah McGuire (SuperEula), Glenn Dixon (Luther), Haji (SuperHaji), Big Jack Provan (Sheriff), Garth Pillsbury (Fisherman), Ron Sheridan (Police-man), John Lawrence (Dr. Scholl), F. Rufus Owens (Rufus), John Furlong (CBS

Commentator), Paul Fox (Tire Thief), Ann Marie (Tom's Other Wife), and **Russ Meyer** (Motel Manager #2—uncredited)

UP! (1976)
Production Company: RM Films International
Producer: **Russ Meyer**
Associate Producers: George K. Carll, Uschi Digard, Fred Owens
Director: **Russ Meyer**
Screenplay: **B. Callum (Russ Meyer)**
Narration: Reinhold Timme (a.k.a. Roger Ebert)
Original Story: **Russ Meyer,** Jim Ryan, Reinhold Timme
Cinematography: **Russ Meyer**
Editing: **Russ Meyer**
Music: William Loose, Paul Ruhland
Art Director: Michele Levesque
Ichthyologist: Charles E. Sumners
Cast: Raven De La Croix (Margo), Robert McLane (Paul), Janet Wood (Alice), Mary Gavin (the Headsperson), Su Ling (Limehouse), Elaine Collins (the Ethiopian Chef), Linda Sue Ragsdale (Gwendolyn), Harry (Carnivorous Fish), Edward Schaaf (Adolph), Monte Bane (Homer), Marianne Marks (Chesty Young Thing), Larry Dean (Leonard), Bob Schott (Rafe), Foxy Lae (Pocahontas), Ray Reinhardt (the Commissioner), Francesca "Kitten" Natividad (the Greek Chorus), **Russ Meyer** (Hitchcock—uncredited), Fred Owens (Rufus—uncredited)

BENEATH THE VALLEY OF THE ULTRA-VIXENS (1979)
Production Company: RM Films International
Producer: **Russ Meyer**
Associate Producers: Richard Serly Brummer, Fred Owens, Uschi Digard (uncredited)
Director: **Russ Meyer**
Screenplay: R, Hyde (Roger Ebert), **B. Callum (Russ Meyer)**
Story: **B. Callum (Russ Meyer)**
Cinematography: **Russ Meyer**
Editing: **Russ Meyer**
Music: William Tasker
Art Director: Michele Levesque
Cast: Francesca "Kitten" Natividad (Lavonia/Lola Langusta), Anne Marie (Eufaula Roop), Ken Kerr (Lamar Shedd), June Mack (Junkyard Sal), Pat Wright (Mr. Peterbuilt), Henry Rowland (Martin Bormann), Robert Pearson (Dr. Asa

Lavender), Michael Finn (Semper Fidelis), Sharon Hill (Nurse Flovilla Thatch), Don Scarborough (Beau Badger), Aram Katcher (Tyrone), DeForest Covan (Zebulon), Steve Tracy (Rhett), Uschi Digard (SuperSoul), Stuart Lancaster (the Man from Smalltown USA), Mary Gavin (the Very Big Blonde), **Russ Meyer** (the Director—uncredited)

Russ Meyer: Interviews

King Leer: Top "Nudie" Filmmaker Russ Meyer Scrambles to Outshock Big Studios

Steven M. Lovelady / 1968

Russ Meyer knows what he likes. "You may have noticed," he deadpans to a visitor, "that all my girls have a couple of things in common."

Indeed, they do. Like Alaina Capri, 42–24–36; Babette Bardot, 42–24–36; Lorna Maitland, 42–24–36; and Adele Rein, 42–24–36. They're all stars of movies Mr. Meyer has produced in the past few years. But now he would like to broaden his horizons. "What I have in mind for the next movie," he says, "is someone along the lines of, say, 43–24–36."

Mr. Meyer doesn't make your run-of-the-mill movie. His bushy-browed, bulldog face isn't often seen in the watering spots frequented by major studio directors and producers. His films never make the ten-best-of-the-year lists. He has never won an Oscar. Rather, Russ Meyer is king of the "nudies." But his influence on American moviemaking is not inconsiderable. Says a Columbia Pictures Corp. screen writer: "You can be sure what Russ is doing today will be done by the majors tomorrow."

If so, get a good grip on your popcorn, movie fans, because what Russ Meyer is doing right now is putting finishing touches on a film that explicitly depicts a series of violent sexual encounters among a plethora of partners in a variety of bizarre settings.

"This one is going to set 'em back on their heels," he says enthusiastically. "Nudity alone isn't a drawing card anymore." As Mr. Meyer sees it, "The public is thirsting for more."

Whether the public really is thirsting for more, some would contest. But the increasing exploitation of sex and violence by US moviemakers is incontestable. It's a well-chronicled fact. And while many segments of the American public may be offended by what they regard as a blatant and tasteless resort to sex and violence in films, the trend suggests a good deal about changing US mores.

"The blatant sex saturating movies today is just part of an exuberant, initial overreaction of a society breaking loose from old restraints and rules," says Gerald Suttles, a sociologist at the University of Chicago.

At any rate, there's no question that Mr. Meyer, a "pioneer" in the field, is cashing in on commercialization of sex and violence. Every one of the twenty movies he has made in the past nine years has grossed at least four times its cost. His first film, which took only four days and $24,000 to produce, has grossed $1.2 million, so far. That return on investment—more than forty to one—has been matched only by *Gone with the Wind*.

That kind of fiscal performance has helped Mr. Meyer win recognition as the undisputed champion at turning out what the trade calls "sexploitation" films—low-budget, quickly produced movies reeking with both sex and violence.

At the same time, he has achieved grudging recognition—by some—as something of a film craftsman. "A lot of people are just plain confused by Russ Meyer, me included," says a Warner Bros.-Seven Arts film director. "Everything he shoots is filled with all those incredibly overdeveloped babes prancing around without their clothes, right in the middle of what is sometimes powerful drama and brilliant use of the camera. You just don't know how to react to that incongruity."

Neither do reviewers. Take a 1965 Russ Meyer film called *Motorpsycho!* It portrays a trio of psychopathic youths off on a series of rapings, beatings, and killings. In some scenes, the twistings of the unhinged human mind are delineated with impressive artistry. But throughout, the viewer is startled by the presence of four amply endowed lasses, all but bursting out of their scanty clothing. A reviewer for a trade daily wrote that the film showed "the touch of a gifted filmmaker" in its excellent photography and skillful drama, concluding that it "succeeds triumphantly" in portraying the more depraved elements of today's society. But he complained that "all the women costumed in plunging, bulging, or bursting necklines" could appeal only to "the slack-jawed trade."

Other critics don't see the beauty in Meyer films. The *New York Post* reviewed *Good Morning . . . and Goodbye!*, the most recent Meyer release, and called it "a smutty sex show" that "can't even be labeled for adults only" It said the plot "moves rapidly down the sewer as it swirls from one sex titillation to another" And it complained that the dialogue "would embarrass a third-rate burlesque comic." The *New York Times* also reviewed *Good Morning . . . and Goodbye!*, the first Russ Meyer film the *Times* has ever reviewed, and found it funny. It is a drama of marital infidelity and lust down on the farm.

The forty-four-year-old Meyer, a big-framed man with a comfortable paunch, admits that he deliberately appeals to "the pant-and-drool crowd." He says he adds quality drama to attract "people who otherwise wouldn't sit still for a girlie flick."

Mr. Meyer dismisses critics who claim the brutality is designed essentially to attract sadists. "Nuts," he says. "The violence is there just to lend excitement, action. The way to succeed in this business is to get that audience whipped up, so they'll walk out of that theater saying, 'Good God, did you see *that*?' When you can do that, you know a full house will be walking in the next day."

Whatever its rationale, the formula works. "Most sexploitation flicks don't really do much business for a theater owner," says Fred Beiersdorf, a Dallas movie distributor. "But when a Russ Meyer flick comes to town, they stand in line."

Right now, they're standing in line to see *Good Morning . . . and Goodbye!*, which opened earlier this year in Statesboro, Georgia, where forty-four hundred students at Georgia Southern College make up half the population. On a daily basis, it outgrossed such major-studio productions as *Hawaii* and *You Only Live Twice*. Result: the film now is playing in more than a dozen college towns.

Partly to meet competition from daring films imported from Europe and partly because Mr. Meyer has shown, as he sees it anyway, that "really raw strong stuff on the screen can make money and rouse surprisingly little public indignation," the big US studios themselves are financing and distributing films with "real shock value," Mr. Meyer unhappily acknowledges.

"It's hard today to stay one step ahead of the majors," he says. "Why should the man on the street shell out to see a Russ Meyer movie when he can see nudity in *Blow-Up* (Metro-Goldwyn-Mayer), lesbianism and masturbation in *The Fox* (Warner Bros.-Seven Arts), and blood and guts in *Bonnie and Clyde* (Warner Bros.-Seven Arts)? I don't have the stars, the name, the cash, or the publicity those outfits have."

Mr. Meyer, a native of San Francisco, began his film career at age nineteen as an Army Signal Corps cameraman in World War II. Once out of the service, he went to work as a freelance photographer, selling his photos to pinup magazines. In the 1950s, he made something of a name for himself, photographing six "playmates" for the then-struggling *Playboy* magazine; one of the playmates was his wife, from whom he is now divorced.

In 1959, Mr. Meyer came to Hollywood and, with $24,000 raised with the help of army buddies, spent four days shooting a movie titled *The Immoral Mr. Teas*. Now considered a minor classic by some screen buffs, the movie follows a day in the life of a timid delivery boy who, to his dismay, sees naked females everywhere he turns.

Mr. Teas drew packed houses wherever it played, and Russ Meyer found himself an instant trend-maker. The movie, according to film historians Arthur Knight and Hollis Alpert, "touched off a whole new wave of moviemaking." By 1962, it had spawned 150 imitations. That's more nudie films than had been produced for theater audiences in the US up to that time.

The movie also won Mr. Meyer favorable comment from some reviewers. The *Los Angeles Times* critic said *Mr. Teas* showed "a subtle, urbane wit." In *Show Magazine*, highbrow critic Leslie Fiedler wrote that he found *Mr. Teas* to be a "profound, funny, and sad" attack on the artificiality of Hollywood, pinup magazines, and advertising.

Mr. Meyer's films have had surprisingly little opposition from local censors. *Mr. Teas* was banned in Pasadena, Philadelphia, and Fort Lauderdale, but since then, Meyer movies have been shown in these cities all but untouched. When he has tangled with censors, he has most often won. Last year, when the Fort Worth film censorship board banned *How Much Loving Does a Normal Couple Need?*, Mr. Meyer and a local distributor went to federal district court, which ruled the ordinance setting up the board was unconstitutional. Most recently, the Chicago motion picture appeal board banned *Good Morning . . . and Goodbye!* Shortly afterward, a Supreme Court ruling caused the agency to disband.

Because of his reputation as a moneymaker, Mr. Meyer figures that up to eight hundred theaters are prepared to play his movies. While that's less than 10 percent of all theaters in the US, it's eight times as many as his competitors usually garner.

Mr. Meyer limits his productions to a $60,000 budget. With a production crew of five, he generally takes two to five weeks to film a picture—usually at rural locations within five hundred miles of Los Angeles, to avoid studio costs. Most Meyer "stars"—whom he refers to as "my stable of tomatoes"—are paid $750 a week and are recruited from burlesque or topless establishments. Some, however, are found in more mundane occupations. Alaina Capri, the star of *Good Morning . . . and Goodbye!*, teaches junior high school in a Los Angeles suburb—under another name.

A visit to the small but plush Hollywood house Mr. Meyer uses as both home and office shows how wrapped up [he is] in his business. On the outside, white columns and a portico suggest an orderly air. But inside, chaos reigns. The walls and floor are cluttered with advertisements for Meyer films, pictures of girls considered prospects for movies, and numerous scripts. Mementoes from past Meyer movies are hung on plaques on the wall. Cut film is strewn ankle-deep across the thick gold rug.

Mr. Meyer often works sixteen-hour days. As he feeds film into a viewing machine and peers delightedly at the small screen, he yells in excitement, "God, look at that babe move! What a sweetheart this scene is! This picture will *kill* 'em!" His eyes never leaving the small screen, he tells a visitor that word of a new movie has already spread among theater owners. He has had enquiries from a dozen exhibitors eager to show the film. "That's what's really exhilarating—to know you're going to have them on the edge of their seats," he says. "That's the greatest feeling in the world."

The King of the Nudie Movies
Is Going Respectable

Marci McDonald / 1971

From *The Gazette*, June 19, 1971. Material republished with the express
permission of the *Montreal Gazette*, a division of Postmedia Network Inc.

Russ Meyer has this problem:

They keep calling him a dirty old man.

It's not the dirty that bothers him, you understand. It's the old. After all, he's
only forty-seven, isn't he? In the prime of his life. Fresh from one career as King
of the Nudie Movies, and puffing headlong into another, fighting back, as it were.

Russ Meyer, you see, is going respectable.

From the hand of the man who brought the world such cinematic milestones
as *Cherry, Harry & Raquel!*, *Vixen!*, and *Beyond the Valley of the Dolls*, now comes
The Seven Minutes, the filmed version of Irving Wallace's bestseller on censorship, a major motion picture for a major Hollywood studio—Twentieth Century
Fox—currently in its final cutting stages.

Now, after years of scrounging around in the underground with a camera on
his back, a shoestring crew at his side, and a bevy of forty-two-inch bustlines in
his viewfinder upon which to build a loose plot, Russ Meyer has finally surfaced
in the bosom of the establishment—with, of all things, a storyline.

As the deadline looms closer for *The Seven Minutes'* release, he is understand-
ably nervous. He frets and sweats over lunch high atop the Beverly Towers.

After all, can Russ Meyer survive respectability? Can respectability survive
Russ Meyer?

"Naturally, I felt very trepidatious," says Russ, who has taken to using big words
now that he's in the big money. "Because it was not my cup of tea. All my other
films tended to be bombastic, fast-moving . . ."

He gropes for the words.

"Well, there's no point in beating around the bush. In all my other films, when there was a sex scene, they had sex."

Then along came *The Seven Minutes*, the bestseller with the storybook ending—the tale of a dirty book on trial for inciting a sexual assault, which turns out in court to be completely exonerated, found to have redeeming social significance and, after a number of relevant romps in the boudoir, prompts everyone to live happily thereafter.

It's an out-and-out Cinderella story for the anticensorship types, if ever there was one. And who better to direct it than Russ Meyer, the moviemaker who has spent a small fortune of his self-made millions on fighting the censors.

"It was," as he says, "a perfect opportunity to answer my critics. An attempt to answer in particular one Charles Keating Jr., head of the Citizens for Decent Literature, who holds forth in Cincinnati. And it's my earnest hope we can preview [the film] in Cincinnati.

"Mr. Keating was one of the two dissenting voices on President Nixon's panel on pornography. To be succinct, he'd like to put myself and [producer Richard] Zanuck in jail. He thinks pornography is worse than war. He accuses me of being a pornographer."

Russ Meyer's voice rises in righteous indignation.

"Now, King of the Nudie Movies—that's fine. And being called a sexploitationist—I don't mind that because I've got a lot of company. But pornographer always comes up.

"Now, it's impossible for the Supreme Court to define pornographer, so how could I? I really don't know what it is. And anyway, I don't think that I am one."

If pornographer ruffles Russ Meyer, however, the unkindest cut of all is dirty old man.

Just seeing how miffed it makes him, one wouldn't dare suggest that it might come from the fact that, well, that—you just can't get around it—Russ Meyer looks like you might imagine one.

Sitting across the lunch table, his 220 pounds loom massive and fleshy, his black hair too slicked back 'til the gray shows, his ears too big, his eyes too small, his nose bulbous and bursting with bluish-red veins, his thick lips parted under a toothbrush moustache in a face both ruddy and pockmarked.

"My wife is certainly more attractive than I am," he says, as if reading your mind. "No doubt I have other redeeming qualities . . ."

His voice trails off, as the reason for his sensitivity soon becomes apparent.

Enter Edy Williams, 37–24–37, in a skintight white hot-pant suit topped by acres of curly brown hair, star of *Beyond the Valley of the Dolls* and *The Seven Minutes* who, last June, between assignments, became the third Mrs. Russ Meyer.

Her entrance leaves the dining room dazzled. They kiss, and he preens himself in her presence, basks in the pride of possession.

"I love her to wear clothes that are very revealing," he says, as if she somehow weren't there, "because I get turned on by it. It's not a vicarious thing. I wouldn't want to make a spectacle out of my wife—her career's her own thing. If she wanted to work with [director Roger] Vadim completely naked, who am I to say no?"

He recounts with relish how he took her to his high school reunion wearing a kind of expanded bikini dress.

"They almost didn't let her in," he beams. "Oh, I loved it. It was great for the ego. Here was this poor boy returning with this fantastic movie queen."

To celebrate, he bought her a red Stingray sportscar, a diamond nearly as big as the Ritz, and a genuine Hollywood mansion with chandeliers in the bathroom and a pool that protrudes into the living room, which might well qualify as a Russ Meyer movie set.

"It used to be a party house," says Edy in her breathy starlet whisper. "It's a very sexy house."

They met, like any other star-crossed couple, in the studio commissary, where she was the perennial starlet, very big at premieres and supermarket openings, not so big on the screen.

He, at the time, was the new boy on the [Fox] lot, the unknown quantity with the sleazy taint of the stag filmmaker about him, son of a mother who'd been six times married and a policeman father he never saw after he was thirteen—a man who learned his filmmaking the hard way, as a teenage combat photographer on the bloody Second World War battlefields of Normandy, Bastogne, and the Saar.

By comparison, in fact, peacetime as a cheesecake photographer was a distinct letdown—until a burlesque manager prodded him into shooting his first movie, *The Immoral Mr. Teas*.

The Meyer-inspired story of a bearded delivery boy who sees all women as naked, it was shot in four days of 1959 for $24,000, somehow slipped by the censors, and grossed over $1 million—the first public nudie. And Russ Meyer never looked back.

In eighteen other films, he refined the formula to a science, transferring to film his wildest fantasies at bargain basement budgets. Until each one—*Heavenly Bodies, Mudhoney, Motorpsycho!*, and *Faster, Pussycat! Kill! Kill!*—became better, slicker, each one a roaring box office success.

"Yes, I came along at the right time with the right equipment." He says, "The public hadn't seen anything like it. It was a chance, and I don't think it'll come again."

Richard Zanuck was impressed enough with *Vixen!* to beckon. If Meyer could make a $7.5 million box office blockbuster on $70,000 what could he do, Zanuck wondered, with $2 million and a title like *Beyond the Valley of the Dolls*?

So did a lot of other people—including Fox's most prestigious producers.

"It was the only time I was really snubbed," says Russ over his steak and Waldorf salad. "You felt that attitude—that dirty old man thing—as if, instead of me rising up to their level, it was Fox sinking to my level. There was definite hostility."

"I purport to entertain," says Russ, changing the subject. "I entertain myself, and what entertains me, entertains a lot of people."

Still, he admits, he is not as entertained as he used to be.

"I used to be wrapped up in the bosom to a pronounced effect," he says. "Until Edy. I'm not in the same bag as I was before.

"I'm really fed up with it, to be honest with you. I've explored this sex thing completely—and exploited it, illustrated it. You get to the point you say, 'What else can I do?' and then somebody else comes along and does it.

"*Vixen!* And *I Am Curious, Yellow* are like Sunday school primers [compared] to what they're showing now. I just feel you have to leave something to the imagination, otherwise it's not interesting."

What? Russ Meyer sounding like a reactionary? He senses it, and is quick to assure, "An awful lot of what I did in my old films is present in this film. I'd be foolish to disregard it. The audience has gotten to expect a certain sexual quota from me."

Still, this time around, the skinny girl gets the guy. There isn't a sex scene that isn't in the book.

Eleven hours a day, seven days a week, he is working at it, whittling away at it in the cutting room, his passport to respectability.

"It's crucial to our lives, this film," he says. "While *Beyond the Valley of the Dolls* was enormously successful, a lot of my colleagues thought, 'Oh, well, just another sex film.' But after *Seven Minutes*, I think a lot of people will start to take us seriously. I mean, it won't win any Academy Awards, but that's not the important thing. Because I will be exonerated—I shall be ripped from the cross."

No more snubs from snobbish producers. No more slights from Hollywood socialites Better yet, no more of this endlessly defending himself. Here it will be, the final defense, the one last widescreen summation:

"Because it's all catharsis, isn't it?" he says. "It's never been proven that anybody, having seen a film, went out and raped somebody. The little man—the mousey man—he goes because he has two hours of escapism. I mean, after all, if it were so hellishly corrupting, then I'd be in a terrible way. And am I corrupted?"

He looks to Edy.

"No," she says, dutifully.

"I'm straight, aren't I?" he asks, assured.

"Well. . . ." She pauses, with an unerring instinct for timing, and says, "What do you consider straight?"

Sex, Violence and Drugs—All in Good Fun!

Stan Berkowitz / 1972

From *Film Comment* 9, no. 1 (January–February 1973). Reprinted with permission of Film at Lincoln Center.

Lexington Avenue runs through Hollywood between Sunset and Santa Monica Boulevards. Just west of where it crosses Highland Avenue, it traverses a district that is noted for its concentration of companies which furnish supplies and services to everyone from student filmmakers to major studio technicians. One of the newer buildings on this street is divided into two stories of offices, fewer of which are larger than a bachelor apartment. Anyone who feels like it can walk up the stairs to the second floor and, without having to worry about guarded gates, card keys, or even surly secretaries, he can go down the hall to room 213. There, as often as not, will be Russ Meyer, standing in front of a Moviola near the open door.

Once, Meyer basked in the exclusive trappings of a major studio, named Twentieth Century Fox. Now, three years and two films later, Meyer doesn't miss any of the prestige. "An editing room is an editing room," he shrugs.

Meyer begins his workdays with a visit to a Hollywood health club; his once paunchy frame is now almost gangling. By 8:00 a.m. he is at his editing room-office, working on his new feature. His tiny cubicle shows a few signs of the draining, time-consuming work that goes on there: a shaving kit, some other toiletries and, tucked away in one corner, a whole case of scotch. On one occasion, Meyer ventured beyond alcohol to marijuana, but he found it lacking. "What's the kick?" he asks. "Nothing happened to me the time I smoked it. But anyway, who needs it? I have my films, and they're a kind of turn-on for me." Meyer's latest turn-on is called *Blacksnake!*

Stan Berkowitz: What attracted you to the story of *Blacksnake!*?

Russ Meyer: I read some legend material from the Caribbean, and I also wanted to dabble a little bit in a Black film. The successful films that I've made have always been in the parody genre, so I figured I would try to come up with something that was kind of irreverent, like *All in the Family*, maybe. I didn't think about *All in the Family*, the successful TV show, to begin with, but it turned out that it has a strange similarity to it.

Berkowitz: In films like *Vixen!*, you've shown a liberal view on civil rights. Are you worried that this new irreverent approach might offend some Blacks?

Meyer: No, I think I've made it a kind of *Joe*. I've been to a number of screenings of *Joe*, and I like the film very much. And every audience I've seen it with, including the Blacks, enjoyed it enormously. They realized that it was a big, broad-ass put-on.

When we were negotiating with the primarily Black Barbadian government for cooperation in the filming of *Blacksnake!*, it finally got down to a question of what the film was all about. I went through my song and dance, and explained carefully and quickly the general theme of the film. The commissioner—he was dressed like a British officer, with pips, swagger stick, walking shorts, a brown belt, and the lot—he asked me, "Who wins?" I said, "Well, the Blacks." And he said, "Well, that's fine." So, from then on, we had no trouble about official cooperation.

This is a very liberal film, extremely so, and it's told in a manner that is forthright, and with my rambunctious style. I think there are a lot of places in the film where the Blacks will get up and start cheering, particularly when they start whipping the white overseer who's been whipping them for a long time. Each slave goes up and takes one crack at him with the blacksnake whip. I think at that point, there's going to be a lot of cheering. But then again, the characters are a lot bigger than life. They're right out of an Al Capp cartoon. There are only two really sympathetic people in the picture, but for the most part, they're all terribly bad people.

Berkowitz: Don't you also try to reflect some contemporary themes in *Blacksnake!*?

Meyer: Yeah, I do that. I've often been accused of making morality plays. But I kind of like to poke fun at history and, of course, current events. When I can borrow from contemporary things, I guess I get some kind of turn-on or particular excitement. Someone might say that there's a similarity between this fellow Isaiah and Martin Luther King, or somehow Joshua reminds me of Eldridge Cleaver, and those Black troopers in Napoleonic costumes and riding horses—who are they? Perhaps they're a parallel to the Tonton Macoutes of Haiti.

Berkowitz: This new film seems to mark a shift in your films from sex to violence.

Meyer: Sure, there's a change. If you want to compare it to *Vixen!*, 60 percent of that film dealt with matters of sex, a very small percentage had any kind of violence. But some of the others had a lot of violence. *Finders Keepers!, Cherry, Harry & Raquel!, Faster, Pussycat!* So, it's not too great a departure.

The basis of this film is sexual. An attractive English whore, low born, has been sold into white slavery—I don't show this in the film—by a pimp in so-called London Town. And she meets old Sir Alec, who owns Blackmoor Plantation, on the mythical island of San Cristobal. He falls in love with her, and he takes her back and marries her and then she literally screws him to death. Now, again, we don't see this, but she's now gone through four husbands, and the thread that keeps our story together is the young Englishman, of the aristocracy, who calls upon an elderly lord for assistance in getting a letter of recommendation so that he may go to this island to find out what's happened to his long-lost brother Jonathan. So, the story is very soapy in one way.

Jonathan, who was the fourth husband of Lady Susan Walker, mysteriously disappeared. There was no more correspondence from him. We find out later in the story that Brother Jonathan has been emasculated and had his tongue removed, because one hangup that Lady Susan Walker has is that any of her men who have some sort of activity with a Black girl—she shuns them very quickly, and in this instance, she really did this guy in. He is what we call a duppy; it's like a zombie, and he runs through the forest. It's a gothic thing we have there. He tries to strangle his ex-wife any chance he can, for the terrible deed she did him.

What I undertook, and I realized it afterwards, was a terribly ambitious thing. I was making a period film, a la *Captain Blood*, Warner Bros., 1934, and we almost didn't make it.

When I was at Fox, I worked with a very large crew, and was able to delegate a lot of authority. When I went to Barbados, my associate, Jim Ryan, and I undertook the responsibility of maybe an entire studio, or a portion thereof, and put together a terribly ambitious film that would have cost at least a million dollars, had it been made by a major studio. We made it for a little over $200,000, and it's a remarkable picture.

Prior to making films at Fox—*Dolls* and *Seven Minutes*—I had gone out with four or five stalwarts and we made pictures for a very limited amount of money, and because they were made at a particular time, they were highly successful. I dare say if I were to go out and make the same kind of film today, it would not be as successful, no matter how much moxie I put in.

Berkowitz: Why not?

Meyer: Because I think that the majors on one side have hacked away at the sexual freedom that I was able to express in my early films; and the porno bunch, the hardcore people, have chipped away at the audience from the other side. So, the idea of coming up with a film which showed simulated sex or eroticism, no matter how attractive or how well acted, I *know* it wouldn't be a success.

So, I have to look toward newer, more ambitious projects. *Blacksnake!* was certainly ambitious, especially in view of the fact that we were making a film in a foreign land, which is not easy. It's not like dealing with a film in the United States, where there are some things you just assume. Every day there was a new, staggering problem that was presented to us. We had a schedule of six weeks, but then we had a contingency of an additional week, and we used that week. And then of course we were down there three weeks beforehand, Ryan and myself. Then I spent one extra week with a very limited crew, just the soundman and assistant cameraman, and we went out and shot material for a montage—which are always very prominent in my films.

Berkowitz: Were you also the cinematographer?

Meyer: No, a fellow by the name of Arthur Ornitz was. He did *The Anderson Tapes*, *Lilies of the Field*, and some others. He's a very capable cameraman. His brother, Don Ornitz, and I were in the service together and we're very close friends. Arthur did a very capable job, although it was far more than he had anticipated. He was accustomed to working with a very large crew, but I made it clear up-front that he was to be the camera operator as well, and he went for it. But it was a very arduous thing working in the cane fields, the humidity and the heat, the uncomfortableness of it, and I didn't provide all the niceties that an awful lot of these English actors expected—tea and umbrellas and folding chairs; there were never enough folding chairs, there was never enough tea, never enough umbrellas. I got caught up in a kangaroo court one night, and it was kind of interesting.

Berkowitz: Were you satisfied by all the performances?

Meyer: No, two did not satisfy me, and I won't go into that except to say that one of the two will probably be the most spectacular person in the film, even though his performance left a lot to be desired. There's the area where the Moviola, the editing, comes into play. I expect this one actor will probably make an enormous impact, and it'll do a lot for his career. I just regret that he could have made it easier for me, but for reasons best known to himself, he did not.

Berkowitz: Since you're the editor . . .

Meyer: No, I'm not the editor, per se. I have an editor—Fred Baratta—who worked with me on *The Seven Minutes*. It's just a matter of getting used to my style, and he's getting used to it. More than that, really.

Berkowitz: Will *Blacksnake!* be cut in the same style as *The Seven Minutes*, with frequent cuts, and no shot lasting longer than a few seconds?

Meyer: Pretty much so. It's a real rock 'em-sock 'em kind of thing. I find myself bored with films that are kind of pedestrian. Maybe that's a hang-up, but my cutting style seems to work. It makes the film move very quickly and informatively. Unlike *Seven Minutes*—which was a very wordy picture in which I had to try to keep this same style going—*Blacksnake!* is an action picture.

Berkowitz: Did you have a lot of trouble casting this film?

Meyer: No. The girl was a problem because she's not the typical girl that I've had—the great cantilevered structured girl. First of all, I had to have a very good actress, which was more important than the physical characteristics. Also, I had to have someone who, like the rest of the cast, could speak with a British accent, in order to make this thing work.

I think that I selected a girl who's very . . . she's got a great ass on her, she's attractive in the same way as Brigitte Bardot. And she's a good actress. She even came up with a cockney accent. I really went through the list in London to try to find somebody, and it's very difficult to find a really spectacular girl. Occasionally, you see someone who can't act their way out of a paper bag. In my next picture, *Foxy*, I'm very concerned about who the hell I'll use.

Berkowitz: Do you have any idea yet?

Meyer: Yes. My wife, Edy Williams, will play Foxy. But I still haven't decided whether or not we can really work together. She looks great, and her acting has improved enormously. In the last six months she's been studying hard, with Estelle Harmon's Workshop, and she wants very much to do the film. She has always been associated with Fox or some other major studio, and I met her when I did *Beyond the Valley of the Dolls* for Fox. She played Edy Williams, and she did it very well. Now, she's a great admirer of this picture *Vixen!* She can see it time after time. It's a curious thing, and I think it's the basis of *Vixen!*'s success, because as Edy pointed out, I unwittingly made a film on behalf of women's lib. I didn't realize it. I was way before their time. I portrayed a woman calling all the shots. Edy's seen it fifteen times and just eats it up every time she sees it. She says, "Christ, I'd like to do a sequel to that." But I don't know about that yet.

Berkowitz: Despite, or perhaps because of, *Vixen!* how do serious women's liberationists regard you?

Meyer: I don't give that women's lib thing a hell of a lot of thought. I get a little bit of it around home. I think that most of the people who are concerned with women's lib are not all that attractive, and I wonder if it isn't a crutch or a cop-out, call it whatever you want. I've been on a lot of panels with so-called women's libbers, I've been on TV with Betty Freidan. Frankly, I'm not impressed, and I don't give a goddamn what they think about *Vixen!*, really. It's like Charles Keating of the Citizens for Decent Literature. He'll take umbrage with anything I do. To me that indicates a kind of inherent weakness in the individual. For want of something better to do, they will attack something that's in the public eye, in order to get themselves their own particular kind of notoriety.

Berkowitz: Don't you think that *Vixen!*'s sexual assertiveness is one attractive aspect of women's lib?

Meyer: I think that women looked at it in a vicarious way. I think an awful lot of women would have liked to have been able to act like Vixen a few times in their lives. To have an afternoon in which they could have laid three guys, have an affair with their best girlfriend—that would straighten a lot of people out. But for the most part, these women do not have the specific courage to do something of this nature, and I think they kind of lived the whole thing vicariously. One interesting thing about Vixen is that, unlike *Naked Came the Stranger*, everything she touched was improved. She didn't destroy, she helped. If there was a marriage that was kind of dying on the vine, she injected something into it which made it better.

Berkowitz: So, you basically approve of what the character did?

Meyer: Oh, I think that every man at one time or another would thoroughly enjoy running into an aggressive female like Vixen. I don't deny for a moment that I like aggression on the part of an *attractive* woman, and I don't think I'm alone in that, by any means. As for the lesbian scene, it's there for entertainment, and for no other reason than entertainment. She was like a switch-hitter. You show this girl as being like a utility outfielder: she could cover all the positions.

Berkowitz: A lot of people tend to condemn both onscreen sex and violence, considering them to be similar. How do you feel about that?

Meyer: In all of my films, I've intermixed the violence and the sex. I look upon violence and sex as two highly entertaining facets of a motion picture.

Berkowitz: In bringing these two things to the screen, have you found that they have anything else in common besides their entertainment value?

Meyer: I don't know. I don't get into it that deeply. For example, maybe early in the game, when I did *Lorna*, if I did a rape scene, it struck me that it was terribly erotic and exciting. Today it would not strike me the same way. I would probably treat it in a much more ludicrous fashion, more outrageous. But then again, even then I was doing that, because I always had a woman raped in the most difficult circumstances, in a swamp, or in six feet of water, or out on a sand dune. I guess my jibes at sex have been just exactly that. I've looked upon sex in a kind of humorous, outrageous way.

Berkowitz: Are you tired of using it in your films?

Meyer: No, but I don't want to get into that hardcore area, having to show explicit sex, except that I am excited by *Foxy* as a vehicle to really tax my imagination insofar as trying to portray current sex in a more explicit, outrageous way, and yet at the same time in a clever way.

Berkowitz: Won't *Foxy* also be a kind of psychological thriller?

Meyer: Yes. I don't think you could make another *Vixen!*, nor would I want to make another *Vixen!*, just by changing the spots, or the numbers or the people.

Again, I'm tuned into violence and mystery, and I came up with the idea of the so-called innocent black widow; she doesn't do it herself directly.

What happens is that she's the kind of girl who chooses her mate. Her sexual needs are gigantic, but they do not linger. She uses her male, and then quickly shuns him and goes on to something else. But unfortunately for her love partner, in a very short time after he's had a relationship with her, he dies in some bizarre way.

The film's got some exciting things. I've got a sequence involving two people balling in the desert in a dry arroyo, and standing nearby are two motorcycles with brain buckets hanging on the handlebars, and the two people are attacked by a von Richthofen–type character with the square goggles and the black leather, and this individual is in a helicopter with a twelve-gauge pump gun. So, an interesting chase ensues with two nude people riding across the desert wearing just brain buckets, and the helicopter firing, and of course, getting the guy. They always go to great lengths to avoid shooting Foxy. One thing that I think will be significant about the film, among other things, is that she'll never get a traumatic thing about the killings. She'll never deal with the revelation that, for example, she's made it with so-and-so, and the next morning, she opens her icebox, and he's in it. So, she'll go, "Agh!" but pow, she'll go into some tantalizing thing, making it with a crane operator. So, it will never linger, otherwise the girl would become traumatic, totally and completely wiped out. So, she's just the victim of circumstance. It's got to be a light thing, and I think I'm on the right track with a very exciting premise for a film.

Berkowitz: You're going to try for an R rating, aren't you?

Meyer: I will get one. I must get an R rating, there's no question about it. I now work in a limited partnership arrangement. I have a number of friends who participate and contribute a small amount of money; there are maybe sixteen or seventeen people. And the way things go now with X-rated films, by and large, it's very limiting. And we must have an R-rated film in order to play extensively in drive-ins. So, it's strictly a matter of economics.

Berkowitz: Does it bother you to see that a basically nonviolent film like *Vixen!* will get a stricter rating than all kinds of other, possibly more objectionable films?

Meyer: Well, you know, I take exception to people who are always hacking at violence. Violence is very much a part of our lives. But there's always that minority that will get up and scream and yell, and put down anything except [producer] Ross Hunter.

Berkowitz: So, you condemn nothing?

Meyer: No, not even Ross Hunter. I'm always on TV shows with Ross Hunter. One time he lost his cool and said, "If I had to make pictures like Russ Meyer makes, I'd go back to teaching junior high school." He admitted that on a *Merv Griffin Show*. And then I also think he said, "If I am ever on another television show with Russ Meyer, I think I'm gonna walk right out." I have no axe to grind with the guy.

Berkowitz: Who are some of the directors whose work you admire?

Meyer: Peckinpah, I love Peckinpah. I like Preminger very much, too. It's just unfortunate that Preminger has selected a lot of New York locale films that don't seem to go. These are two of the directors who stand out in my mind. George Roy Hill I like very much. Don Siegel, very good. He's excellent, just sensational. I thought *Dirty Harry* was a totally engrossing film. If I had cut it, I would have tried to make it move a little faster, but I admire him enormously. I think Siegel and Peckinpah and Preminger are my favorites. They're "doer" directors. There's an action thing, a vitality about the three of them.

Berkowitz: Isn't *Vixen!* an example of how you occasionally use your films for the purpose of politicizing?

Meyer: Oh, that was a personal thing. We're all influenced by things. I was influenced by a couple of very good friends who kept trying to get me to join the Communist Party. They took me to a cell meeting once . . . I mean, Jesus Christ, of all people, they should have known that I wouldn't be taken by any of that garbage. Not that I was offended, but I said, "I take it as a personal affront that you thought I had such a small degree of intelligence and dedication." So, I storehouse that stuff.

I am kind of concerned about the Democratic ticket, though. I've always been a dyed-in-the-wool Democrat, but I don't feel terribly sympathetic to what they've put up at home plate. And I'm not in love with Richard Nixon by any stretch of the imagination. But I'm not about to grind any axes while I'm waiting for favorable decisions on *Vixen!* from the Supreme Court, this so-called conservative court. There have been some interesting opinions handed down by a so-called conservative court that indicate no push-button thinking. There have been some very liberal opinions that have been passed down. My attorney, Elmer Gertz, in Chicago, was telling me that he was very enthused about a number of opinions. So, we'll see what happens. There are going to be some important decisions made in the next three or four months, I believe, about whether or not a private citizen in the privacy of his own home can look at anything. Medical photography, pornography, anything, you name it. These are terribly tough decisions that the court has to come up with.

Berkowitz: I'm surprised that you're still worried about that kind of thing.

Meyer: Well, *Vixen!*'s still in the Supreme Court. It's been there for a year. No decision has been reached. Charlie Keating has been pushing this attack on "the King of the Nudies." What has come and gone after *Vixen!* has no bearing. If they can get a judgment against *Vixen!*, literally everything else could fall. Here's a major flaw in our judicial system, letting something go on as long as this. And then, say they came out with an adverse decision. Why, there are major films that have things in them that are more explicit than *Vixen!* So it would be, as they say, a dirty shame.

Berkowitz: You don't really expect an adverse decision, do you?

Meyer: Well, I don't know. We have lost in every court with *Vixen!* We've lost on the city level, the county level, and the state level, in Ohio.

Berkowitz: In your films, you've presented characters who were in the vanguard of the new morality, yet your own personal life seems to be fairly conservative, despite it all. You're married and you spend a lot of time taking care of your elderly mother. How do you reconcile that apparent contradiction?

Meyer: Well, my wife thinks I'm promiscuous, but I can't convince her that I am following the straight and narrow. I have a great deal of feeling for my mother, because I think she was probably the best friend that I ever had. She was strong and long on momism and all that, but I was strong enough to circumvent that. From the moral standpoint, I would probably take exception to any friend's *wife* who might stray from the straight and narrow, and at the same time, I would take exception to *his* small or slight deviation. So, I suppose in that instance I am kind of a prude, and a lot of that has to reflect back on my upbringing. Yet there's that kind of paradox with the films I've made, wherein I have glorified the swinger, as in *Vixen!*—the deceit, which was kind of bland and barefaced. The perfect fool, the husband, is totally believing, and totally giving, and totally good, but he's a cuckold. It's a strange thing, and I suppose my imagination has a lot to do with the whole thing.

Berkowitz: So, you see your films as being only fantasies?

Meyer: That's exactly right. I can fantasize and I think that's what the public wants to see, an hour and a half of escapism, total fantasy. I think that's what I have in *Blacksnake!* I've taken a very serious subject—intimidation of the human race, cruelty, and outrageousness—and I've treated it in a tongue-in-cheek manner. The sum total of the film will tell us whether it's going to be a successful film or not. I don't know. I'm so close to it at this point, it's difficult for me to say.

Berkowitz: When will *Blacksnake!* be released?

Meyer: We'll release it around Christmastime. I was just talking to the Chicago distributor, so we'll probably release it there. Uniquely this time, I have four subdistributors who are investors in the picture; each one of them put in $15,000. I've shown them clips, and it's been very exciting for me because they've all responded in a very positive way. I'm spending an enormously long period of time cutting this, and I want to get away from the editing because it can be a real time-consuming thing. I've got to spend more time in story development and casting, things of that nature. But I know that if I do not cut it myself, it will not have the same moxie that all the other Russ Meyer films have. And I'm just blessed by the fact that my films play and play and play, they just keep going. And I've got to make that same kind of film. Unfortunately, *Seven Minutes* was not that film.

Berkowitz: Is there any chance that your next film, *Foxy*, will fall through?

Meyer: A very few projects that I've had have fallen through. Every time I depend on somebody else, it's not so sure, but if I depend upon myself, it's less unsure. My associate and I had two projects that did not materialize, and in each instance, those projects were dependent upon someone else raising the money. And it was just fortunate that we prepared the third property, *Blacksnake!* We had obtained the money, just like I have obtained the money for *Foxy*, so I will make the picture. I will make it in January, no question about it. I will also do a film called *Beyond Beyond*—it's a two-picture package. It will be of the *Beyond the Valley of the Dolls* genre. It will be no sequel, but it will be a similar picture. I'm going to use as my central theme a successful rock 'n' roll singer and an older advisor. And this thirtyish young man will have sampled all the fruits of life, and become a kind of recluse. But every now and then he will come out of his shell to throw an exciting party. But there's a vicious, evil basis for this whole thing. I just think it's a great vehicle to show the drug scene in a pleasant, kind of entertaining light, and sex in a pleasant, entertaining light, and violence in an unpleasant but very entertaining light, climaxed by maybe a little *Doctor Phibes* at the end. And you can guess who our man is. Is it Howard Hughes when he was twenty-two, or is it Elvis Presley at thirty-one? Who can say? But the basis is there, and I think the audience will associate with me and what I've done before. I think it's the basis for a very good film.

Pensées of a Porno Prince

Scott Eyman / 1976

From *Take One*, August 1976. Reprinted courtesy of Scott Eyman.

During the war, MGM—and, I suppose, the other studios—entered into a kind of unholy alliance with the military and, in order to defer their personnel for six more months, said they'd use them to teach amateur filmmakers.

"We'll teach them technique and we'll enroll them at Kodak and teach them theory."

It was all a lot of crap; we didn't learn a thing. We did learn how to thread a studio camera, which none of us would ever see again. We each shot a hundred feet of film, and they would judge us on our aggressiveness. The final determination as to what kind of rating you would get was based on how close you came to what was called a "printing light." Absolutely perfect exposure was twenty-four, and those that came closest to that got the highest rating. I came second closest, so I got a staff sergeant's rating. I was nineteen years old and no more deserved that than flies.

After World War II, I did a lot of still photography and industrial 16mm stuff, mostly titty-boom nudies. Then I did some motion picture coverage, then some architectural stuff, all of which has been beneficial.

I worked on *Giant.* I was supposed to get a picture for the Hearst supplement of the time, *The American Weekly,* I believe, of [Elizabeth] Taylor and [Rock] Hudson on their horses in front of an enormous herd of cattle. I had known [the director] George Stevens during the war, so there was a rapport there, which certainly didn't hurt. The one cover I had on *Life* was also shot during *Giant.*

Stevens was a brilliant director and a fascinating guy. On some scenes he would run three cameras; he had a technique of taking his hat off and putting it over the lens of any of the cameras that would shoot something he didn't like. He wouldn't have it stop, but he'd see things he would know he didn't want and make an instant editorial decision.

Jimmy Dean and I became quite friendly; Robert Altman's film *The James Dean Story* used a lot of the stills I shot during *Giant*. Dean was a curious guy, very much a loner. I remember I had a very heavy tripod that I was using with a view camera to get the picture for the Hearst paper. Jimmy had a Bolex and would go out on Sundays to shoot pictures of these wild burros they had out there. He asked me—quietly—if he could borrow my tripod and I said yes. So, he would always cooperate with me, but was very hostile to everybody else.

I remember the scene where he paces off the ground around his oil well. There must have been fifteen stillmen hovering around, as well as the regular crew, and you could just see his concentration flagging. Finally, he blew up and started yelling, "No pictures! No pictures!"—and then he spotted me—"Except for him."

When I was shooting the regular stills on *Giant*, I was using a Hasselblad, which was a very noisy camera. One day I let it go right in the middle of an intimate dialogue scene and there was this enormous "Clank!" Stevens turned around, looked at me, and immediately everything stopped, waiting for the explosion. All he said to me, very sweetly, was, "Russ, please watch it with that thing." Now, he could have laid me out and he would have been perfectly justified in doing so, but he didn't. And then afterwards, when he saw the cover on *Life*, he sent me a note saying the whole thing was worth it. Gestures like that are the mark of a man, you know? In George's case, his graciousness was the measure of his greatness.

A few years later I made *The Immoral Mr. Teas*. It cost me $24,000, and I had a ball. Time magazine said, "*The Immoral Mr. Teas* opened the floodgates of permissiveness as we know it in these United States." Right out of *The March of Time*.

I take great pride in the fact that I've made a contribution to cinema. Trite as *Mr. Teas* was, it changed things around. You've got to put that film in a context. When *Mr. Teas* was made, foreign films were very big and they all had scenes of people hopping into bed, and the camera panning to the sky or crashing waves, and then the next morning Lollobrigida or Loren is either bouncing around happily because she's been well-laid, or morbid and depressed because the guy didn't know what he was doing. Then they'd wait for the big, brutal escaped convict to come and have them. Lousy, unfunny films. I did that plot in *Lorna*, except I had them screwing in two feet of water in the middle of a swamp. I love to put sex in outrageous locations. Up a tree, in a canoe, behind a waterfall . . . screwing under tremendous odds strikes me as both erotic and funny.

Up through *Beyond the Valley of the Dolls*, all my films made money. And then came *The Seven Minutes*.

I thought *The Seven Minutes* would be an overwhelming success, just as Dick Zanuck and the rest of them [did]. When they saw the rough cut, they were all salivating. I now know what happened. I really do. The worst thing I could have done was to have gone out and sold the picture with my old lady (Edy Williams). My fans expected a certain kind of picture, something wild and bizarre like *Beyond the Valley of the Dolls*. I should have sent out *The Seven Minutes* with somebody dignified like [cast member] Yvonne De Carlo, and used a more sedate approach. I turned off the audience for the picture, and my usual audience didn't go. The first night was packed, the second night half full and the third night there were seven people in the audience.

Fox was terrified of getting another X rating, so I made it an R, which was a mistake. There were some good things in it, but a lot of garbage, exposition that should have been excised. A lot of it was in the writing; I should have gotten Roger Ebert, who did *Beyond the Valley of the Dolls*. Roger laughs at the same things I do. He's into big tits, too.

After the Fox films I was awash in my own vomit. A number of things happened: the Supreme Court's 5–4 decision, an uptight situation in my own marriage, my continued fat head, a lot of things. Just after *The Seven Minutes* was released, Zanuck got booted out and went over to Warners; I went with him. Then Zanuck got into a power struggle with John Calley. He and Calley were the two vice-presidents under Ted Ashley. But then *Klute* came along, which was Calley's picture, so they decided to kick Zanuck out again. As part of his stable, I was asked to leave; the way they told me was to paint out my name on my office door. Zanuck went over to Universal, where he's been sticking it to them ever since. I thought about going with him, but I don't think I'd fit in over there. Universal is PG at the worst, you know?

Anyway, after that I decided to make *Blacksnake!* on my own. It was a period picture that I thought would have an appeal to Blacks, an interesting premise, shoot it in Panavision. . . . Right down the tubes. Lost a lot of my own money, some friends' money, and further alienated my old lady because I wouldn't put her in the film. We're divorced now.

Then I decided to do *Supervixens*, which is, thankfully, doing very well.

I photographed, wrote, edited, and directed *Supervixens* because I wanted total control. I wanted to do the umbilical thing again, to see if I could still cut it at age fifty-three. I mean, since this is all my money, I might as well take it all the way. Dubbing alone cost me $28,000 and lab costs are very heavy. Work prints, opticals, titles, negative processing adds up to $75,000. I pay my people well, order fifty prints, and the whole thing adds up to $400,000. That's a lot of money.

Next time, though, I'm going to simplify it. I'm going to shoot it silent and dub in all the lines. It's silly to lug this enormous Mitchell camera up a mountain every day and not be able to use any of the direct sound because the actors have to step on gravel. I'm going to get a couple Arriflexes and strip it down to the essentials.

It's going to be a good movie; six people who are all fucking each other without any of them being aware of each other's existence. Four women, two men. Strictly heterosexual, except I'm going to have a Black chick make it with a white dildo. She's a truck driver, so nobody'll mind. I'm going to call it *Russ Meyer's Up!* It's all marvelously excessive. I'm going to get into what I'm doing very heavily. I'm going to do the ultimate sexual parodies, the ultimate violence parodies. I enjoy obsessive grossness.

I think I'm entering upon my richest period. I've overcome that entire hard-core thing. *Supervixens* proves that. When hardcore was at its peak, I was making R-rated tragedies, two of them. Losers.

Hardcore porno—and I don't put it down—is not the way to go for anybody that wishes to make pictures that can play legitimate theaters and enjoy a really big profit. People who go to a hardcore go to a specific kind of theater. People who go to see my movies go to the same theaters where they'll see *Tommy* or *Funny Lady*. I'm in direct competition with the majors.

You see, in order to attract a wide audience, you have to do something that's palatable to a female. And a woman, in her most vulnerable state, is not very attractive for a woman to look at.

My old lady and I went to see *Deep Throat* and it fucked her up for a week. She wouldn't go down on me anymore, and she's a sex freak, for God's sake. I don't think it was the act itself, but the fact that she saw herself in a very secondary position. Almost in mute supplication, servicing the male. And pictured in a way that's most unflattering. Of course, they say that the picture was great therapy and everybody's now out cocksucking like mad, but I question that.

I don't get anywhere near as much flack from the women's lib thing as I'd like. They always expect some shambling slob in a pool of drool. Whenever I do get involved with any feminist groups, they're always very surprised that I can cope with anything they can throw at me. The trouble with those confrontations is that they're so contrived and the people are so angry. Easy pickings.

A few weeks ago I was showing *Supervixens* in Austin, and one girl went into a long diatribe about my filthy, sexist propaganda, my fetish about big breasts, the whole list. I asked her to step out of the shadows, which she did, and then I said, "You're much more attractive than I thought you'd be." Well, she lost all control, yelled that I ought to have a stick of dynamite shoved up *my* ass [referring to a scene in the film], and stormed out, which is exactly what I figured she'd do. No sense of humor. Those female liberationists are mostly a pretty linty bunch, like they slept in their sweaters.

I personally will never make a hardcore picture. That would be the end of the line, just what people have expected me to do. I know Radley Metzger, for reasons of his own, is now doing them, and Metzger made the most erotic films

I've ever seen. But he made *Little Mother* and *Score*, which was very heavily into bisexuality, and they both bombed. Maybe he decided to make some money again, I don't know. But it's not for me.

Oh, maybe when I'm ready for my swan song I might do something with pigs, goats, elephants, and pole-line construction men throwing themselves off of Coit Tower and impacting on a mattress, but it would take a series of really massive failures to push me that far. It would be very sad. Perhaps I would open a bar-restaurant near the mountains so I could get some fishing done. I can't conceive of myself ever quitting, though. More than anything else, I would like audiences to find humor in what I do. I'm into the female form and I think my audiences are, too, but I think of myself as basically a humorist, and I think there's a large new audience for my kind of film. I'm a great admirer of Mel Brooks, for instance. I didn't think *Blazing Saddles* was worth shit, but *Young Frankenstein* was wonderful—genre parody as well as it's ever been done.

Besides, there's a great security in knowing that, if you make a film for three or four hundred thousand, you can't help but make out unless you're a total fool. Maybe I won't make eight million bucks anymore, but I'll make enough to keep my hand in, to stay in the game. And staying in the game's very important, you know?

Russ Meyer Thinks Big

R. Allen Leider / 1976

From *Porno Movie Girls*, no. 1, 1976. Credit to the late R. Allen Leider.

He's the legendary creator of *Lorna*, *Vixen!* and now *Supervixens*; he's the courageous director who singlehandedly invented the slick, soft-core cinema; he's the man whose box office bonanzas feature the bustiest beauties in all of America!

Russ Meyer has the distinction of being the pioneer of American blue films. He didn't plan it that way. It just happened. It happened to a guy from Oakland, California, whose modest ambition was to be happy in his chosen field. Now, that "guy from Oakland" is one of the top-rated photographers, cameramen, and directors in the film business, both major and independent productions. On a recent trip to New York to promote his latest erotic effort, *Supervixens*, with his newest discovery, Shari Eubank, freelance writer R. Allen Leider made a point of getting a long chat with this pioneer of the erotic cinema . . . Mr. Russ Meyer.

R. Allen Leider: When did you first decide you wanted to make films as a career?

Russ Meyer: I didn't do it as a boy, certainly. I was fascinated by home movies. I badgered my mother until she got me an 8mm Univex camera outfit, and I shot things like fishing trips and pets and local sports events . . . not even scripted things. My mother was great. She saw how much it meant to me, and pawned her engagement ring so I could get enough film to keep happy for a while.

Leider: Was yours a large family?

Meyer: Just my mother, my sister, and myself. My stepfather was in the hospital a lot.

Leider: I take it money was tight.

Meyer: That's putting it mildly. I learned how to squeeze a dollar. I still do. That's one of the secrets of films . . . bringing them in under budget.

Leider: Did you get any formal training in filmmaking . . . college courses?

Meyer: No, I was just interested in film as a hobby, then. I went to college for a degree in chemistry, oddly enough, but I didn't have the funds to continue, and I had to leave after only six months at junior college . . . a two-year one.

Leider: When you made your home films, did you plan them?

Meyer: No, not really. I was more into technique . . . making the film, not writing it or directing people.

Leider: Did you go to the movies and watch the great directors of the day, and try to learn from their styles?

Meyer: Oh, nobody. Hell, I can't even remember what was playing back then. I wasn't into filmmakers at all. I was not interested with theory or the dramatic aspects. I was into film as a medium . . . technically.

Leider: How old were you at that time?

Meyer: When I started to get into film, about sixteen. I got influenced in my later years by some of the big film directors, but not back then.

Leider: How did you survive after the college career went bankrupt?

Meyer: I took the only thing open to me—a government job as a messenger boy for the Corps of Engineers. I took a civil service exam for it. That lasted until I became an accounting clerk. I worked my way "up the ladder." Then the war came along.

Leider: Did the experience you had as an accountant help you when you budgeted your films?

Meyer: Not at all. It's a different animal . . . budgeting films.

Leider: But the army did help?

Meyer: Definitely. I saw an ad in the paper at the accounting office for young men interested in film to sign up for a hitch in the army, and get a Hollywood studio training course. Then they put us in the army as combat photographers. My heart jumped. Here was a chance to train in Hollywood at something I had always been interested in. It certainly beat accounting. So, at age eighteen, I signed up for the course and the Signal Corps.

Leider: Was the course everything it promised?

Meyer: Yes and no. It was very instructive. The whole idea was a joint effort by MGM studios and Eastman Kodak. It served as a gimmick to get deferments for their own cameramen, who cranked out those musicals each month, as instructors for the kids who went overseas. That was the prime reason behind the course. We did get good instruction. The bad part was that when the war was over, the studio didn't hire a single one of us "kids." We'll get to that later.

Leider: Your instructor was something of a legend in his own day, wasn't he?

Meyer: Yes. Art Lloyd . . . bless him. He directed the *Our Gang* comedies. I also had lessons from [cinematographer] Joe Ruttenberg, who shot *Mrs. Miniver*. They liked me because I was "aggressive" and finished what I started. I always said that what I lack in the talent department, I make up for with determination.

Leider: Was the ad in the paper your lucky break?

Meyer: Lucky break? Well, I was in the right place at the right time.

Leider: Did you find that in your experiences in Hollywood . . . especially with the major studios and name stars, that their success was also a case of being in the right place at the right time?

Meyer: I think you make your breaks. True, the situation must be there for you to take advantage of . . . but largely *you* do it . . . it isn't given to you. It isn't simply being at a place at a time. For example, in the war, I felt like Tom Swift in his Electric Underwear . . . very dedicated to his job. It was a great and wondrous game. It was exciting. I've never done anything in my life, to this day, that compares to the things I did and experienced in the service. It's what you make of the situation. Other guys did practically nothing if they didn't have to.

Leider: What sort of combat footage did you take?

Meyer: Oh, stuff for training films, newsreels . . . propaganda films.

Leider: What was wondrous about that?

Meyer: The thrill of sticking your neck out. Americans have become soft in this respect; no one takes a chance anymore. We used to go out into the thick of the battle, creeping and crawling up somewhere, all alone, no supporting people. You didn't have to be there. You could have faked it, and many people did. But doing this gave a sense of real achievement. No one knew about it. There were no awards. Maybe a "thanks for the good work" from one of the officers. You could get together with your unit—in my case, one or two other guys—and chat about what we did. "Gee, Chuck, that was fun! We coulda got killed, but we didn't, did we? We got out with all the film, and they liked it." It was just great!

Leider: Why didn't you stay in that line of work after the war? Newsreels or TV film or something?

Meyer: There were no jobs. The newsreels were all union; so were the studios, as I was to find out. You had to be born into it. Father and son. That's been the problem all along. There's no chance for an outsider, no matter how good his stuff.

Leider: So, after the service there was nowhere to go. What about the great MGM studio that trained you?

Meyer: Are you kidding? It was the same thing. The unions. Their guys were deferred as teachers . . . remember? They worked, their sons got in. I was outside, Now, they're running into trouble with that, because the government is taking a dim view of such practices. One cameraman sued the union to get in, and succeeded. It's the all-powerful IATSE, the union.

Leider: Well, having had a taste of the system in Hollywood, where did you go from there?

Meyer: I got a job from a friend of mine. Well, I went to San Francisco. I then approached an industrial filmmaker who said, "Maybe." Then he said, "No." I took my old accounting job back because the government is very good about giving veterans their work back. Suddenly, one day the industrial guy called up and told me he needed me. I was thrilled. I *hated* that old accounting job. So, I went to work for him for five years, making industrial films.

Leider: You really liked the work?

Meyer: I could have kissed his ass. I think it was my second favorite assignment.

Leider: All this has been exceptionally interesting, Russ, but how did it all lead you to girlie films, the busts, and the big return to Hollywood?

Meyer: I got into shooting pictures for girlie magazines . . . in the early days of *Playboy* . . . mid-fifties . . . when I needed more money. A friend of mine named Donald Ornitz, who was a photog with me in the war, steered me into it. So, I started shooting sexy girls for extra money.

Leider: Did you like the idea, other than working with the girls?

Meyer: Other than. It was all one thing. Not a lot of things. I was happy. It, too, was a wondrous business. I made a *lot* of money at it.

Leider: When you started with the girlie magazines, how did you get models to pose nude? Were there agents, or what? This was in the beginning, when there weren't models out hunting for nude work.

Meyer: Well, other photographers would steer them to me and vice versa. Then, when I found attractive girls in places, I would approach them with the idea of posing for me.

Leider: How?

Meyer: The approach? I'd stop a woman in the street sometimes, and I'd flatter her, tell her how beautiful she was . . . that I was a photographer and that she was just the type I was looking for. I'd tell her that I was prepared to pay her a realistic amount of money to pose, and so forth. It's all a matter of how you present yourself. You have to move quick, though, so that she's not turned off. If you come off as a creep, forget it!

Leider: Is that where most girlie photographers fail?

Meyer: Yes. The amateurs. They practically broadcast that they want to get into the girl's shorts and blow the whole thing . . . no pun intended.

Leider: How many centerfolds did you do for *Playboy*?

Meyer: Six . . . a record, of sorts.

Leider: At the time there were no X-rated or sex films like we have today. What was there?

Meyer: Mostly nudist films—health and sunbathing. It was all people playing volleyball and games, or swimming or exercising. And there was always this terrible sonorous narrator who went on and on and on.

Leider: And you decided to do something about it. How did that idea take form?

Meyer: I knew this man, Pete DeCenzie, who ran a top-notch burlesque house called El Rey in Oakland. I had used his girls in the girlie magazines, and I had an idea to film an entire burlesque show, which I did. It was called *The French Peep Show*, and was very successful. In fact, it shocked people even though it was just look . . . no sex or action of any sort. DeCenzie was, incidentally, responsible for the success of Lili St. Cyr and Tempest Storm. After *The French Peep Show*, he was after me to do another film. I knew that America was into voyeurism—it was very big—the sexual awaking was just beginning. I told DeCenzie that I wanted to make a film like *I* wanted to . . . no strippers, no nudists . . . a story! He trusted me, and anted up half the budget, and the result was *The Immoral Mr. Teas.*

Leider: That was a classic, of sorts.

Meyer: It's still around. It's just a dirty old man looking at girls, but it's believ-- able even without any sexual action. In fact, it's rated R today, but when it was released back then, we got busted every time we opened it.

Leider: How much did *Mr. Teas* cost?

Meyer: We shot it, with my signal corps buddy, Bill Teas in the lead, for $24,000 in four days. It's now in the Museum of Modern Art's archives, and has become a classic, without hardcore. I think we've grossed millions on it.

Leider: The big thing *Mr. Teas* did was open the gates of permissiveness. How many copiers of your style have there been?

Meyer: I've lost track. I don't even care.

Leider: How was *Mr. Teas* accepted?

Meyer: It was considered to be so frank and so nude and so shocking, that no distributor would handle it. It was what they call a jeopardy film. No one wanted to handle it. It was busted everywhere. There was no contact, no attempt at lovemaking, no sex . . . just a bearded delivery boy who was seeing clothed women as if they were naked . . . everyone's fantasy.

Leider: Do you put your own fantasies into your films?

Meyer: Always!

Leider: Why so many busts, though, and why the big deal over them?

Meyer: You may have been young then, but this was the *first* one of its kind. No one had ever thought of filming a man leching at women before. There was no attempt made to present the women in any phony light as sunbathers. These were chesty, buxom, hefty "Russ Meyer" women, like Al Capp's girls. The character Teas goes to a psychiatrist because he thinks he's sick . . . and a few prosecutors thought I was, too.

Leider: You made a number of films after *Mr. Teas* with the same formula. In fact, eight of them. Didn't the films get monotonous?

Meyer: No. The technique was getting better . . . being perfected. The market was so big then that there could not be any saturation point.

Leider: Then came *Lorna*.

Meyer: Yes, it was a big step forward because it had a comprehensive script. In essence, it was a loose morality play of a kind . . . based on the biblical story of Lot. I think it had a poor man's Erskine Caldwell quality about it. I used a *very* voluptuous girl. It was a simple story: a knockout wife married to the novice husband. He worked in a salt mine all day. She bathes in a stream, very pastoral, and meets a convict on the lam who takes her in the grass. He rips her blouse off, then her shorts, and jumps on her with his soggy clothes.

[Editor's note: the original article in the magazine was supposed to jump to another page but, likely due to a technical problem at the time, there was no other page. The piece just stopped here.]

Russ Meyer

Nat Segaloff / 1979

This is the full transcript of an interview conducted on May 15, 1979, a portion of which was broadcast on WEEI-AM, Boston. Printed courtesy of Nat Segaloff.

Nat Segaloff: I think we should make a distinction, right away, between the porno pictures and your nudie cuties. If the MPAA had applied a rating to your film [*Beneath the Valley of the Ultra-Vixens*], what do you think it would get?

Russ Meyer: It would have an X, no question about it. They base it upon if you're dealing with matters sexual, whether it's explicit or Olympian—as I choose mine to be called. It's the degree or the amount—that would be the best way of putting it. There's a lot *of* it, a lot of funning in the picture.

NS: But there's nothing of what you would call sexual activity. Well, I've gotta split hairs at this point . . . nothing explicit, but certainly everything is there. You keep a very good thumb on the taste button, if you'll pardon the expression.

RM: It's fantasy. Everything I do is an extension of my own fantasies.

NS: But you began the whole thing twenty years ago. You personally liberated the motion pictures in this country with *The Immoral Mr. Teas*, and now you're carrying it even farther, but in a fun way. I don't think that's been done since Mae West . . . really having fun with sexual matter. Do you have to think about it, or does it just happen?

RM: Well, it's longer than twenty years ago. I started this thing, I think, in 1958. So, twenty-one years. Why split hairs? I started it because I was into shooting pictures for magazines like *Playboy*, when they first started, and I had a very pretty wife—Eve Meyer—who was the number six Playmate. And I was also gainfully employed as an industrial filmmaker for oil companies and paper companies, and so forth. So, I suppose that's why a lot of my films bear the indelible stamp of an industrial-type approach to sexual behavior.

NS: Well, mechanical, maybe . . .

RM: It's a style. You know, narration and voiceover and things of that nature.

NS: But what you've got in your films is some incredible pyrotechnics. I'm thinking specifically of *Beyond the Valley of the Dolls*. There's an enormous number of set-ups, an incredible electricity of the editing. Now, this is a film-making style that very few directors would *dare* to use. And you tell a story and get people aroused at the same time.

RM: Well, I've refined the so-called art, almost to the nth degree with *Beneath the Valley of the Ultra-Vixens*. It has a rhythm that I've developed, I suppose. I've had musicians say to me that it's almost musical. That style of editing, although I like it personally, I wouldn't make a film any other way. But it evolved out of working with very abundant young ladies that didn't have a great deal of thesping ability, in the old days. So by cutting them very short and tight, and always cutting away to the man—the male actor generally was a very good journeyman actor—I was able to make them look a lot more professional than they really were. But now I find that people who do have some ability—that have been on television or variety shows or quiz games or whatever it is—they have that presence that at least comes through. And I certainly wouldn't select a girl unless she was really cantilevered. There's a lot of *girl* actresses around that just don't have the qualifications to appear in a Russ Meyer movie. So, I do pick women essentially for their physical overhang, so to speak.

NS: So, the measurements are the first things you look for on a woman's résumé or picture.

RM: Right. The uppermost dimension. The bosom. I am very much into bosomania, both on and off the set.

NS: Do you think it's safe to use the words tits and ass when we talk about this kind of film?

RM: Oh. I would prefer that. I was just being a little bit reserved here. Yeah . . . big bosoms, square jaws, tits and ass. But essentially tits, more so than anything else. I find young ladies, too, don't find that objectionable anymore. It was at one time kind of course, but I know my girlfriend, Kitten Natividad, who happens to be the lead in this film, is very proud of her big tits.

NS: She's 43E, according to the handout?

RM: That's right. She's like a 7 5/8, like a hat size.

NS: So, obviously you've gotten past the point of being reserved in discussing sizes and such things.

RM: Oh, generally when I'm dealing with print media—newspapers and so forth—we go way off even further than that. We discuss our own personal lifestyle, and the continuity of sex and how often and how much fun we have. There are a lot of residuals with what I do in my work. I meet great-looking women, and I'm able to make a great deal of money, and I have a lot of fun, going out like this, selling my wares, so to speak.

NS: It's the American male sexual fantasy, and you're living it out. But is it something which you consciously think of as being what every red-blooded American man wants, or just something Russ Meyer wants?

RM: I think the reason that my films have a really good direction is that I'm dealing essentially with my own fantasies. But I also have the confidence, having made some twenty-two films, that there's a lot of other red-blooded types that think very much the same way I do. So, I think whatever I like, there's gonna be a lot of people out there liking very much the same thing. We shouldn't ignore the women; more and more women are coming to my films, because my films do really put the woman in the position of [being] very much in command. They're the ones, like, for example in *Beneath the Valley of the Ultra-Vixens*, the women are all the bosses. They're the ones that run the junkyard, there's one who runs the radio station, one young lady is really calling the shots to correct her old man's deficiencies. I can't see where any Equal Rights Amendment person would take umbrage with my films. If anything, I'm championing their cause.

NS: That's true. I guess, except for the headline issue, you've got women in the man's position, really. That certainly is the other side of it.

RM: They're all bigger than life. And they're the ones that call the shots: this is the way I want it; you're my willing tool; do what you have to do for me; let's get on with it, and then go about our business, or do something else, or find someone else to grapple with.

NS: There's a lot of humor in your films, too, and I've been told by other erotic filmmakers that the humor gets in the way of arousing the audience. I think you manage to fix that.

RM: If my films would generate more togetherness, I think that would be the greatest justification for making my kind of film. I find with this new picture that more people, particularly young couples, are very complimentary about the gymnastics that I portray on the screen. I think humor also makes sex a lot more comfortable for people that haven't been exposed to what would appear to be on the screen—explicit sex. My films look very much like that the people are having a real good time; it also looks, too, to a degree, that they might be qualifying for the Olympics.

NS: I hope I don't destroy the picture by saying you've made a clean sex picture.

RM: No, I think you're saying it just right. It's not the kind of thing with people sneaking and skulking in and out of the theaters, because we play the mainstream. I think I've helped that image, as far as sex films are concerned, sex-oriented films. I call *my* films really raucous comedies. I think that's a lot more appropriate. And as I pointed out, more and more women are being intrigued into the theater because they find a certain amusement. They don't find that these women are competitive with their own particular configuration.

NS: Have you found that women, by and large, who haven't seen your films, will be opposing them or picketing or anything along these lines?

RM: Not nearly enough. I wish they would come out in force and picket against the film [*laughs*]. Anything at all that we can do to sell a ticket, attract some notoriety.

NS: The women in your films run a very thin boundary line between being exploited and being actresses.

RM: Well, they're being exploited for a very good reason. And it is a two-way street. Nearly all the women that appear in my films are professional dancers. Very simply put, they are strippers. But premier strippers, I choose to call them. Women that make $2,000 to $3,000 a week. They work in Vegas. Most of the girls I use in my films are drawn from the ranks of what I call premier strippers. They are young ladies that work in Las Vegas in good clubs. Certainly, in the case of Ann Marie—she works throughout the Midwest, and from what I understand from her manager, she can make as much as $8,000 a week. Well, it is to her advantage to be in the film, it is to her advantage to be exploited. She can say, "I am starring in Russ Meyer's *Beneath the Valley of the Ultra-Vixens*. And that probably would ensure even a better booking than she would normally get.

I have made some twenty-two films, and they've all, I think, progressed pretty much along the way. The new one is, I think, as far as the girls are concerned, I have really gone off the scale. I do not know where I will *find* girls with bigger bosoms than I found this time. I have searched a great deal of time for *this* casting job, and it was not a simple one. I usually find girls based on recommendations, meaning girls that have worked for me on other films, and that is most helpful.

NS: They are supernatural, in this case. Does America have a gazing fixation?

RM: I think the whole world has a bosom fixation, very definitely. They may say that French women are not really very busty. But I know, having traveled extensively, and usually on the arm of some very cantilevered young lady, that wherever you go—Rome or Paris—when she's walking down the street, in a tight sweater, there's a lot of hooting and yelling. And that would indicate that tastes are not too much different anyplace you go.

NS: What strikes you first when you get a film project together? Is it story or having women you can show off or attitude . . . what?

RM: I have to have a story idea. I'm the one that usually comes up with the original idea. As a rule, it comes to me at a specific time. It's not the product of a lot of thinking and searching. I get an idea *handle*—an angle to base the picture on, and then I hire a screenwriter to work with me. Generally, it's been Roger Ebert, a newspaper critic from Chicago. We're kind of a poor man's Rodgers and Hammerstein [*laughs*]. We do words and music. But essentially the idea has to come from me; I work on the auteur principle. It's a fancy expression for being a jack of all trades. I like to be the one who calls the shots just about every place, whether it be casting or exposure or the choice of a lens or how to edit or cut a scene. It's my baby, and to make it really work, it has to be that way all the way through.

NS: Is there a temptation when you're on location to screw around with the actresses while everybody's making a movie, or is that just inefficient?

RM: This time I had a very heavy affair, and continue to do so, with Kitten Natividad. We would repair to the convenience of a bedroom during the course of the day, usually at the lunch hour. We'd hurriedly eat lunch and then go in there and have a lot of horizontal activity together. And that helped me a lot in the film. Normally, I would be concerned about bleeding off the vital juices. But if anything, I think we invented new ways to portray the most pleasurable thing there is in the world, and contributed to the variety in the film. Because this is the first film I've made in which I dumped all violence. I've always been into portraying outrageous violence, but I've found, of late, more and more criticisms of this, so naturally I had to fill up the gap with more horizontal fun. That's the reason for it. I suppose one has to, in his own mind, seek a reason for anything we do. So, I'll just say that was my reason. Aside from the fact that the girl couldn't see her feet when she looked down, which is a particular turn-on for me. And she's wasp-waisted, and a girl who's been married three times and has incredible experience in the art of love. And it's not bad for a guy in his autumn years to have someone that's twenty-seven years of age that's abundant and outrageous and inventive, exciting, and a turn-on. Why not?

NS: How do you get people to not know there's a camera and a camera crew there?

RM: Well, there doesn't seem to be a problem. The question never comes up. They know, first of all, we're going to make a film, and by and large they're not supposed to look at the camera at any time. Except in the case of the narrator, we had this man from Smalltown, USA; it's kind of a take-off on *Our Town*. It was one of the most difficult things for this actor. I've used him in a lot of films—he's Stuart Lancaster, who is an heir to the Ringling circus fortune. Someday, before too much longer, he'll end up with 49 percent of the circus. He's worked with me in six films. He was the dirty old man in *Faster, Pussycat! Kill! Kill!* I used him in *The Seven Minutes* at Fox. He played a psychologist. [In *Beneath the Valley*] he worked as the cuckolded farmer that was married to the Austrian SuperSoul, portrayed by Uschi Digard. One of the most difficult things that *he* encountered was to have to look directly in the lens, which is the very thing he was trained *not* to do. Particularly, when we're shooting out of doors, we use a salmon-colored filter that converts daylight to a tungsten value, meaning that all color films are essentially produced for shooting indoors—professional films. So, when you go outside, you reduce the speed of the film by adding this filter [an 85 filter], which corrects it to the proper color balance. Well, when you look into the camera, you can see your image there, like in a mirror. And an actor tends to be fascinated with his own appearance. It took him three or four days to really get into this whole thing of being able to look directly into the camera without being flustered.

NS: What sort of a shooting schedule did you have for *Beneath the Valley of the Ultra-Vixens*?

RM: I think principal photography and pickup photography was about fourteen weeks. The long time that I spent on the film revolves around cutting. I spent seven months editing this film. Then the sound effects took another four months. So postproduction took more time than anything else.

NS: That's something else. The sound effects, especially in the first couple of reels of the picture are bizarre, as if you've got your ear right up there against everybody. Was that just done for fun? I had trouble figuring that out because it was effective in a bizarre way.

RM: Let's break down some of those things. A lot of activity does take place on beds, and I've always found that putting in what we call a wrought iron bed [works well], because it has all sorts of accoutrements—like pipes, and so forth, that one can hang onto. I searched for some time to find a real obscene spring noise, and I found it in an old '58 GMC pickup, with that RANK RANK kind of noise. And the sound effects did continue. For example, when the superabundant Junkyard Sal would take a deep breath—she's wearing overalls because she's running a junkyard—I used the sound of a rusty nail being pulled out of a piece of Douglas fir, and got a great kind of raucous noise. Also, every door that opened—whether it was the casket that Martin Bormann got into and became the voyeur of the superabundant Ann Marie—anytime anything opened, there was a horrendous squeak—whether it was a car door or a house door or a casket lid. Whatever it was, there was a big squeak. So, I've tried to make, in a cartoon sense, everything very overdone. I think the sum total of all that contributed to the effect that I was seeking.

NS: When you go into production, do you storyboard, or do the normal, everyday thing—shoot in masters and then break it down?

RM: No, I never have any really long shots, because you know that with the frenetic pace with my filming, generally there's no room for a master. I'll establish a scene occasionally, but as a rule, I'll open a sequence with an insert and then pull back. I just run very short scenes, because I want as much variety and as many angles. Otherwise, I think it might tend to be—if you lay on a scene too long—kind of tedious.

NS: You also seem to shoot nonsync sound, except for obvious dialogue scenes. You must have an awful lot of freedom if that is, in fact, what you do.

RM: We shoot a cue track all the time. I use a very portable camera called an Arriflex BL. This isn't unique. Every major film is done much the same way.

Most of the sound one records—even dialogue—is stuff that you loop later. You replace the voice, because there are extraneous noises; the sound effects are not really strong enough, or they conflict, for example, with dialogue. And in the case of those two [things] conflicting, that presents a problem on a foreign release, because the foreign distribution companies are only seeking music and sound effects. They replace the dialogue with their own tongue.

NS: So, you will work with the cue track and then drop in your loops as you need to.

RM: On occasion I'll use—like in the case of Lola Langusta, when Lamar Shedd knowingly is being solaced and succored by this young lady who's trying to correct his unique problem—we'll call it a rear window problem—that was all natural sound. The girl spoke in her native tongue—Spanish. Kitten was very comfortable doing her speech, and because there was *so* much speech, we just made a point of using shotgun microphones that would get us in very close and record the actual sound. And we were able to retain most of that dialogue, by and large. The young man, Lamarr Shed, I met him at UMass two years ago when I was on a college tour. He came out to work with me on my previous film as a grip, meaning one who handles the reflectors and lights and so on. And this time, he presented me, as he was wont to do—he always gives me a letter, and in great detail and fine penmanship, spells out what he would like to do the next time. He offered his services as an actor, and I think he did a remarkable job. He's a very handsome guy, and on a personal level, he's very good with the ladies, and very professional in this instance. I think he did a remarkable job. I'm hopeful that he may find other things. And that brings up a point. A lot of the men that have appeared in my films have done well. But the women generally just *marry* well. They're so outrageously developed, particularly in the bosom area, that there's no place to go. Having been in a Russ Meyer film, there's nowhere else to go, I suppose, in this area, to improve themselves, except if they're show people. But the men have done pretty well. Harrison Page is a Black actor who was in *Vixen!* He was the first banana to Rickles in *CPO Sharkey*, and he worked for years. Charles Napier, who was in *Supervixens*, did *Handle with Care* and *The Last Embrace*. He's a regular man on the tube with the Radio Shack commercials. He has a very square jaw and a lot of teeth. And he's been in *Barettas* and a number of things.

NS: You've mentioned that Kitten Natividad is working for Roger Corman on a film now.

RM: Yeah, she's doing an expensive film for him. She plays a big-busted hooker in a bordello who gets shot. And she's got a film coming up in New York, based upon *Snow White and the Seven Dwarfs*—not at all like Disney made, I'm sure. They'll be using a lot of comics as dwarfs. I know Rich Little and Irwin Corey are two of the dwarfs. One of the girls in *Beyond the Valley of the Dolls*—Dolly

Read—married Dick Martin of Rowan and Martin. Erica Gavin, who was in *Vixen!*, owns a boutique store. Alex Rocco, who was Moe Green in *The Godfather*, has also done a couple of miniseries for Disney. He works all the time. Steve Oliver was on *Peyton Place*. So, the men, by and large, find things to do. Napier, of all of them, I think has made more of a career for himself than any of the others. But a few of them are not too far behind.

NS: You've had your films shown at the Museum of Modern Art and you've been studied on campuses. Does that sort of put a crimp in what you try to do? You find out that you're being taken very seriously by people who maybe don't have a sense of humor?

RM: No, there are some things that are laudatory. There's no question about it. The New York Cultural Film Society a couple of times, the Museum of Modern Art—I spoke with the museum when I was in New York and they said, "Yes, we will be doing another thing on you." That's fine. Next Wednesday I'm getting a fellowship at the USC cinema department, and they'll be showing a number of things from my films. That's recognition. It's nice. There's two levels I work at. One is tongue in cheek, and the other one has kind of a serious aspect. My nature today is not to be serious. Frankly, I'm into this business for two reasons: lust and profit. I have a good time, there are a lot of residual benefits, and I make a lot of money.

NS: That's a great combination. Do you take on disciples?

RM: No one seems to have the dedication that I possess. You know, I think I came up through the good school. Meaning I had an opportunity, many, many years ago, to learn how to do filmmaking with all the facets. I was a cameraman, a half-assed director, I did editing, I did sound, and so on. And those opportunities don't seem to be around too much anymore. Everything is a lot more specific. There's a tendency *not* to be a one-man band. So, when you bring up the idea of a disciple, it's do you want to be a disciple in a specific area or do you want to make films? I don't think one or the other, individually, would satisfy your needs. It has to be a collective thing. Because whatever we do in life, we have to make a profit.

NS: Your films appeal to audiences, which sounds like a very dumb thing to say. But when you look at all the spin-offs and lunch boxes and cable and television sales and guarantees and advances in theaters, you find that many producers seem to thrive on the deal, and not on making the picture. They don't seem to need audiences. But your films do. Do you see the T&A market becoming one which is so commercialized that it forgets who's watching the pictures?

RM: Well, I think that if anything, there are fewer T&A pictures being made today. I think hardcore is very much . . . I won't say on the way out, but it's like water that seeks its own level. There's a coterie of people that will go, week in and week out. But they're not in the great, inquisitive numbers that hardcore once benefited from. In so far as doing what we call softcore, which is simulated lovemaking, replete with a lot of nudity, there are not too many craftsmen left in the field that want to spend the time that I would spend on a film, to make it as slick as I *do* make them, and hope to go out and play in the better theaters. Now, with the majors coming on so strong with their product, it's increasingly difficult for us to find the theaters to play in. And you've gotta have a quality piece of product to compete.

NS: That's true, but there was a time, as you well know, when you'd make a picture for as little money as you could, because you wouldn't be sure of making your collections from the theaters, since they might be in communities, and you'd have very little chance for playoff. You'd have to glean your profits from a handful of big cities that might show the pictures. Now you're big time.

RM: My films do play widely. But I also will say, and I reiterate, that the competition is a lot steeper now. Stiffer. It doesn't come from other sex-oriented films. It comes from the likes of Robert Redford and Jane Fonda and Oscar-winning pictures that move you too much down the line. Because, you know, *Coming Home* made a buck or two.

NS: It's sometimes difficult to get independent films into theaters. Because the majors have eight-, sixteen-week guaranteed runs, and you can't really find screen time. Has that been a problem with *Beneath the Valley of the Ultra-Vixens*?

RM: I always seem to be able to find a screen somewhere. But I find that, during Oscar-time, if I have a booking, it may be shifted back two or three weeks because of a picture like *Coming Home* that won [the Oscar]. But it's not a great problem, because I have kind of a casual approach to release, and that is I want to personally handle the publicity with every engagement. And there are just so many places you can cover. So I just as soon look upon *this* effort as something that will extend maybe way into the fall. And I'll go most anyplace, wherever it is. I'll go to Charlotte. Next week I go to Louisville, for Redstone Theaters. I just got word that I have a break on June 8 in Chicago, which is a great town for me; they're really into tits, and into my kind of art. My great success occurred there in 1968 with the picture *Vixen!* Just the other day, the *Guinness Book of Records* contacted me, and said, "We understand that you may have a picture that holds the world's record for the longest run at a drive-in. And I believe that is the case. *Vixen!* played in Aurora, Illinois, at the Starlight Drive-In, for fifty-four consecutive weeks. And when you consider the population of Aurora—I believe it's around thirty-four thousand—that would mean that everyone in that town had to see it and saw it more than one time.

NS: And now you'll probably have a couple of prudes who have houses around the periphery of the drive-in claiming that their privacy was violated by having it onscreen. Has that ever happened? Have you ever had to cut film for certain regions?

RM: Years ago. In fact, I have a picture called *Mudhoney*. Originally it was called *Rope of Flesh*, but people thought it was a picture about lynching. They didn't realize that the term "rope of flesh" made reference to a man's appendage. There was a lynching sequence in it, but we changed the title to *Mudhoney: A Taste of Evil*. We borrowed that from Mr. Oscar Wilde. One print of that is impounded in Longview, Texas [since the midsixties], and they will not release it. We'd have to have a tremendous court action to get that print of *Mudhoney* back, and I'm sure films like *Vixen!* and *Cherry, Harry & Raquel!* have played there. But it's an example of why the people there—it was some Bible Belt kind of thing—were uptight about a preacher we had in the film—Brother Hansen—who wasn't really their idea of a good preacher, and he didn't necessarily bring a lot of good attention to that experimental kind of Baptist religion—a lot of shouting and yelling. It's the kind of fundamentalist stuff—immersion and born-again stuff and all that. I like to have fun with that. I've done it in *Beneath* where we have a radio evangelist who makes Dolly Parton look like a boy. She's probably the biggest-busted girl I've ever used. But she's pretty, she does quite a job, and she fit right in there pretty well with that kind of evangelism. What I consider to be tax-free religion. I take exception to the fact that [those churches] don't pay a great deal of tax for the money that they do collect. There's a giant exemption there. It's a real moneymaking proposition now, no matter how you slice it. All religions demand certain funds to keep going. Now, I'm not saying that all religions are problems, or difficult to live with, but some of those fundamentalist religions I think get a little bit more than their share. And they certainly take advantage of people that have nothing, and they're able to extract their life savings or money that could be used to put food on the table for the sake of buying somebody a fancy haircut and a custom-made suit, as we are often seeing now on UHF television.

NS: I'm going to dwell on *Beyond the Valley of the Dolls*, because I was turned on to it on a 16mm print that we had to squeeze through a prism to stretch out to Cinemascope proportions, several years ago. It was the most alive and vital film I'd ever seen, up to that point. How are you and Fox getting along on that film?

RM: The present regime—which I choose to call the San Marino regime—is totally and completely embarrassed by *Beyond the Valley of the Dolls*, and no effort, to my knowledge, is being made to really reap a tremendous profit from that picture. It's become a very important cult movie. To my knowledge, there is only one print—a badly scratched print—in the Fox Library in Hollywood, which we sometimes manage to get out for a repertory showing. But it's almost embarrassing to show it in that condition. I think that film could easily be another *Rocky Horror Show* that plays around the country. They ignore it, they turn their back on it, it had an X rating, and it was made at the time of the Zanuck regime, which was always looked upon with some disfavor by the present management. But I'm surprised to learn that Zanuck and Brown are going back to Fox, a return back to the scenes of their crime. But I guess time heals everything, including an X rating. When I finished *The Seven Minutes*, which was the second film I made there, Zanuck was not welcome on the lot, and I had to smuggle a print out, and take it to his outrageous Malibu beach house, which had its own projection room, so that he could see a print of the picture. Now, it's all wonderful and good, but I'm very sure Zanuck is not gonna have anything to do with bringing back *Beyond the Valley of the Dolls*. It's something they'd just as soon have silently and quietly go away. It frustrates me. I would like very much to be able to distribute the film myself. We've even used subterfuge in the sense that my distributer in California even contacted the Fox distributing department and presented a plan that would be very beneficial to them, on a financial level. Totally ignored. I know it wouldn't do any good, but it would be nice to get up at a stockholder meeting some day when Fox is not doing as well as it has. I hope all of those executives have got a picture of George Lucas on the wall in each one of their given dens, and go over there every morning and bow and genuflect to this thing. Because that brilliant man is the real reason that all those people are working. Because I don't think they've had anything but stiffs compared to *Star Wars*. That's carried them through. And now they're gonna get lucky again with *The Empire Strikes Back*. I hope George has got a real good tough deal. I'm so proud of that picture [*Beyond the Valley of the Dolls*]. And I would like very much to have many more people see it. It's an important film. Of all the films Fox has made, probably in the last twenty years, it's the one film that is more often referred to and commented upon, and that frustrates me more than anything else. I really don't know how to take up the cudgel and make that known. Because still, within Hollywood itself, it's common belief that the film was a total failure. This is the way they spread a myth around. That the film was a loser and didn't supply any cash flow, and that I personally found it impossible to really have a good time making a film, which is completely untrue. I had one of the greatest times of my life, going over to Fox. They gave me George Stevens's offices because he was no longer there, and I had my own Murphy bed, which was my casting couch. I didn't use it to cast with, but I met so many young ladies, I had tremendous opportunity to do so. But an assistant of mine would come over—Uschi Digard—who's been in a lot of my films, and we'd do a lot of activities, right on the rug, right in that lofty office. And when I got married, I could get away from my old lady—Edy Williams—who would be on the warpath every now and then, and I could always retreat there. And the guards would indicate that I was not there; they were always kind of super protective. When I got there, they gave me two cars. They gave me a Corvette and a Chevy, and I had my own two parking places with my name. I had access to Darryl Zanuck's [the old man who was there before] own private bar and his steam room. And he had a swimming pool with a kind of a fireman's pole that came down from his quarters. I remember Edy and I used to go into the steam room at night. We'd drink Cold Duck and then we'd participate on the warm yet slippery floor. I often wondered if she wasn't doing that trying to induce a heart attack. But it was a lot of fun; it was a great experience. And then one day they came by, after Zanuck got kicked out, and they painted my name out on the parking lot and they said, "Give me the keys to the cars, and get your furniture out of there." Which I did. It was sad to leave those circumstances. It's not at all bad to make $150,000 a year, get 10 percent of the picture, free meals, free booze . . . good lord!

NS: Did you work with a union crew on that?

RM: Oh, yeah. It was great. I had fifty-five people. It's the best way to make a film. But not for an independent. It's not feasible anymore. The cost of production is so high. Unless you have a big name and a lot of money behind you, and a really impressive distribution company, with a great deal of funds to sink into TV spots, forget it. I think the day of the independent, to a large degree, the end is not too far in sight. I think the price of producing films is getting way out of hand. And with the majors taking over the distribution, with great vigor, and having great sums of money to spend, and acquiring independent films that normally an independent distributor would get a hold of. But now they're acquiring them and they're selling them very much the same way they'd sell a major picture. There's not much left in the way of films for independents to distribute. The cost of production is a factor. I'm fearful of the plight of the independent. I'm glad that I started when I did. I would really dislike having to start now.

NS: There are two things they don't do, that I imagine you do. One is you go to various cities, and you see how the pictures are, and you talk with the local people. They don't seem to do that, save through their branch managers. And they don't sit in audiences, and watch how the pictures are playing. They watch them in their own little Bel Air circuit. But *you* know what the pulse of the audience is. So, won't that destroy them eventually, when they really don't know what the public wants?

RM: Well, there are still filmmakers of Woody Allen stature. There's Don Siegel, Martin Ritt. If the man really makes a good commercial film, I think it's going to survive pretty well. Because of the system, with all the publicity hype. They put out stuff right from the very beginning. Granted, they'll handle coverage only in major cities. You know, they'll come in with Jane Fonda and they'll line up all the press people, and say you have fifteen minutes with her. But it indeed does pay off. It isn't quite the same thing that I do. But I *have* to do it. I have to do it to compete.

Porn King: Russ Meyer Still Upfront with Films and "Fillies"

Karin Winegar / 1979

From the *Minneapolis Star*, July 2, 1979. Copyright © Star Tribune Media Company LLC. Used with permission. All rights reserved.

Russ Meyer and I have nothing in common. I grew up in Minnesota believing in meaningful male-female relationships. He grew up in California with a fantasy of monstrous breasts with women attached somewhere.

I marched against the Vietnam War and cry at art flicks. He speaks fondly of World War II as "the last good war" and only cries watching Bogey in *Casablanca*.

My ideal of feminine beauty is a gristly, aerodynamic runner. His fantasy women are "zaftig," as he says, bosomy to the point of causing traffic accidents.

I met Meyer, the king of American softcore porn and master of the "T&A" film genre, out of curiosity and because he is at it again. He's on tour to promote his latest slapstick sex film *Beneath the Valley of the Ultra-Vixens*. (Good grief!)

Meyer's new movie is racist, sacrilegious, and scatological, as well as sexist. It slanders women, men, gays, Blacks, Mexicans, and Germans. Its one-dimensional characters with giveaway names (Mr. Peterbuilt, Dr. Lavender, Mr. Semper Fidelis) frolic with gusto through an overlong cartoon in which heroes bleed blue and cowards spit up yellow blood. Every sexual encounter is fraught with crossed eyes, funny noises, and violent jiggling. Meyer describes it as "outrageous football scrimmage sex, water buffalo and wildebeest sex."

So, what's new?

All Meyer films, from *The Immoral Mr. Teas* (1959) to the forthcoming *Jaws of the Ultravixen*, have as themes the sexual shenanigans of females with bovine brains and beachball breasts. Meyer is just capitalizing on the fact that Americans pay well for freak shows—witness the attention paid to the bounteous mammary fat of Dolly Parton (real) and Carol Doda (silicone). And Meyer had made a fortune trading on female (and male) deformities.

His first film, *Mr. Teas*, earned more than $1 million, and a print of it rests in the archives of the New York Museum of Modern Art. His top-grossing films of the twenty-two he has completed are *Vixen!* (1968), which has earned more than $14.5 million, and *Supervixens* (1975), which has made $13.4 million. And then there are *Cherry, Harry & Raquel!* (1969), which earned $7.2 million, and *Beyond the Valley of the Dolls* (1970), which grossed $6.8 million.

Sexist doesn't begin to describe his tongue-in-cheek work: his films are corn porn and constitute a film category all their own, somewhere between greasy Super-8mm stag films and big-budget high-flown love stories.

Meyer is rightfully acclaimed for his extraordinarily clean shooting and crisp editing. He has a wonderful satiric way with a camera that makes silly, carnal significance of simple objects such as bedposts, napkins, and augers.

Knowing his fondness for his GI buddies (he was a successful newsreel cameraman in World War II), and for big-breasted, small-brained women, I go to the interview on guard. Meyer, however, is instantly likable, courteous, articulate, and looks like a sportsman—Ernest Hemingway, perhaps, with Clark Gable's eyebrows.

He wears an open-throated dark green silk shirt, a Western belt, and tan pants with stains down the front. He is tall and sturdy with a medium paunch, fair skin, and long, strong-looking fingers. I wonder where his pith helmet and khaki safari suit are.

Meyer has been known to hold press conferences with his current starlet answering questions in the nude. She once charged into the men's showers at a college for an impromptu publicity stunt. So, I decide to be direct.

"What is your attitude toward women?" I ask. "And do you find most women hostile to you?"

Meyer looks at me calmly; he is not leaping onto the soapbox on this one. "Most of the females I've been close to have always tried to change me in some way," he says. "I represent someone that must be changed for the better—except my current lady, the star of this film, who thinks that what I do is just fine."

"Are you bored with sex?" I ask, pressing on. "I mean, I suppose bakers get tired of pastries—doesn't your work make your play redundant?"

"No," Meyer says. "The leading ladies are all to my own personal taste and my films are all extensions of my own personal fantasies. I make films essentially to please myself."

"Then, what's your attitude toward women generally, and women's liberation?"

"I knock everyone in my film. I knock gay people, too. Everyone's fair game. I'm honest about my own fetishes and shortcomings," he says.

Not exactly a thorough answer, I think. Maybe I'll catch it later.

"What Freudian or other interpretation do you have for people who are fascinated with breasts like this? I mean, if you had to analyze yourself . . ."

"First of all, Roger Ebert, who does the dialogue, is even worse than I am; he's into boobs like you wouldn't believe . . . an all-engulfing kind of thing. The point is, there's so many people who think as I do," says Meyer, with complete conviction.

"You mean people or men?" I ask.

"Men, I mean. I exploit women," he says. "But the women I exploit really enjoy that, see, because it adds to their own personal coffers. Because all the women I've used, with the exception of one, have come from the ranks of strippers.

"Number one, I have a fascination for strippers. I like them. They're in the business of selling or projecting sensuality in a manner that I like and that other people like. . . . They have no inhibitions, they lose their laundry at the least provocation, and they can use a relationship with one of my films to earn more money."

"But you don't consider it a purely business relationship?" I ask, sensing from his remarks that his onscreen ladies have been his offscreen ladies.

"It's not bad for a fifty-seven-year-old to be with a twenty-seven-year-old with the kind of figure that he most ardently desires," says Meyer, referring to his current starlet, Francesca "Kitten" Natividad.

"What happens to old Russ Meyer stars?" I ask, remembering mom's warnings that brains last and beauty doesn't.

"The women, because of their outrageous abundance . . . well, there's really nowhere to go except marry someone. Kitten is an exception to that. One girl married the assistant district attorney of Los Angeles. Dolly Read (*Beyond the Valley of the Dolls*) married Dick Martin, of Rowan and Martin. Erica Gavin (*Vixen!*) has her own boutique; she's probably the most interesting girl I've ever used in a picture—she could project a sensuality that I don't think any of the rest of them could have."

His films are clearly his family. The women come and go, and he has a son (who doesn't know him) by a married woman, a former Meyer star who had what he calls "a lapse in her marriage." He is eager to talk about his favorite child, the ten-year-old film *Vixen!*

"Women in great numbers came to see that film; it was my all-time most successful motion picture. Recently the Guinness Book of Records contacted me after having learned that *Vixen!* played longer than any other film in a drive-in—fifty-three consecutive weeks.

"I think women found her noncompetitive. And she had an ability to portray sex in a kind of possessed way . . . it was like watching a championship wrestler.

"Do you know that I have four pictures in the top hundred grossers of all-time?"

Meyer is not smug about that success. This is just business for a Casanova of the Camera, I think. What's going to happen to him when he's too old to do what he loves best?

He overrides my remarks at times. I can see he's a forceful man, not boorish but very sure of himself.

"What kind of feminist reactions have you had to your films?" I ask, thinking this should bring on a raft of stories.

"Not nearly enough," says Meyer.

He claims he's had only three confrontations with angry women. Once at a Princeton screening and lecture, a woman told Meyer what he could do with a stick of dynamite, and ran out of the theater to the applause of more than two thousand people. "The women I use are really caricatures of women, and that's why a lot of women are not offended by them," he says.

"So, feminist criticism doesn't upset you very much?" I ask.

"No, I wish they would get out in force; I'd sell more tickets," Meyer says emphatically. "They could picket the theater and say I'm a dirty old man—which isn't true, in truth—and the exploiter of women."

"But how much money does one man need?" I ask.

"You're asking me to defend what I do. I enjoy the limelight. I'm called an auteur, and I do everything myself and I go out and compete with the big boys," he says. "It's very satisfying to make a film that has no-name [actors], a picture that cost $233,000, and play very favorably next door to a film that cost $9 million. I make the best Russ Meyer films that are made."

"Is there a limit in your filmmaking?" I ask, thinking of a scene in a past film in which a woman is blown up with dynamite. "Would you do a snuff film or anything like it?"

"No, that doesn't turn me on," he says with disgust.

That's an interesting professional barometer. I note that there's a sort of chivalry even in the porn business: they are "ladies" to him, or his "girls."

"I am not anti-intellectual; I'm antisophisticate," he says, which might be why he prefers the company of strippers. "I have no desire to do other kinds of films. I'm not sensitive enough to do any other type of film, like the definitive woman's film . . . I don't know enough about much, really. I don't read. I don't like stage plays. I can build a great birdhouse, and I'm a good fisherman. Basically, I make comic strips."

Meyer lives for today. He is, for example, not overly possessive about Kitten Natividad. He frequently says how much he admires her "honesty, how much she's very upfront about satisfying her needs . . . she has the most healthy attitude of all." And there is not much he doesn't tell me about her sexual life.

"Would you say that you love her?" I ask.

"As much as I guess I could love anybody, any woman, but I've loved a lot of women. Eve Meyer (his wife of twelve years who was killed in an airplane crash) was a fantastic woman, a really fantastic woman," Meyer says with genuine awe.

"What I've done is not conducive to a good marriage. It's not that I'm going to be unfaithful; that isn't it. It's that with my fantasies, you can't quit at six o'clock and go home and make dinner. You've got to be thinking all the time, editing, and so on."

"When was the last time you were embarrassed?" I ask.

He is silent for a moment, then says, "When I cry, I'm embarrassed. I think it's a very personal thing. When I watch *Casablanca*, it always makes me cry; it's my favorite film. And I lost my mother, who was a very important person to me, and I can generate great grief. Of course, then I prefer to be by myself."

It's probably silly to think of America's major pornographer as a sugar daddy, but as he walks me to the door, talking about Kitten again, I catch a fatherly fondness in his voice.

"Would you like to try shooting war footage again," I ask.

"No, I'm not interested in getting shot up by people hiding in a jungle. World War II was the last good war, it really was. We had wine, women, and song and honor—you knew who the enemy was, sweetheart," he says, leaning on the doorframe.

As I walk down the hall, the nasal "sweetheart" reminds me of *Casablanca*. It's been giggle-porn for the main course, and a bit of Bogey for dessert.

Russ Meyer

Craig Reid / 1981

From *Adam Magazine*, May 1981. Reprinted with permission of Bentley Morriss, publisher and president.

The word genius is often misused when describing a man or woman of accomplishment. However, that certainly is not the case with Russ Meyer. Meyer is a genius at what he does; and what he does is make adult films that feature the most outrageous tits, passion, and social parody in the business. Popular moneymakers like *Lorna*, *Vixen!*, *Up!*, and *Beneath the Valley of the Ultra-Vixens* have made Meyer millions of dollars in the past two decades, in an America that had not officially come out of the X-rated closet until fairly recently.

Furthermore, as a remarkable footnote to the lucrative standard that Meyer has set for adult films, every one of his movies is softcore, featuring very few actual insertion scenes and no wet faces, rope shots, etc.

Over the years, Meyer's detractors have lambasted some of the gruesome violence in his pictures—a characteristic of his penchant for overdoing things. But Meyer's critics are more than evened out by the legions of his admirers who range from the "Average Joes" who go to see his movies almost religiously, to his fellow filmmakers in the so-called legitimate end of the business, who hail his talent.

Adam Magazine: You disagree with critics who contend your films are too violent, although you admittedly gave in to their criticism in *Beneath the Valley of the Ultra-Vixens*, which seemed passive compared to your other efforts. Would you agree that the bathtub scene in *Supervixens*, where a woman was stomped and electrocuted, and that the chainsaw and axe fight between the big brute and the lawman in *Up!* left you open for legitimate criticism?

Russ Meyer: No, because the main criticism is that scenes like the chainsaw fight encourage people in the audience to go out and cut someone up or commit an act of violence. Well, you could say the same thing about a lot of motion pictures. The *Texas Chainsaw Massacre* has been playing in theaters for years now, and I haven't seen any reports of anyone running out with a chainsaw after the movie and committing any crime.

There wasn't that much criticism of the bathtub scene, in the early going, after *Supervixens* was released. I think a lot of that had to do with the excellence of the actor, Charles Napier [who played the part of the gruesome murderer]. Napier is one of these actors like Alan Hale or Ernest Borgnine. He can play comedy, or he can be the worst heavy in the world. Very few actors can do that.

AM: But not even Napier's acting could hold down the furor among certain women's groups over what they felt was your condoning the brutal murder of a woman. On the other hand, Napier took part in an equally bloody murder scene with an Indian in your film *Cherry, Harry & Raquel!*, yet there was no protest.

RM: Yeah, I remember that scene with the shotgun under the car [*laughs*]. It was a different thing. It wasn't sexual. I think if the Indian had been a female with a big bust, I would have had more criticism. Right. Instead of an Apache with long hair. That's astute, I must say. Very good.

AM: Thank you. You advertise at the conclusion of *Beneath the Valley of the Ultra-Vixens* that your upcoming film would be titled *The Jaws of Vixen*. Tell us about the next film.

RM: I changed the title to *The Breast of Russ Meyer*. I think it provokes more humor. In *The Breast of Russ Meyer*, I'll be recreating some of the scenes from my past films, and using old footage, as well. I want to review my old films and encapsulate a given film in a very short period of time. One thing I'm going to do with *Vixen!* is show a concentrated version of it as it was and then show how we would do it today. It would be an "Arch-Vixen"—everything overdone, you know. I think I would do some shots of religion—commercial religion, which I did a little bit of in *Beneath the Valley of the Ultra-Vixens*, with the stacked psalm-singer of the airwaves.

I would do something now on Masters and Johnson, for example. Maybe have a couple of preachers. One, Herschel Schwartz, who is a rabbi, and the other, Sidney Brenshaw, the evangelist. And maybe, the Mountie in *Vixen!* might be a Catholic priest. He puts on the collar and says, "Wow, you're the funniest father I ever saw." It's bound to get some reaction.

AM: It often happens in our media-dominated society, that the credit for pioneering movements often doesn't go to the doers. Instead, it goes to those who are discovered doing it after the fact. A lot of credit goes to Harry Reems for fighting in court to preserve the rights of Pussy Cat Theaters and hardcore moviemakers all over the country. In fact, though, aren't you the one who fought the battles in court and spent the bucks on lawyers that made it possible for X-rated adult films to flourish?

RM: I wouldn't want to come off in some heroic way, but let me just jump ahead and say, "Just wait a couple of months, and we're going to be right back in the same kettle of fish with dear ol' Ronnie [Reagan]. He's in a position to stack the court now with a bunch of conservative judges. And I heard a rumor that he's also going to get this guy [federal attorney Larry] Parrish back on the track. The one that was prosecuting Reems.

Getting back to my legal battles, sure, everyone took their lumps. I spent a quarter of a million dollars in the state of Ohio defending *Vixen!* Recently, I went back and I was doing some filming there, and I had a nice piece in the paper about "Cincinnati Revisited: *Vixen!*" and it was interesting to me that Hamilton County is still a bastion unto its own. There is no hardcore, there is no softcore, even. It's bust time if you try to show anything like that.

I must say that even *Vixen!* is now R-rated in some versions, and we approached the prosecuting attorney in Hamilton County and he reportedly said, "If *Vixen!* was G-rated, I would bust it again." So, we still have some of those enclaves in the country that we have to contend with in that area. So, sure, I've been in the trenches and I've fought some battles. But they were all largely personal and selfish just as anything else is.

AM: How do you feel about the accusation that movies like yours playing in respectable local theaters have opened the door for tits to be shown in soap operas and nighttime TV features, which in turn has led to increased promiscuity among the nation's youth?

RM: I think there was more promiscuity on the part of the mothers of those children back in World War II. I mean, there was more infidelity, I believe, in World War II than we can even begin to approach today. And people do change. They change tremendously.

I have friends I knew in the service that had relationships with anybody and anything. Today, they're all preaching conservatism and "Why do you do this?" And I can say, "I remember you when you had a social disease that you caught from some ballet dancer in Prague, Czechoslovakia. What are you talking to me about? I didn't have a social disease. Now, here you are an archconservative."

Today's kids certainly know far more than any of my films represent. Also, kids by and large do not gain admittance to any films that are X-rated or adult oriented. And for the most part, in that they have so much companionship readily available to them, why would they want to go to a film and get titillated? I think adult films would be more of an amusement than any kind of perversion that would occur to them. The outcries come from the parents to cover up their own inadequacies and guilt feelings.

AM: If you are right about the political climate becoming antiporn, will you try to speed up the production on *The Breast of Russ Meyer* in order to get it released to theaters before the conservative tide takes hold?

RM: No. I don't have any fear of that because my film will be loaded with socially redeeming significance. I'm concerned about my colleagues who are making hardcore. And hardcore is not spreading as it once did. It's reached a point where it's like water; it seeks its own level and there's a certain number of people that go to see it week in and week out. But, as I've said, we'll find more and more prosecutions once this conservative attitude takes place.

It's such a great political chestnut to make busts. It keeps a pretty high profile for some sort of crusading politician who wants to say I did this or I did that. And really, all that they're interfering in is something that is pleasurable for people. There are a lot of lonely men in this country, or the world for that matter, and they can find an hour or two of escapism in adult films, where they are reveling in their personal fantasies. They skulk into the theater and kind of rush out so as not to be noticed. What's wrong with that? It's bad to curtail pleasure, whether it be drink or whatever. So long as it is not forced on anybody. People are not forced to go into bars, people are not forced to smoke pot, they're not forced to see dirty movies or read dirty books.

It's that minority that we're dealing with, and they're ultrasensitive, and they want to make sure that no one else enjoys the pleasures of the flesh, simply because I suppose they might be uptight about it. Maybe they are unhappy and feeling terribly inadequate. It's like people who protest all the time; I always question their motives and makeup and mentality.

AM: Describe the kind of guy that comes to see your movies.

RM: It's difficult to come up with a category because there is no category. I could not have done as well as I did if I didn't have women come to see my films. Women more and more are coming because of the fact that they like the jokes, they like the outrageous screwing, the kangaroo pouch, the commuter, whatever, and they like the humor. Women find that the picture is not repugnant, there's no roping sperm and the open-faced oyster.

Certainly I have the tit freaks, right? God bless them. [Meyer is a world-renowned connoisseur of the big boob.] I have the film buffs, which is very important. I have Joe Gas Station and his old lady, they'll come. They're not really young people. They're starting to get a little over the hill. They come in and they want to look at something and, as one Mexican guy said to Kitten [Natividad, who lives with Meyer in connubial bliss] and me when we were promoting a film in Dallas—he said, "God, we liked that film. You know what me and my old lady are going to do when we go home? We're going to fuck our brains out and try the wheelbarrow."

It's so gratifying when people say things like that. So, I would say, by and large, the people who go to see my films are pretty much the same people who go to see Paul Newman and Robert Redford in a film. I won't say that they're in the same numbers, but they are the same kind of cross-section. It's a known fact that today our theater-paying public range between seventeen and maybe twenty-nine. And you see fewer and fewer old men attending my films.

AM: I know that a lot of our readers would like to know what some of the luscious ladies who've starred in your films have gone on to do. For example, what did Lorna Maitland (*Lorna*) and Alaina Capri (*Good Morning . . . and Goodbye!*) go on to do?

RM: Well, let's start with Lorna. Lorna was a Las Vegas dancer, and she was pregnant when I did the film. That accounted for her tremendous superstructure to a large degree. She had the baby and then she came back and did *Mudhoney* for me, and then she disappeared. I have no idea where she went. That seems to be the case with a lot of the girls.

The girls are always so outrageously constructed, there's like nowhere else for them to go because they can't play a straight role in a film. They're a caricature of a woman. Some of them marry well. Then again, a lot of them are what I call premier strippers that make a couple of thousand a week. There are still women that can make that kind of money in Vegas, at the Cabaret and some of the good clubs, which Kitten enjoys.

And the girls have to take care of themselves. I've found that so many of them don't. Kitten, if she's got a crease or a wrinkle, she'll be in the other room [*he groans*] working it out, exercising, you know, while a lot of them sit around and just go to shit. A girl has such a short time of it. There was one exception to the rule. I saw her the other night. Her name is Tura Satana, and she was in *Faster, Pussycat! Kill! Kill!* Half-Japanese and half-Cherokee, I think. That girl looked just as good as she did eighteen years ago. A mutual friend of ours had a stroke and he was in Veterans Hospital. She showed us her body, and it was great for our friend. He had been through hell with the stroke, and she just took off her sweater and the rest of it and said, "Look at these." He loved it and I thought it was a nice gesture.

AM: What ever became of the beautiful girl in *Finders Keepers, Lovers Weepers!*, who did the fantastic pool scene?

RM: She's missing. I don't know where she is. She was a lovely chick. She was Canadian, from the province of Manitoba. She was married to some guy who tried to conduct some sort of makeup school. They just go away; you never hear from them again.

AM: What about Cherry and Raquel?

RM: The girl that played Cherry was a Miami Beach chorus girl, when Miami Beach was doing well. She worked in *Cherry, Harry & Raquel!* but she quit before the film was completed. And it was actually a godsend because I then had to go out and reach and find Uschi Digard. I used Uschi as Soul in *Cherry,* and everything worked out fine and, as you know, she has done a lot of work for me since.

Raquel, I don't know. I used her in *Beyond the Valley of the Dolls,* and she was upset with me because I didn't give her a bigger part. You never do anything really right as far as that goes.

AM: Haven't you used Uschi to recruit buxom starlets for your films?

RM: She has. She's found girls but she always admits that it's tough. There are not many women like that around.

AM: In *Supervixens,* why didn't you use the fantastic-looking girl in the gas station scene in a balling situation?

RM: She wouldn't do it because of her father. He was a very wealthy man in the state of Indiana, and she was fearful that he would see her. Then she wrote me a letter and said, "I want to do a big nude scene in the next picture." But, when the time came, she had married and the husband said no. So, you have to grab them when they want to do it, even if you don't know at the time what you want to shoot. You just can't wait because the opportunity isn't there long. That particular lady looked like the USS *Missouri* when she's slippin' into port. People often ask that question.

AM: Last but not least, what about Shari Eubank of *Supervixens?*

RM: I had a great deal of admiration for her. Of course, she played the shit and the nice girl in *Supervixens.* She inherited about a million bucks from her grandmother. She's had a child and she's married to a guy that she seems to go for. I had to admire her very, very much. Her family was strongly opposed to what she did. We were in Chicago together pushing the picture, and I had to go to Milwaukee next, which was near the town where her family lived. So, I told her that she didn't have to come with me, but she insisted that she come.

Then she told all of her family: "I don't want you to come and see the movie because you won't like it." And they all showed up, like fifty people plus her father, who was an ex-GI. So, she sat next to him in the theater, and when the scene came when she was on top of the pinnacle, he turned to her and said, "My God, Shari!" You could hear his voice throughout the theater. And she says, "Dad, I told you I didn't want you to come to the theater." The audience, of course, loved it; they heard this banter between father and daughter. But she had courage, and I take my hat off to her. I owe her because she had not only beauty, she had enormous spirit. The way that she was dragged over that damn mountain in the movie, she never complained. And every rock just reached out and bit you. It was volcanic stuff. She was just a great person.

AM: It has been theorized that there is a thin line between mental prowess and eccentricity. Are there any ways that you know of in which you are "off-the-wall" or "out-to-lunch?"

RM: I don't consider myself in any way eccentric, because I'm a real good businessman. That's one of the things that I so enjoy in what I do. I not only handle production and make the film, I also sell it. I run a very tight ship. Before, I had a couple of girls working for me. But I got rid of them and I have just a man now. And I go out. I went to Australia a few months ago and set up distribution there and did publicity and so forth. So, I can wear more than one hat.

And these films are personal to me. They are a very personal part of my life. I take great pride of ownership. Also, it's very important to have achieved something in your life. I can think of some of the women I've known that did not really achieve anything. I'm sure they've had a lot of guys and have jewelry to prove it. But they never really did anything with themselves. Nothing really significant. Now, that may be a little hypocritical of me, but I believe that not everybody gives that extra, extra effort. You know what I mean?

One of my best mentors was a man named Donald Ornitz, who was a very famous magazine photographer. He's passed on. We were in the service together and I said, "I think I've got to do something, Don. I've got to shoot stills, I like girls, and I think I might make a buck." And he says, "That's the field to get in, but what do you think about your ability in that area?" And I said, "What I lack in ability, I will make up in enthusiasm."

And I have always gone by that philosophy. I have developed a flair for shooting women, and the proof is in the acceptance of what you do. Whatever it is, if it's accepted, if someone will lay down a few bucks to buy your pictures or come to the theater to see them, that's the proof.

The Breast of Russ Meyer

Anton Rush / 1983

From *Blitz*, February 1983. Reprinted with permission of Simon Tesler.

"I have a feeling for tits that I won't entrust to anybody else," says Russ Meyer, a week before his Guardian Lecture on Film. "I like tits, and I want to present them in the best possible light. In a way that titillates me, and gives me a stirring in my groin."

Russ Meyer is just completing his twenty-fifth film, it's called *The Breast of Russ Meyer*, and he promises that it will do credit to his lifelong obsession—women with impossible mammary dimensions.

Breasts will feature in every scene of Meyer's autobiographical opus. Because the film is going to be a condensation of everything he's ever done, he says he's going to give it his best shot, presenting his own psychological make-up in a definitive statement.

"I hope the film will show how I think, my joie de vivre, and why I did what I've done over the last twenty-three years. It's going to be a very personal film."

Nobody makes a film like Russ Meyer. His formula of square-jawed young men with an IQ of 34, huge cantilevered heroines, and plots that race along with the speed of an express train are what he calls "fleshed-out cartoons." His formula has caused him to be considered as a persona non grata in Hollywood—where he's thought of as a pornographer—and as one of America's foremost satirists in New York—where he's thought of a something close to a "true artist."

A Meyer film appeals to a cross-section of society, to "rednecks, college students, and middle-aged couples"—and here Meyer pauses for maximum effect— "and also to a lot of serious film buffs"—a comment underlined by the National Film Theatre's decision to screen a full Meyer retrospective last year. Meanwhile, the newspapers and magazines content themselves with referring to him as "The Titan of Tits," "King Leer," "King of the Nudies," or "The Glandscape Artist."

Meyer laughs off the name-calling, and points out that despite what people say, he's "put a lot of asses in a lot of seats in a lot of theaters," and the success of the Meyer formula has enabled him to compete directly with the product of Hollywood's major studios.

He claims never to have lost a dollar on any of his films and, in fact, *Cherry, Harry & Raquel!*, *Vixen!*, and *Beyond the Valley of the Dolls* have made it into *Variety's* list of the hundred top-grossing films of all time. *The Guinness Book of World Records* has also given Meyer the dubious accolade of having the longest run ever at a drive-in movie.

"*Vixen!* played for fifty-four weeks in Aurora, Illinois," says Meyer, "and that town has a population of only seventeen thousand people. They must have seen it quite a few times!"

Whereas many Americans might only confide secret fantasies to their analyst, and pay for the pleasure, Meyer likes to see his own quirks and obsessions writ large on film acetate, where the world can share them, and *he* gets paid for the pleasure. Describing his own films, Meyer says they are "fun and sex, tongue-in-cheek comedy, satire, and put-on." Describing the characters, he says, "My girls are all very pneumatic. My heroes are all Dudley Do-Good. And my heavies are real evil. It's becoming quite a cult."

As might be expected, Meyer has very strong views on film censorship. All of his films so far have been severely abridged for viewing in British theatres. "*Supervixens* had 137 cuts here, and in Ireland they had over three hundred," says Meyer with an air of total disbelief. "I think you have really shitty censorship here in England. If you cut that many scenes out of a picture in order to protect the average adult filmgoer, it's insane. It's offensive."

The thought of a Meyer film being edited or cut by any other than Russ Meyer is like showing a red rag to a bull.

"*One man* does this," says Meyer. "Mr. Ferman, the film censor, and he does it with a straight face! The problem is now that when you see one of my films, you can never tell what the censor cut or what the projectionist has cut out for his own private viewing!"

Russ Meyer knows what sells his films, and he tries hard to ensure that every film he makes is an "X."

"The United States has a deceitful form of censorship," he says. "It's not the fucking they dislike, it's the accumulation of the fucking. If you have a film that's seventy minutes long, and there's forty minutes of low body blows, you're going to get an X. Now, if you cut it down to thirty minutes, you'll get an R. Now, if I got an R, I'd go right out and shoot some more film so that I could qualify for an X. People associate me with X-rated films. If I made an R, they'd stay away; they'd assume, quite rightly, that the film wasn't very sexy."

It has been said that Russ Meyer is a very moral man. Whether or not the morality in his films is honest, or just part of his tongue-in-cheek parody of

American life, is hard to decide. At the end of *Beneath the Valley of the Ultra-Vixens*, there is a moral résumé given by Meyer describing what has become of the characters in the story. The bad characters get their just deserts, and the good characters live happily ever after.

"If you don't make the characters pay the piper, then you lack an ingredient that a defense attorney must have. It's called Social Redeeming Significance. The characters can be bad, evil, but they must pay for it in the end."

However, Meyer's outlook has changed since the days of *Ultra-Vixens*.

"Now I have it in the back of my mind to do a parody of my own parodies. The people would have a great time; the woman would make a cuckold of her husband, the convict would get away without having to pay with his life—he'd continue to be a bad guy. The girl would continue to be promiscuous, and the husband would continue to be a cuckold. Times have changed. I think that I could get away with that now, but in the beginning it was different. I'm not personally moralistic, it just occurred to me that it was the way to do it; it could circumvent a lot of problems in a courtroom—it's a formula, nothing else; it's theater."

Meyer insists that there is no message in his films.

"Why should I have one? I purport to do nothing but entertain. Maybe it's better to have people write in all kinds of undercurrents, but I don't do that."

On the occasions when Meyer did try to put over a moral point, he feels that he made a huge mistake. The box office reactions were very bad, and both films only just squeezed past the winning post from loss to profit.

"A couple of times, I fell on my ass. Once was with *The Seven Minutes*, Irving Wallace's supposed bestseller. I thought that I should be a spokesman at the time because I was in the courts of Ohio, involved in a case with the Citizens for Decent Literature league, defending *Vixen!* which was the *Deep Throat* of its day. I felt I should be the one to make the statement about freedom of expression, First Amendment rights, and so on. So, I made *The Seven Minutes*—a courtroom drama about the defense of a supposedly pornographic book. But the audience wasn't used to that kind of thing from me; they expected the same old kind of zip-a-dee-doo-dah that *Beyond the Valley of the Dolls* had. Then I went on and compounded the mistake with *Blacksnake!*, which was about the slavery question in the 1880s. I thought it was great, but everybody else hated it. Even the Blacks hated it."

If you're a feminist and concerned about the gratuitous exploitation of the female form in the cinema, then Russ Meyer will provide plenty of meat for your arguments. Meyer claims that he has never been satisfied by the extent of the feminist criticism he's received, "but it has helped a lot; it's generated activity. But that's all old hat now. I don't think that people really give a damn anymore. I certainly don't give a damn about feminist arguments. I counter any feminist criticism by simply agreeing with anything they say.

"If I'm accused of exploiting women, I'll say, 'That's true. I exploit them with zeal and gusto.' If I'm accused of using women, I'll say, 'I've always used them for my own selfish ends.' If I'm asked what I think a woman's place in society is, I'll say, 'The kitchen or the bedroom.' And after a while, what have they got to say? Never try to defend yourself with women; they're all wound-up gramophones!"

Meyer's heroines, on the other hand, are often very strong women who exploit men, or are very independent, commanding people, who get what they want, and want what they get, which, in its own ironic fashion, is supporting women's liberation.

"A lot of [my] films are pro-female," says Meyer. "They put the women in control. The men are just used by them; they are willing tools, klutzes. The women are the ones after their own physical pleasure."

The best example of the theme, argues Meyer, must come with the antics of SuperSoul, SuperLorna, SuperCherry, and company, in *Supervixens*, which he describes as the sum total of all his films. Meyer has seven large ladies in the film, which is an odyssey inspired jointly by Horatio Alger and the darker side of Russ Meyer's personal life, in which all seven women are on the make for a young man who works for Martin Bormann, who plays a friendly gas station attendant in the desert.

It's hard to say exactly what makes a film "cult" viewing material, but *Beneath the Valley of the Ultra-Vixens* serves as a good example of the qualities that have made Meyer's movies compulsive viewing for those who enjoy his quirkiness and satire. *Ultra-Vixens* is a pastiche of *Peyton Place*, in which a narrator, complete with check shirt, baseball cap, and pickup truck, gives us a documentary-cum-travelogue commentary on the sexual behavior of the inhabitants of "Smalltown," USA—behavior that only just falls short of sex on an Olympic scale.

The men in the film even bleed in symbolic colors when they receive a solid right to the jaw, and the colors respond to Meyer's idea of them as people.

"We used different colored bloods to show that a man was either a fag or a coward or had an anal fixation! The only character in the movie that bleeds red is Mr. Peterbuilt, because he's the only one that fucks straight."

Needless to say that the Black man bleeds white, the gay bleeds pink, and the coward bleeds green.

"The colored blood is intended to ape the violence; it's just another exaggeration."

Several of Meyer's films have been very violent, but not, as he points out, in the serious, Peckinpah, exploding-chests-and-fountains-of-blood style. In *Up!* for example, a character gets a double-sided axe buried in his chest, then plucks it out, runs a hundred yards, and kills a giant with a chainsaw.

But the women in Meyer's films always show less physical evidence of violence than the men, a fact that enhances the cult quality of his films.

"A woman would not have a cut lip or black eyes according to my *Playboy*-centerfold approach to cinematography. If a woman bleeds, then she bleeds gracefully—it's all concerned with their physiognomy—hills, valleys, and mountains, you know? A good example is in *Supervixens* where SuperAngel is reincarnated as Good, and she's atop the mountain like Zarathustra, with carefully placed blood lines that extend down over her breast, and follow the line of the breast and the hip and the waist. It's like a costume, a Daliesque approach, I suppose, to create an impression that she had bled in contrast to the last time we saw her, in the bathtub, after Harry Sledge had jumped all over her."

Sex is also often placed in strange and exotic situations in Meyer's films.

"Up a tree, behind a waterfall, in a bathtub, or, as in *Lorna*, in two feet of fetid water in the middle of a swamp. It's screwing under tremendous odds that strikes me as both erotic and funny. When they're screwing, it's like Rodin has happened on the screen. Every crevice, crack, and bulge is scripted. It has to be presented as if you're doing a layout for *Strength and Health*. In anything I photograph, the women have to look great. In real life, it's not like that."

Meyer likes to think of himself as basically a humorist, and is a great admirer of Mel Brooks. Sex and violence have been a successful cocktail in the cinema for a long time, and Meyer has added excess, and parodied the violence and sex.

"I enjoy obsessive grossness," he says, but I'd never make a hardcore film, or at least I certainly wouldn't do it in a way that is normally expected."

For Meyer, it would be the end of the line if he made a pornographic film as an independent producer and director who distributes his own product, sharing the same venues as *On Golden Pond* and *101 Dalmatians*. It would literally be the kiss of death, and would place him in America and Europe where he has been in this country from the beginning—"in the scumbag cinemas."

A few years ago, Russ Meyer was asked to shoot a film with the Sex Pistols, which was to be called *Who Killed Bambi*? Meyer describes the script as *A Hard Day's Night* a la *Valley of the Dolls*. It was to feature an ageing rock star who made sorties into the Queen's Reserve to shoot deer, which he then presented to the poor. The ageing rock star was based on Mick Jagger, and the story was to be loosely based on *Robin Hood*. Meyer shot three days and then folded the show.

"The only problem with the Sex Pistols movie was called Malcolm [McLaren, the band's manager]. That was the only problem. We could have made a hell of a film, but he wasn't really qualified, or in a position to call the shots on the film."

Just to prove that he can still give what it takes at fifty-eight, Meyer is planning a new film which will be set in Germany. And is destined to be a *Dirty Harry* spoof.

"The film will star Charles Napier (arch Meyer villain) and three abundant ladies—the Brazilian Bombshell, Anna Popov, and Brunhilda, the buxom accomplice to Mario Fettuccini, who's trying to get his hooks on a lodestone that will turn a warehouse full of sugar into cocaine! The film stars Harry Sledge (Napier), and he's constantly being drugged, bludgeoned, and falling into circumstances that involve the ladies. It's going to be an R-rated film, but we can stretch it. It'll still be a Russ Meyer movie. Big tits and a lot of low body blows.

Tit for Tat

Tom Teicholz / 1986

Russ Meyer is one of Hollywood's most successful independent filmmakers. He is involved in all aspects of producing, promoting, and distributing his work. His tried-and-true formula for cinematic success is, in a word, "bosomania," or, as Russ describes it, "outrageously buxom women and dumb, muscular men, laying their sexual prowess on the line." He has produced twenty-two money-making films in his long career, from *The Immoral Mr. Teas* (1959) to *Beneath the Valley of the Ultra-Vixens* (1979). To give you some idea of Russ Meyer's commercial success, *Supervixens* was made for $219,000 and has grossed more than $17 million. Almost all his films are currently in release; most are available on videocassette, and a few, such as *Faster, Pussycat! Kill! Kill!*, *Mudhoney*, and *Motorpsycho!*, have become midnight movie cult classics. Over the years, his over-endowed stars, Kitten Natividad, Raven De La Croix, and Erica Gavin, have become bedroom, if not household names.

In 1983, Russ Meyer took time out from filmmaking to write a chapter on independent film production for Jason Squire's *The Movie Business Book* (Prentice Hall). For years, Russ has maintained a house high in the Hollywood hills which contains the offices of RM, Inc. Originally used as the interior sets for *Ultra-Vixens*, the house is now filled with memorabilia from floor to ceiling, so much so that John Waters has dubbed it "The Russ Meyer Museum." Movie posters and plaques abound, and there are, of course, beds in every room, including the kitchen.

Tom Teicholz: This is from the Yale Film Society?
Russ Meyer: Yes.
TT: And these?
RM: These are all the mementos from my films. I mean, they were things that were important to them . . .

TT: What's this?

RM: A cup. The guy wouldn't . . . he was supposed to be nude, and we couldn't show anything, but he didn't want to run around with his doohickey flopping, so we taped it to the front of him, which was kind of difficult to get off later on. Just shows how times change. Five years later, he said what the hell . . .

TT: Anything from *Faster, Pussycat*?

RM: Here's Tura Satana's glove, the actual glove that she committed mayhem with. Mr. Teas's hat's up there.

TT: *Mr. Teas* was really the first film that brought your name . . .

RM: Well, it started the whole nudie movie thing. It was the one that came along at just the right time. So, I bought this house originally as a place to shoot *Ultra-Vixens* because the ceilings are tall; I could get up high and shoot. In fact, we shot it in that front room there. All the sets were in there. Upstairs were all the offices. Cutting rooms were in the back. . . . So, now these are books and memorabilia. I also have shrines to dear departed friends. This man gave me his camera. This guy was a cameraman.

TT: What is this camera here?

RM: That's the kind of camera we used during the war. It's an Eyemo 35mm. And that will go on a plaque, once I get the plaque.

TT: Well, that's actually how you got your start in film, in the army.

RM: Pretty much. I was nineteen, but I was an amateur from, I guess, fourteen. The camera came out that did so much for amateur home movies; it was called the Univex. Universal Camera Corporation. It sold for $9.95. It used single-eight motion picture film. So, I got hooked on it, and the war came along. I had to get away from home, for one thing. Not that home was unpleasant; I just wanted to get away. I was fortunate to get into the Signal Corps. I saw an advertisement in one of the photo magazines, and went down and was interviewed. All they hoped to get were amateurs, anyway. So, I was enrolled at a school of Eastman-Kodak down there on Santa Monica Boulevard, a technical school, and then we went to MGM, and we were supposedly taught how to thread a camera or two. There were all these cameras that we would never see again, like studio Mitchells and so on. But nonetheless, the whole thing eased us into the service very gently. It was marvelous. We were enlisted people, but we were still able to buy four or five more months at home base. To me, the service really represented the high point in my life. Whatever I've done, it was the most exciting and adventuresome.

TT: I see here that you have the newspaper *Stars and Stripes* from when Paris was liberated.

RM: I was there on the day of liberation with the Second French Army Division. I've gone back many times, always trying to seek out my youth. I'd much rather go there than anywhere else. In fact, I went to Germany and toured twenty cities to promote two of my films that opened last month.

TT: Which ones are those?

RM: *Supervixens*, for the second time. Something about my films, they never seem to die, they just keep playing. It was originally released years ago, with some cuts, as *Eruption*, and it played in really terrible German theaters, which they called Bahnhof cinemas. You know, train station cinemas. And my picture *Beneath the Valley of the Ultra-Vixens* is now in its fifth year in Germany. Amazing, really amazing, when you stop to think about a film that can play five years and go back to the same theaters all over again. It's opened up a whole first-class distribution network.

TT: What did you like best about the military?

RM: I had so much zeal and drive that my devotion was entirely to duty. I felt this was going to be a really important, formative time in my life—not wine, women, and song. Though, finally, it was, with the aid of Mr. Ernest Hemingway, outside of Paris. My first piece of tail was in a town called Rambouillet, in which he sent us over to a bordello. It was closed.

TT: Hemingway sent you?

RM: Yeah.

TT: Well, how did you meet him?

RM: He was over there. He was there running guns and, I don't know, doing a lot of drinking and so forth. He was with the French Resistance forces—trying to write a book or wanting to write a book. And so we just stumbled into the town before our division arrived because the front was so fluid, and we had three delightful days. I didn't become a close confidant of his, but he acknowledged our presence and would have a drink with us and made reference to us in a *Collier's* article. "There wasn't any room, so the three Signal Corps cameramen had to sleep out in a tent in the back." But then, in the course of those three days, he had a Portuguese lieutenant who took us to this marvelous whorehouse. It had, I think, around sixteen girls with their children, and a madame right out of de Maupassant, with a bun in the back. We were in a toy factory. It was my first intimate experience with a lady. It was a great way to kick it all off.

TT: And when you returned to the States . . .

RM: First we went to North Ireland, played soccer and went drinking, and then we went to England, and it was the same thing, so we gradually got into the war. And then the war was suddenly over the next hill. So, we were glad, we were really tickled, when the bomb was dropped—just as about everybody else in the world was. Now you have all this antinuke stuff, and to everyone his own, but I'll tell you, you couldn't have found one GI who regretted that bombing, or bombs, I should say.

TT: Now, how did you segue from there into the film industry?

RM: Well, I came back, tried to get a job in Hollywood. Forget it. No way. Unions. I wasn't hostile to them, because they had to give the jobs back to their own guys; they were entitled to them. So, I went back home to northern California and thought I would find some work up there, and damned if I didn't, through a representative of Eastman-Kodak.

TT: And you started doing industrials . . .

RM: Yeah, I think the war prepared me insofar as being audacious and taking a chance, whether it be with your skin or with money. My associates and I were in a position to do everything: sound, lighting, camera. We had marvelous accounts, like Southern Pacific Railroad and Standard Oil. So, we'd made these pretty fair, not bad, films—employee relations, straight propaganda, whatever the case was. But in that area, I was able to get a good, sound basis for, in essence, becoming a one-man band. It stood me in very good stead with most of my fellows because they were all shot with a very small crew. Then one of my army buddies, who was a great magazine photographer, said, "Why don't you take pictures of girls?" And I thought, "Well, I don't know anything about taking stills." And in a great line, he said, "Well, what you lack in ability, you'll make up in enthusiasm." And sure enough, I started shooting stills of chicks, and I found it to be quite interesting.

TT: For magazines?

RM: Yeah, for magazines. Then I married one lady whose pictures were around the top. My second marriage. And I shot a centerfold for *Playboy*, and she became probably the most well-known model of the day.

TT: Eve Meyer.

RM: She perished, regrettably, in an airplane crash in the Canaries. And so that was it. Finally, to make a long story short, I've had a great friend who was one of the last burlesque entrepreneurs, Peter DeCenzie, and he was always after me to make a nudie movie, a kind of "nudist" film. I was not too keen about that sunbathing type of thing. So, he finally said, "Do any damned thing you want. I'll match you: $100 for $100." So, that's how *Teas* got started.

TT: And where did you find the whole notion for it?

RM: Well, I'd been doing layouts for magazines, a couple of them for *Playboy*. The girl next door, the boy next door, the lech, the voyeur, you know.

TT: Can you give me a sense of what *Playboy* means in the 1950s to a young photographer?

RM: Well, everything. Cars, literature, but still, the most important thing was that big fold-out center. I don't think so anymore. It's kind of commonplace. I don't mean to put it down, but at that time, being in *Playboy*—whether you were the photographer or the model—was something special. Hefner did a marvelous thing; he made his magazine respectable. So, I ended up doing four or five centerfolds. But I shot for a lot of *lesser* magazines. And I made a lot of money out of it. So, it was the marriage of industrial movies and shooting tits for magazines that brought all of this about.

TT: But there was a certain point when you really had the market on these sort of exploitation films.

RM: I've always been kind of the leader, certainly up through *Vixen!*, that being the nineteenth film I made. I always was kind of ahead of the pack. Because of *Vixen!* and its outrageous success, I went to Fox and did *Beyond the Valley of the Dolls*, which was a very important thing to me, and turned out to be an important film, as well. And I did another one there, so I was able to cushion the shock of hardcore.

TT: Just as *Playboy* has cornered a certain market and maintained a standard, it strikes me that you also have never strayed out of your limits and gone hardcore.

RM: Well, it's nice to be in the company of Hefner. We have, I would say, a good acquaintanceship. I'm flattered to have the association. There are a number of reasons I always give, and I think they're logical and honest. Number one, the ladies I work with wouldn't *do* hardcore. Number two, hardcore is of course now pretty much on the wane in theaters, per se. Video still goes, but no theaters. If you made a hardcore picture, you had to play in a scumbag house. I've always prided myself on playing in the first-class theaters around the country. Number three, the joke wouldn't work with me. My whole thing is to try to make sex *so ridiculous*, and, oh, almost like qualifying for the Olympics, that if I ended it on a very *actual* note, I don't think there'd be anything left to the fantasies of people who watch my films. Number four, more important than anything else: hardcore movies are just something I couldn't care less about. They're not interesting to me. I had five girls that were in them that I know. I've never even bothered to look at the damned films. Well, I've looked at a few. I don't put it down, but it's not for me. I don't like the looks of the films, the way they are made; I don't think they're humorous. It's taste, that's all. So, there are a lot of reasons why I haven't done it. I can't say I wouldn't have done hardcore no matter what, but I think I was helped to some degree by having gone to Fox, which all of a sudden elevated me onto a whole new plateau. And I could probably look down upon a lot of things I did before, because all of a sudden, here I was with the establishment. And then when I came back, I did the same damned thing that I'd always done, on a broader scale, with *Supervixens*.

TT: Your films are all spoofs.

RM: All tongue-in-cheek. They're not comedies, they're satires. But I like to generate a laugh. That's terribly important. To personally turn me on. I deal with women who are archetypes; in fact, *they're beyond women*. They're caricatures of ladies. I love that kind of woman. I mean, I don't really have anything to do with a woman unless she is that kind of lady. She's got to be stacked like cards. I would not be bothered with a woman who is slim, on a personal level. See, I'm really opinionated in that area, and I've been fortunate in my life to have found the women that I've been close to. It's also a little bit of a curse, because once you set your standards, there are not enough of these women to go around, you know? I'm fortunate now to have a lady that's like this, and she works for me, too, and it's great. And we also have a great time.

TT: Was Edy Williams really the prototype?

RM: No, no. Edy was not at all. Edy had a great ass; she did not have the giant tits. Now, *she's* looking great [*points to a photo on the wall*]. Here she is, probably forty-five years of age, and she had a great figure, but she was another kind of a lady that I was taken with. The starlet and the dirty old man, the film producer. Oh, it was fine. I mean, I have no negativism about any lady that I've been with, that I've been married to or divorced from. It was a great moment in my life. I wouldn't exchange it for anything. I probably never fully intended to stay married to anybody, for that matter. By and large, I had to finally say the film was more important than the marriage. More often than not, ladies would take exception to what I did, even in spite of the fact that that's how I met them. "Why can't you do something more artistic? Why don't you make a better movie?"

TT: And what would you say?

RM: Well, I would say, "So long." I don't mean to say that my separations were frivolous or flippant. There was a lot of heartache, a lot of problems and all that, but in the final analysis, and I quote, I think, Mr. Coppola, "There is nothing more important than the film."

TT: Which of your films are you most satisfied with?

RM: The most satisfying is *Beyond the Valley of the Dolls*. First of all, it's probably the only cult film Fox ever made. It continues to be a success in spite of the fact that there was a lot of opposition to its release and distribution.

TT: How did Fox get involved?

RM: It happened because of *Vixen! Vixen!* made so much money, and cost only $61,000. And because of *Vixen!* I am right at this moment so financially secure with my retirement program that I . . .

TT: I remember reading that *Supervixens* was made for $200,000.

RM: $219,000, and it's grossed a ton.

TT: Made $17, 18 million?

RM: Box office gross, I would guess that. And *Vixen!* is greater than that. But *Vixen!* made it at a time when the dollar was something else, and my wife and partner at the time, Eve, a really clever businesswoman, invested it so successfully, that when I'm ready to retire, which I hope is never, I think I could enjoy an income of maybe $25,000 a month for the rest of my life. So, *Vixen!* really represents Chicago—the town that made me bigtime. *Vixen!* played there fifty-two weeks in 1968. But of all the films, the one that I can just sit down and lust after and thirst for and enjoy is *Beyond the Valley of the Dolls.* Not because I consider it the best film, and I don't consider any one film the best. It represents my having gone to the mountain. I went to the mountain, and I did a movie that was hellaciously successful.

TT: What did the film cost?

RM: Oh, I think about a million seven. It's in the top two-hundred grossers. It's hard to get true figures as to what it's made, but it's still in demand.

TT: What was the other film you did for Fox?

RM: Irving Wallace's *The Seven Minutes.* It was *not* a success. I got conned into getting an R rating. The other one, we slipped in there, and Roger [Ebert, who wrote the screenplay for *Beyond the Valley of the Dolls*] and I made the film just the way we wanted it. It turned out to be an X, and we said we can't have that but there was no other way. They had to release it as an X, otherwise it wouldn't have been commercial. So, it did well; they made a deal with me. The next time, they made it very clear—meaning Brown . . .

TT: David Brown.

RM: Yes, David Brown got to make it an R. And I was so full of shit then, and fat-headed, that I figured, well, whatever I do is going to be great. But it didn't work that way. There wasn't enough tits and ass in the movie. If it had had a lot of that, and less courtroom action, it would have been a great hit.

TT: Would you work with a studio now?

RM: Yes. I've got something cooking now with my agent. It's a spoof on the cocaine business. But I would shoot it X. When I say X, it's the MPAA X, not the hardcore X, not the purple X. But you know, a lot of preoccupation with screwing and all that sort of thing, nudity. I would shoot it that way for Europe. Germany is a giant market, it can go strong; France is strong. See? And then over here, they'd probably have to tame it down.

TT: Why do you think that in America, which is supposed to be so sexually liberated . . .

RM: Well, let me just go back again. First of all, there's a problem on the German front. It's a throwback to fascism and everything else. The violence now is kind of getting to them, they're becoming concerned about it, not so much with sex, but violence. The only really wide-open country in the world is France. France *loves* that violence: the more bloodletting, the more tits, the more fucking. But you can't get by with hardcore in France. So, the United States still, on a complete basis, is freer than any of them. The MPAA developed an attitude that X is poisonous in the United States, and it has affected the distribution and advertising. That's the problem.

TT: Well, what do you think about sex and violence? Can you have one without the other?

RM: Well, my sex, my violence, is so ridiculous. It's meant to be a caricature, a cartoon. I frankly enjoy films with violence that have no sex in them. I love Clint Eastwood. I don't particularly care for Stallone. I admire him, but I'm not a fan.

TT: You saw *Rambo*?

RM: I care more for Chuck Norris than I care for Stallone.

TT: With breasts, does it ever get too big?

RM: No, bigger, bigger, *best*. They've got to be gravity-defying—they can't be penduloso, pendulous. And she's got to be wasp-waisted and with small hips. They've got to look like something out of Al Capp.

TT: And when did you sort of seize on this?

RM: "Seize," that's a good word, great word. Seize. I was about thirteen. I had taken up with a stripper from a distance in San Francisco. Marjorie Sullivan was her name. I thought that to spend the rest of my life cradled in her arms would have been the best.

TT: What about some of your stars? Were these breasts all God's gifts or have they been aided by surgery?

RM: Well, Kitten was natural. And Raven was natural. In fact, this girl, Tami Roche, she had her breasts reduced. She's in the movie *The Breast of Russ Meyer*. She had her breasts *reduced*, and this photo is after they'd been reduced.

TT: Aren't there problems associated with it?

RM: Kitten would occasionally complain, but she had a good hammock she kept them in during the day, and then she'd take it off at night.

TT: Where is Kitten Natividad today, and what is she up to?

RM: Well, she's not far from here. She's doing well as a stripper. We were together for some four years, which I really think, from an erotic standpoint, was my best time. It was totally erotic, tits and fucking, you know, every night. There wasn't a night when you didn't get laid. And if you didn't get it up, you really had a problem the next day with the lady. I can't speak too highly of her. She had *imagination*.

TT: How do you discover these women, your stars?

RM: Well, one gal recommends another.

TT: In a lot of your films, it's really the women who run the show.

RM: Ah, the women are the superior beings. I have gotten so little static from the feminists. Women are the smart ones. The men are klutzy and muscular and willing, but the women call the shots. I like a strong, aggressive woman.

TT: You've been able to take your own personal tastes and sort of make a movie career out of them. Have there been women who've starred in your films and now repudiate their association with you?

RM: Well, Erica Gavin, who was the star of *Vixen!* She shouldn't have done that. She's even reduced her figure to something that's extremely slender. The trouble is that no matter how you deal with someone like this, they really show the chink in their own armor. But those who defend themselves really get in trouble. That's why years ago I stopped defending myself, and I could deal then with almost any kind of interview by agreeing.

TT: Have you been exploiting the videocassette market?

RM: I have a very good business with them. I just handle my own. I have thirteen titles. I don't advertise at all, the reason being there's no place really to advertise my style of film.

TT: And you distribute them yourself?

RM: Oh, yeah, and they're word of mouth. I go to trade shows. What else can I show you here? This painting was done by a friend of mine, the assistant who's working out in the back there now. This is my mother, grandfather, and grandmother, and my father here, whom I only saw once.

TT: You only saw your father once?

RM: Yeah. He was a policeman in Oakland, and my mother and he separated before I was born. I never knew why, and I never bothered to ask. I figured that was privileged information. My mother always was very nice about him. Interestingly enough, he had to pay child support even while I was in the army. And this here is an important day; I arrived at the National Film Theater in London. We had a tribute, and they showed the films.

TT: Well, it really is a museum.

RM: I never realized I could do it quite as well as I've done it. Everything is adverb upon adjective. I like punctuation that never ends; dot-dot-dot, dash, going and going until finally, paragraph.

TT: Well, your movies are a little bit that way. Everything is larger than life.

Russ Meyer

Jim Morton / 1986

From *Re/Search Publications*, no. 10, Incredibly Strange Films, 1986. Reprinted with permission.

Jim Morton: I've heard a lot about *The Breast of Russ Meyer*. What's that?

Russ Meyer: Twelve hours of unfettered beauty, great history, and humor! I've been working on it for five years, I've got a million and a half dollars of my own money in it, and it's going to be a sensational film. But I refuse to stop fishing and womanizing and having epicurean meals and generally having a good time, so it'll be ready when it's ready. I estimate in about two to three years—there's a big job ahead of me yet.

JM: Is it going to be released as a movie or a video?

RM: It's too long—it's twelve hours. See, I'm making a film for myself. It's an enjoyable position for a filmmaker to be in, to make a film just for himself. What I mean by that is I don't have to make any money; it's not necessary. It *will* make a lot of money in video, but that is so far off, just with what it takes to make a video master the way I go through it, with scene-by-scene color corrections. It will show at festivals like the Cinemathéque Francais or the National Film Theatre in London; already I've been invited to a number of them. So, it will be my song. I think the unique thing about the film is that, to my knowledge, no filmmaker has ever made a film of himself.

JM: Probably not intentionally, anyway.

RM: No, not even intentionally or unintentionally. It will have a ring of truth about it and, I think, also interest and entertainment value. Usually, films about a director follow a format; it's generally: get six or seven of John Huston's associates together and we'll shoot 'em and they'll tell little vignettes from his life, and then show the beauty of John Huston's story—some great film clips. The beauty of George Stevens is not his military footage or his friends, it's the great film clips. I have great film clips (which aren't clips, they're condensations of all my films) but I have more—my own particular brand of humor . . . World War II footage . . . footage of me revisiting the places, photographing friends that I've known through the years. Instead of having them stare at the camera—if the guy's a farmer or if he's a painter or if he sells hamburgers, I photograph him doing that while he's reflecting and talking in voice-over. It's an amazing picture; it's mind-boggling to think of the number of scenes I've shot, in addition to compressing twenty-three films down to ten to fifteen minutes each.

JM: So, the film will be almost like a book?

RM: Exactly. I'm writing my song. Curiously, a German chap—I've known him for a long time—had obtained an assignment to do a book on me, and came over and spent a long time here. I've got ninety volumes of clippings (which we built this cabinet for). But I'm afraid he didn't do a very good job—I'm rewriting it. He was incorrect in the synopses and like most Germans, he has no sense of humor. He also did a little bit of the *Philadelphia Enquirer* (which we had an understanding wouldn't be done) in that he assassinated a number of characters in the book—friends of mine—for the sake of trying to get into the Teutonic mind something that's sensational. I think it's really bad, so we have levied upon them: publish it and be forewarned! [*Laughs knowingly*] Anyway, that's the end of the story.

However, the point I'm making is: it's going to be a good book. I have three publishers who want it: one in France, one in England, and one here in the States. I'm doing all the synopses, and I'm writing them in a very florid style that I didn't think I could pull off. The writing is like the films, with adjective upon adverb, unending punctuation, dots, dashes, etc. What I've been doing is in a sense writing the narration for my big film. So it has value.

JM: Your films usually have fairly heavy narration.

RM: That's because I have a very strong background in documentary films. After the war, I worked for four years doing—we can call them documentary, but they were more employer-relations films for oil companies, paper mills, railroads, things of that nature. I worked for a producer in San Francisco, and it was a great training ground for me. I've always loved the documentary format with the serious, intoning narrator. And generally, at the end, there'll be a scene where we try to straighten everything out by reviewing the film and pointing out where a character went wrong, or point out the characters' shortcomings and frailties—things of that nature. It adds to the whole tongue-in-cheek aspect of the movies.

JM: Educational and industrial films can be quite wonderful.

RM: They don't seem to make them like they used to. They're too loose now; I think television has had a lot of influence. The older ones were really marvelous, *well* structured, maybe hambone by today's standards. A lot of my stuff seems almost unintentionally funny now.

JM: John Ford directed an old "training" film called *Sexual Hygiene*.

RM: I'm familiar with it—remember the guy with the soft chancre in his throat! It was always *dreadful* to look at. In the army, they would terrorize us with that—remember the short arm and the chancres and the guy in the crib: "Honest, doc, I won't do it again!" I often thought it would make an interesting film: to take that and intercut it with my kind of drama, then cut to these [venereal sores]. I'm afraid, though, the military wouldn't release it to me for that purpose.

JM: You could show lots of terrible slides interspliced with *Playboy* bunny pictures. Incidentally, where do you find your women? I walk down streets all the time and never see anybody quite like . . .

RM: There's only a very few, and I've been fortunate to find a few of them. Those that I find and can't use, it's either because of a difficult boyfriend or a husband who doesn't want the bird to flee the nest, as it were. That's the most-asked question in interviews. That, or "Does your mother have big breasts?" They kind of go even Steven.

By and large the girls are from the show business world—premier strippers that make four or five thousand a week, or others that someone will recommend to me. They're not easy to find; in fact, I'm arduously searching for two more. I've got five superwomen in the new film, intercut throughout the opening, which is seventy-eight minutes long, and I need to find two or three more. Hard to find, very difficult.

JM: They also have a certain larger-than-life quality to them. I remember watching *Faster, Pussycat*, and you had Susan Bernard, the Playmate, in it, and she looked like a tiny, dinky thing compared to Haji and Tura.

RM: She was a little squirt, very definitely. In *Playboy*, when you get that foldout, it's pretty hard to tell how tall anybody is unless you look at the specs. By and large, women are not that tall, you know. If you get a woman that's five foot seven, that's pretty tall for a lady. In the instance of Tura, she was wearing boots and she was so voluptuous—big hat, big pair of hips, big boobs—a great Juno-esque looking lady.

JM: She takes on a kind of mythical quality in that film.

RM: A lot of people draw all sorts of conclusions about it . . . *Gotterdammerung . . . Flight of the Valkyries*. She's part Cherokee and part Japanese; her father was a well-known chef in a restaurant in Chicago. That was one of the few times I've really lucked out in casting a role. I couldn't have found another girl that had the configuration, and really knew judo and karate and was as strong as a fucking ox, and had never acted before. She'd been a stripper. Another time was when we found Z-man, who played Superwoman in *Beyond the Valley of the Dolls*. We could never have found another man who would have done that whole Shakespearean shit and the whole works. He still to this day believes that

I ruined his career—he didn't have much of a career to begin with, but—he's another one. I don't mean him any disrespect, because he *made* that part.

And again, with Charles Napier, the guy with all the teeth who was in *Supervixens*. Without him, the film wouldn't have had anywhere near the kind of success it had—I'm certain—in spite of the big boobs and seven girls. Napier, I think, has a quality that few actors possess. Wallace Beery, Borgnine, Alan Hale. There can be just a thin edge separating evil and humor, and they can work both sides of that line. Napier's got that quality: smiling on one side of the mouth and sneering on the other. He's had his good shot now with a picture called *Rambo*, and I think he may be off and running. He wants very much to be Clint Eastwood, but I think he's just a great character type. Who knows? Who would have known that Bronson would have such great success?

JM: It was a rather long time before he made it, too. People always talk about your women, but I notice that certain male characters show up in your films, like Napier and . . .

RM: Stuart Lancaster. I have a band of players. Lancaster was in *Mudhoney*—Uncle Luke, with the bad heart, kindly and totally good, always rising to the defense of his niece. He played the narrator in *Ultravixens*, which was a take-off on *Our Town*—remember the man who would sit on the corner of the stage and say, "Well, I don't know what's going to happen. We'll see what's going to happen tomorrow when the sun comes up." I didn't use him exactly that way, but that was what it was patterned after. Super guy, but never having done anything, largely because he inherited a fortune from his mother. But she was wise enough to set it up in a trust so he gets, I think, $8,000 a month. He spends it every month. If he had gotten all the money, he would have made/produced two hundred bad plays—he's *really* into theater. Dave Friedman said that the first sum of money he got was $400,000, and it all went in like two months, producing plays.

JM: Another male character that comes to mind is Hal Hopper. What a sleazy guy!

RM: Poor Hal. He's passed on. Hal wrote an all-time great song, *There's No You*. He was one of the Modernaires [Editor's note: actually, a member of the Pied Pipers]. It's hard to imagine him sitting there by the microphone singing. He was brought to my attention by an actor named James Griffith. Hal made a great nasty son-of-a-bitch, but he was also the guardian of little Jay North of *Dennis the Menace*. So, here's this whole other side of him. He's gone now, regrettably. In *Mudhoney*, he had *no* redeeming qualities; at least in *Lorna* he did an about-face—he realized that he had met more than his match. I wanted to use him again in *Beyond the Valley of the Dolls* but he was very ill. I've always felt comfortable using certain people, like Haji—she's been in a lot of my films. She's just a great standard-bearer. Even today she really looks great.

JM: She's one of the few women characters that crop up again and again in your films.

RM: She's been in *Beyond the Valley of the Dolls, Motorpsycho!, Faster, Pussycat! Kill! Kill!, Good Morning . . . and Goodbye!*—very substantial part in that. She was in *Supervixens* and *Up!* With some of these people I feel *comfortable.* Trouble is, with girls—generally I use them once and not again. It's almost like having a wondrous affair, even though I might not have one—I have an affair with the camera with them. I think I've extracted all the vital juices that are available for a given film, and I think there's a great shot in the ass if you have someone new to work with for the next picture. But in a supporting role it isn't quite the same thing. I've only used Haji as the main lady in one film—*Motorpsycho!* The others, she was always in a secondary position.

The girls often don't have the same kind of freshness and newness; often they don't have the same kind of dedication. There's a tendency to not take it as seriously the second time. Maybe they're thinking a little too much; maybe they're listening to too much pillow talk—I don't know what it is. That's a tough one for a director that's dealing with matters sexual—to fight off that pillow talk when they go home at night. The "ace" I call it—the husband or boyfriend who is terribly insecure himself, and has got to give them a lot of advice. In the morning, when you start up again, you can sense that someone's been feeding that chick's computer, and you've got to try and work around it—listen and discard things.

Anyway, to put it very simply, it's a miracle that these films are ever completed. Just a miracle. I mean, the emotional problems, the insecurity, the loss of interest after three or four days, and all the cajoling and bullshitting and ass-kissing and ass-licking—it's a miracle the films are finished—certainly mine.

JM: Is that your camera there?

RM: No. I have a couple of shrines in this house. This house was bought to film *Beneath the Valley of the Ultra-Vixens*—you can see some scars on the ceiling. I bought it because of this room—we built all the sets in this room. It did not have that big bookcase; it was just a completely big room and then I converted it into an office and a work area, and now it's my second home. I stay here occasionally and edit films.

That shrine there is for a Chinese chap; he and I shot movies together when I was fourteen or fifteen years of age. He recently passed away. He was instrumental in my getting my first job before World War II. His wife gave me this camera, and that's my little shrine for Henry.

Over there I have another camera that belonged to an old army buddy, who just passed away, who was more brother-like than just about anybody I've ever known. The one below, with an exposure meter in it, is for the cameraman who was in the service with me, who shot a lot of series like *The Twilight Zone* and

Hatari! He also shot my *Seven Minutes.* He was a combat cameraman in the Spanish Civil War.

They're my little shrines. At their husbands' behests, their wives have given me these things because we were so terribly close. It's nice to walk by them and stop for a moment and reflect on the individual. Displayed is the one object—or objects—that really represents the basis of our friendship—the one identifying thing that can bring it to a point immediately. I think about Henry . . . I think about that camera.

JM: When did you get your first camera?

RM: I think I was fourteen. My mother got me a Univex—it's the camera that probably did more for home movies than anything Eastman Kodak ever came up with. It sold for $9.95 and the film was sixty cents a roll—orthochromatic single eight (meaning sprocket holes down one side). The projector was $14.95. By today's standards, that might be $50, but it was the thing that got me by the short hairs. I tell you, when I got that camera, from then on, every nickel I could get my hands on went to upgrading and so on. It got me into the service as a GI. cameraman, simply because of my very strong amateur background.

JM: Getting back to the leading ladies—Edy Williams . . .

RM: Edy Williams plays Edy Williams better than anyone else in the world! She did a pretty good job with *Seven Minutes.* The film wasn't so successful because I was told I had to have an R rating (and when I say X, I mean an MPAA X; not hardcore, but softcore). It just doesn't have the content, and people do react to it in a poor way, but Edy did a pretty good job on that.

We were married for four years, or so. I think the best thing she ever did (and not just because I was involved) was *Beyond the Valley of the Dolls.* She gets a great reaction in the theater every time it's shown. She's been in a lot of other, much lesser films, but I have to admire her—she's in there trying all the time, and does her publicity and—here's a recent picture—she still manages to look very good. But I couldn't have used her as leading lady because you've got to have a little more control over a person than your wife. There's a tendency for things not to go as smoothly as when you're working with a stranger.

I have to take one exception: that's my wife Eve—a wonderful lady whom I lived with for twelve years. She was killed in Tenerife in a terrible airplane crash. We did *Eve and the Handyman* together. There were just four of us: the guy who played the handyman, my assistant, and Eve, and she cooked for us and we really had a tight thing. She said, "OK, half of this is my money, I like the idea of doing it, and let's do it." And she broke her ass; there was never any static from her. She just said, "Look, whatever you want to do, let's do it, OK? I'm here. I'll get up early in the morning and I'll look right," and so on. She was special in that area and in many other areas as well. But with her, I could do it, you know.

But I would never have given Edy a shot at being a lead; there would have been head problems, definitely. There's a tendency to have a wife take advantage of her position, and I'm not talking just about her, but I'm sure any filmmaker—there have been occasions where they've used their wives and it's not been a good idea. I guess that's one of the reasons why I've tried to be at arm's length with the leading lady, and not have any hanky-panky. A couple of times I did—three times, four times—and it really wasn't best for the picture.

The last lady was Kitten Natividad—we were very close, we lived together for four years, and she was fine, because she was a total sex object and a sex machine, and she knew that what we were doing was going to be beneficial to her, and it's proven to be because she was able to get more money. But she liked it, she liked that whole thing of turning people on; it was a big game, and it was fun, you know. She never had any real big aspirations of becoming some kind of "actress" or anything like that, but she did fine, she did very well. She came equipped with what I need for a leading lady more than anything else. She had a great body, and she had done a lot of fucking in her time, so she knew all the positions and everything in the way of turning on a guy—two necessary prerequisites for the success of any leading lady's performance in one of my films. But, when you get that passionate intimacy, there's a tendency (I think) that either person will take advantage of the other. Best to be at arm's length, I've found.

A great lady [Rena Horten] I really cared for—we'd been together quite a while—played the deaf-mute in *Mudhoney*. Very pretty lady. We had become intimate years before when I was in Germany shooting *Fanny Hill*. That's where I met her, and then I brought her over. One night she decided she didn't want to appear naked in front of the whole crew, and no matter what I said, like, "You did it in Berlin and there were fifty Germans hanging around," she would reply, "Well, it's different now."

I ended up very angry. There's an example of being placed in a position where you're getting your nuts wrung out. Sure, you could do several things—you could punch her out, but then you fuck up your picture, and I'm not prone to punching women out, anyway. Or, you can have a giant fight, somehow managing to force her to do what you wanted, and not getting the results. The only best way, then, is to break your ass and do the best you can. Anyway, it worked out, but it affected my feelings toward the lady for as long as we were together from there on out, because it represented a deep-down solid lack of trust.

JM: When you work with a person all day long, and then come home at night and see them there, as well, sometimes . . .

RM: No, no, the women I've known have been turn-ons; I'm lusting all day for them. Even if I'm not having them, I'm lusting for them. It's very healthy to feel that lust. They're great enough—we can bear witness that it's difficult to tire them early in the game. Unless you're a fuckin' wooden Indian.

JM: When you started making films, did you come up with a story and say, "Hey, this would make a great sexploitation movie?"

RM: I didn't know what sexploitation *was. The Immoral Mr. Teas* was the first breakthrough film in the sense that it popularized and established the "nudie." It was number one. As Time Magazine said, "It opened up the floodgates of permissiveness as we know it in these United States." *Teas* simply was an idea which I scripted out in a document and we shot it in four days. I knew exactly how it was going to begin, I knew how it would be in the middle, and I knew how it would be in the end. It was based on my experiences doing stills for *Playboy*. There's a lot of stuff on the girl-next-door, the common man, the voyeur—little nude photo essays. So, *Teas* was a film that was imitated by so many people—*I* imitated it, in a sense. I did *Eve and the Handyman* and I made other nudie films, but *Teas* was a huge, huge success and it's still a collector's piece. *Teas* came out in 1959 and it's still kicking.

JM: There's a certain almost "GI" quality to your humor.

RM: Best time of my life, I'll tell you that. Never had a better time. I was sorry to see the war end. People say, "What?" But I was sorry to see it end; I was ready to go to Japan, the whole shot, you know—the damn bomb interfered with all that. 'Cause I had a feeling like, "Son-of-a-bitch, I'm having such a good time, I'm doing just what I want to do, it's exciting; what kind of job can I get when I get out? How can I get some kind of job?" And it worried me: "What if I have to go back to that same job I had before?" I liked very much that whole living by your wits, with each day being a new piece of excitement. I had mixed emotions about coming home; I probably was the only one in my group who felt that way. Everyone else wanted to go back to Alabama and start a family and all that. Not me. I was just, "Gung ho! Let's do it again!" Just like I feel about my art now: I'd like to start it all over.

JM: When you got out of the army, you went to Hollywood?

RM: I just got off the train here. With the other guy that was with me—just fishing—we went over to the studios. We went to the union to see about getting a job, and they said, "Forget it, we got guys that are gonna get their jobs back." So, I went home to San Francisco/Oakland—I even went back to my old job for about a month. Then I managed to find this industrial job which was great for me. However, I have the feeling that I would not have given in—that I certainly would have been persistent.

JM: Well, your memorabilia here is a testament to that.

RM: You haven't even seen the other room, yet, with props from each picture. As fast as I find something that I want to put on a plaque, I will. I'm starting to put them on the ceiling now—great ceiling for that purpose, slanted like that. My films are having a great rebirth in Germany, France, and England now.

JM: There's a French book on your films.

RM: It's a book by my distributors; Jean-Pierre Jackson wrote it. The captions are all wrong, but otherwise, it's great! There was one photo of that great big Black woman, June Mack, titled "Erica Gavin."

That's why I'm so concerned about this new movie [*The Breast of Russ Meyer*]; it's damn well going to be right. I like the video aspect of it, too—projectionists can no longer cut scenes out of it. Projectionists are great slide collectors—they cut out two or three frames and then crudely splice it so the action goes WHAAP! And the soundtrack ends up harsh. But in video, you can't do that. You buy it, and you can go over the juicy roles over and over again.

JM: Video seems to be opening up a whole new market for sexploitation films from the 1960s.

RM: For me, there aren't many that hang in there. Fortunately, I have a big, strong following, and it grows. Not many softcore—not many hardcore films, for that matter—have become real classics. You can count six or seven hardcore films that are steady sellers—Radley Metzger's stuff (he goes under the name of Henry Paris or something like that), and *Deep Throat*, of course, which is like *Mr. Teas*. It started the whole shooting match.

JM: The hardcore pretty much drove out the softcore.

RM: I never suffered, but of course there wasn't really much good softcore except mine. There were some things like Jonathan Demme's *Caged Heat* and so on—films that prefer not to be called softcore, but there's nudity, a plot, and whatever.

When hardcore came in, I was over at Fox making $150,000 for five months' work and doing a couple of films. All those other guys were jumping in there making these hardcore movies, and I was making a film that was so-called bigtime, you know. When hardcore was at its strongest, I made a picture called *Blacksnake!*, which was the only unsuccessful film I ever made. I thought it was a great idea, but it was about two or three years too late with its slavery aspect. It played mainstream houses.

Hardcore has always been at some shadowy little place where you skulked in and out, with the exception of *Deep Throat*. Women went to that because it became so popularized. The others were all guys in raincoats. That's one good thing about hardcore now—people can take it home. You don't have to parade into a theater.

JM: I've been to a few adult theaters. They're kind of depressing.

RM: Now they're really falling by the wayside—folding very fast. Video, of course, is killing them off. People can rent it rather than go to the theater. But still, there's nothing like looking at something—I don't care what it is—on a big screen in a dark auditorium. It's great! And until they get video in some *size*, you're always going to have that comparison. People like to sit at home and be lazy and look at video, but it doesn't have the *quality*. My stuff I dub from the negative, with scene-by-scene color corrections, but even so, there's nothing to replace something being projected on the screen. This *Breast* will be a monster, just considering the scenes there are in it.

JM: Are you going to have somebody else playing yourself?

RM: Oh, no, it's me. Throughout, I introduce films in a kind of P. T. Barnum way, and it's not bad. If it's me, and I'm doing it, it works, you know—I'm a type, I'm a character, I'm not acting; I'm just introducing. In the beginning, I'm driving a car, and I go to Europe and retrace my steps from Ireland to England to Normandy, Omaha Beach, and so on. I'm driving a Mercedes, then I cut back to my black-and-white GI footage. And there's always a girl like Kitten in the back seat playing with herself, naked, but I'm not aware of it. And I have a narration (which I haven't written yet) which has got to be unpretentious, just matter of fact—not trying to be funny or anything—just reflections. I've got some pretty good photography of me driving the car, stopping and looking, and then I move down to the city . . . go down the road, and there's Tami Roche—now *there's* some cups! Great lady! She's intrigued watching the Mercedes go by. She represents the guardian angel. Then you cut to a room/window and there's Candy Samples doing something to herself. It's for the audience to realize that they are in the right theater. There's this referral, this new stuff all the time.

JM: Tami Roche—did you use her in any films?

RM: No. She's a great stripper. I met her through Kitten. She's got a great body. She'll be awesome in the picture.

JM: I just got a magazine from France called Nostalgia. It seems like the French picked up on what you were doing quicker than the Americans.

RM: Yeah, but they had a lot of time to get ready. If it wasn't for my distributor—a real film buff—I don't think we'd be playing as well as we play. He was a schoolteacher; he got out of teaching and decided he wanted to distribute these films because he believed in them so strongly. Now, we get calls from people wondering if there's any others where the rights have not been given to Mr. Jackson . . . so I owe him a great deal.

JM: Tura Satana is a woman that everyone likes.

RM: She appeals to gays, lesbians, the whole bag, everybody. She has a very strong following now with young people. Musicians look upon *Pussycat* as a remarkable film. Warner Bros. wanted to use an excerpt for some new female group on MTV, but I turned it down, period. It's gratifying to have young people today see and hear it—I get phone calls, asking, "Where can I get the soundtrack?"

or "I heard there were T-shirts," and so on. Tura's developed into a real heroine, or antiheroine. Whatever.

JM: A group called the Cramps does a cover version of *Faster, Pussycat*. There's something about Shari Eubank that really appeals to me.

RM: She wasn't so outrageous in her body (although she had a great body and a real presence), but. . . . She got in with some guy that kind of screwed her around, but she did end up pretty well—she inherited an awful lot of money from her family. I admired her; I liked her very much. She had balls, she had real guts.

We were travelling—promoting the film in the Midwest—her home was Farmer City, Illinois. I had to go to Milwaukee and I remarked, "Well, they got an opening in Champaign," and she said, "I'll go." I said, "That's awfully near to your home, isn't it?" She replied, "I might as well." And she went down there and it turned out a huge share of the audience knew her.

She sat next to her father (who is an ex-GI) and I said, "You've got guts!" (*I* didn't want to sit next to him; he'd probably punch me out.) She did something where she's sitting up on this peak, nude, and her father shouted, "MAH GOD, SHARI!"—you could hear it all over the auditorium. She retorted, "I told you you weren't supposed to come see the film!" She could handle it, you know. I never met the family, but they probably would have stoned me or something.

Shari was gung-ho. There was never an ounce of trouble with her. She just loved doing what she was doing. We always had a lot of privation, difficult conditions—no showers, sometimes—and she was there. She carried water, carried the battery up the road. I'll take my hat off to her.

Uschi Digard's another great trooper. She was in a number of films—a very special lady. I've really been privileged to know some great people.

Most filmmakers are generally not one-to-one on a project; they have a lot of people who are sharing responsibilities. Whereas I've always done a kind of one-man band, where there's something like an umbilical cord tying me to one or two of the people, where you have that tight feeling and that dependency on one another to make the whole damn thing work—and I think how fortunate I've been to have had people like Shari Eubank or Uschi Digard or Kitten Nativided. All these ladies and I had a communion, a marvelous communion, and a meeting of the minds. It went beyond just being an actress in some kind of little television show, because we were doing so many little things together. It was like qualifying for the Olympics every day—it was the 440 and the high hurdles and everything all rolled into one. And they performed, they did it with a minimum of complaints, and rebounded at night when we had dinner and enjoyed the evening, then got a good night's sleep and got out of bed at 5:00 in the morning, and they're putting on body makeup.

Once we were up in this cabin where I had shot *Vixen!*; we went back there to do *Up!* Makeup always has kind of a heady odor, and I walked in and both Uschi and Kitten were naked (Uschi just sleeps in the raw; she had a great body), and I said, "God, it smells like breasts in here!" It broke them up; they never forgot that line. There was something about this musk odor that was permeating the entire room, and here were these two women with giant tits making them up and so on, and I was smelling breasts—sounds like a W. C. Fields line.

This umbilical cord thing—I don't know if I explained it quite the way I feel it. I've always been my own man, but when I worked at Fox I was dealing with an awful lot of boyfriends and outside influences, and I was in town—which made it very difficult to isolate these people from bad influences, because they go home at night. You can't sequester them there on the lot. When I'm in Miranda, California, we have an arrangement: no boyfriends come up, no husbands come up. We're up here, we're going to do it in three weeks, hang in there until we get the film done, OK? And that's what I meant by becoming close (and I don't mean it in a purely physical sense): working together, arguing, fighting, cooking, eating good food, having a drink, swearing, whatever. Nobody to really cater to them and kiss their ass as they do in these major productions. It brought out the best and the worst in all of us.

JM: Sounds like good times.

RM: You just felt it down there in your own scrotum when you're shooting a scene. I know when I was shooting *Vixen!*, the scene with Erica Gavin and her brother was the best of them all. She really displayed an animal quality that I'd never been able to achieve before—the way she grunted and hung in there and did her lines. It was a really remarkable job; I have to point to her always. I've done a lot of jokey screwing, but there's something about Erica and her brother there that was just remarkable. Nothing made the adrenalin flow like that—that was a great experience.

JM: The whole movie seemed more intentionally erotic; your other films are more like ribald humor.

RM: I wonder about the word "erotic." A German I know uses the word all the time. I said, "Do you mean filming through a bunch of dirty wine bottles . . . people caressing each other?" Europeans have a kind of feeling for this kind of eroticism; it's totally unlike what I feel.

When I was rewriting the synopsis on *Vixen!*, I'd just finished that particular part about her brother and I said, "Strangely enough, what I've achieved on film with her and her brother really represents the kind of way I like to screw—I mean like a football scrimmage. That's the way I like it—I don't want all this funny stuff or all this cocksucking and everything else—I just want to get in there and whale away at it." And this is what her brother was doing. If you're going to thrust at the woman, I want her to meet me halfway! You know, just strong physical fucking. And here it is, and that's the thing that I like—it's part of me.

When you see her in that scene when she's hanging on to the iron bedstead (I love the iron bedstead because that *really* represents the basic workbench in life, with the rungs you can hang onto), and she was just grunting almost animalistically, like the mating of the wildebeest and the water buffalo—wonderful, wonderful stuff.

JM: I think "erotic" means it gives you a hard-on.

RM: Exactly. The Germans and the French—it's not the same feeling. I get tired of them when they talk about, "Well, this isn't really erotic." Maybe "erotic" is *sick* or something! Give me the good ol' American way, with lots of grunts—you know, get in there and whale away at it.

I have a girlfriend now that's that way—no foreplay, nothing, just climb on and do it. That's wonderful. You feel great about it . . . I say you need a girl who just yells.

I told this one lady, "I read where women need something like four minutes to get ready for sex," and she says, "Well, I'm more like twenty-two." And even now she'll do it; she'll call, "Twenty-two! sixteen! twelve!" You're walking upstairs with a hard-on, and she's like a viscous sponge. She's so in tune with her whole mind—remarkable lady to get laid. And that's transferred to me as a person. So I'm living a film fantasy, right then and there. It's marvelous to have that kind of union with somebody, where you just *have* each other and then you (exhales deeply) say, "OK, let's do something else here, take a swim, whatever . . ."

JM: Were any of the women in these films difficult to make movies with?

RM: Every one of them had a moment of some difficulty, just as I'm sure I came off as being one son-of-a-bitch at times. When I said earlier that it's been a miracle that every one of these films was finished, well, every damn film I ever made had monstrous problems, there's no question about it. For example, after three days of filming I was looking at one girl through the reflex, and she stuck her tongue out at me—not in a jokey way, but really pissed off. And I remembered what Preminger told me one time: "You treat these actors like cattle; don't treat them like human beings," And from then on, I was really a very difficult guy: never said anything rewarding about her performance, never complimented her, I barely spoke to her. I would use my assistant to say, "This is what we're going to do." And that girl did such a better job; she became so apprehensive about me, and whether or not she was *pleasing* me from the standpoint of doing a good job on the film. See—it worked. It wasn't a master stroke but I *had* to do something. I knew I was losing grip there.

Sometimes people get a little too merry or too funny, laughing it up, so I'll have to say, "C'mon, we've got to be serious about it. I want you to break your ass; now stop it—enough of this lunch break!" So, each woman presents a problem—no question about it, and they wouldn't be special ladies if they didn't have some sort of problem to present. If they were some kind of mush-bag that you could . . .

One time I had a girl quit in the middle of the film. She quit because she couldn't handle the privations—she was used to Miami Beach. We threw her into *Cherry, Harry & Raquel!* and we used her as a wraith-like character who ran through the scenes and did strange things. A guy named Cohen, who is a critic for *Women's Wear Daily*, wrote, "I can't explain the presence of Uschi Digard cast in the role of Soul . . . but thank God she's there!" [*Laughs*] That was exactly right. I mean, he said what I felt so much better than I could have ever said it. Thank God I had her, you know.

So, they all present a little bit of a problem, there's no question about it. Actually, Shari Eubank is one person that never presented a problem. I have to say that in her behalf, rather than to say, "Well, such and such was a real bitch at times." In the final analysis, we were always able to look at it square in the face and kind of joke about it and laugh and say, "Well, we did it, it's OK, everybody's friends." But Shari never let me down, she was a super lady, and Uschi was the same. Uschi never presented a problem, she would extend herself beyond the limit. So, I have to say those two ladies are above and beyond any woman I've ever worked with, who are 100 percent.

Anyway, I have to go.

Some of My Brest Kept Secrets

Paul Sherman / 1987

This is the full transcript of an interview conducted on September 18, 1987, and later edited down for Filmfax, no. 28. Reprinted with permission of Paul Sherman, author of *Big Screen Boston: From Mystery Street to The Departed and Beyond*.

Paul Sherman: I saw *Amazon Women on the Moon* last night. [Meyer has a cameo in it.] Have you seen it?

Russ Meyer: I haven't seen it. I've been in Europe. My lawyer is going to see it tonight at the Cary Grant Theatre.

Sherman: It's very funny.

Meyer: I'd like to get the girl [Corinne Wahl, wife of actor Ken Wahl] for my new movie. But she's being obstinate.

Sherman: How would you describe your films to somebody who's never seen one?

Meyer: Big bosoms and square jaws. And then they say, "What's the square jaws?" And I say, "That's Harry—Charles Napier." He has seven more teeth than Burt Lancaster. Oh, I don't know. There's other ways of describing them. They're cartoons of fleshed-out characters.

Sherman: So, what's taking *The Breast of Russ Meyer* so long?

Meyer: It's just a monster. I almost, a couple of years ago, decided to forget it. I've never been on anything that's had me by the short hairs so long and with so much intensity. It grows and grows. It's seventeen hours long, now; that's the anticipated length. What has really saved me is that I've decided to bring it out in sections. The idea of trying to complete seventeen [hours] is almost too much to contemplate. So, I'm in the final sweep through doing what I call the autobiographical section that will be *Breast 1*, and that will be about three and three-quarters hours. We'll release that to theaters, limited theaters. The others will be truncated versions of all the films, my last chance to really make them great.

Sherman: It seems that you're putting together "The Legend of Russ Meyer."

Meyer: Yeah, in a sense. *Breast 1* has four hours dealing with year one, as it were, up to 1979, with just little excerpts from the films at a given time, chronologically. But it's remarkable. I think this film is worthy of submitting to the Academy for Best Documentary. I think it's going to be a remarkable picture. It's a tone poem.

Sherman: Something for PBS?

Meyer: Nah. It's a lot of great pictures, but without the dialogue, it wouldn't mean a damn thing. The dialogue means narrative. It's nonstop, wall-to-wall narration. Humphrey Bogart, Edward R. Murrow, Richard Burton, and George C. Scott, with a man that does all of those voices expertly. Unrelenting, unstoppable, nonstop. That's one of the things that's taking a long time in the final sweep-through—to write all of the narration. Because it must be written to the exact length of the sequence, and it's being spoken at a pretty good clip. Three words per foot; it's possible for a good narrator, but nonstop. It's a lot of sound effects, a lot of noise, a lot of music, rap rap rap rap rap rap. And the scenes are cut, by and large, three feet, four frames each. So, you get a rhythm. It will either lull you to sleep or give you nightmares.

Sherman: Have you discovered some new women for this?

Meyer: Yes, I have six remarkable women, one of whom is Tundi, a girl I got from Hungary. Tundi Horvath, she makes all other women obsolete.

Sherman: Is Kitten Natividad in it, too?

Meyer: Yes. I've found others, too. Tami Roche, the scourge of New Orleans. A marvelous girl. And now I need four more women to complete it. They represent women that I knew many years before. I photograph the women in sort of a *Playboy* mode, only with a motion picture camera, by themselves. It's intercut with motels and bouncing Pontiacs and things of that nature. I'm going to England Sunday night to shoot the place where Patton made his speech—near Birmingham, in Stourport. I have some good contacts. I think I may have two large girls in Germany, and one in England. It's tough to find these ladies. Just a bitch.

Sherman: Do these women contact you?

Meyer: No. Usually the worst part of making an RM film is the casting. It's so frustrating to find that girl each time, and luckily you just manage to find her each time. I'm going through a lot of frustration now, and I have been over the last two years. Boyfriends—"aces," I call them—talk girls out of doing it. They're threatened, they're insecure people themselves. You got somebody and then all of a sudden you don't got her anymore. And hardcore, of course, presents its problems. It's made it even more difficult. People always think in terms of "Uh-oh, what do I have to do?" And that knocks off a lot of good potential talent. There's no way to get critical of hardcore, but I get mad at it every now and then, when I have someone literally in my clutches, and someone says, "I know what he wants from you, he wants you to be balling this guy." And no matter how sincere I come off, it's sometimes not too believable.

Sherman: What about *Mondo Topless 2*?

Meyer: That's the scraps from the cutting room floor of *The Breast of Russ Meyer*. I went over and toured with Tundi. I got my seven aluminum suitcases, and with the aid of a friend of mine from Nuremberg, found some great suites to shoot in, and I just set up shop. We toured in Southern Germany for seventeen days, and I had her totally under my control, and I just shot a ton of film. If I never had another nickel, I could retire an incredibly wealthy man just by releasing half-hour clips of Tundi. Because there is nobody—nobody—around like her. Nineteen years old, looks like Eva Gabor when she was young, with the biggest tits you've ever seen in your life. Awesome. Just awesome. People I've sent photos of her to just beg me to come out with the footage. But it's got to come out when the time is right, when she's being integrated in the film. I would probably even use her for the other women, because I'd say this really typifies the Russ Meyer woman. I can't find anything better.

Sherman: Does she speak English?

Meyer: No. I had to take a crash course in Hungarian. One-word sentences. But we got along well, very well. I had a lot of trouble getting her out of Hungary, but I had some help. She enjoyed it very much, really had just total abandon. All she needed was a minibar in the suite which she could raid all day—except for the booze—and consume all these nuts and popcorn and chocolates, all the soda water and tomato juice. And listen to Tina Turner—totally, completely, with rapture, full board. And in the Mercedes with the eight speakers, it took a lot of ability to keep driving on the Autobahn and still retain your cool. But it was good because she could dance, and it just made her come unglued. And that's essentially what she's doing all the time—dancing.

Sherman: What are her measurements?

Meyer: I don't know. I don't walk around with a tape measure, but you can certainly do away with the long, low whistle for this one. Though one of her breasts is, hat size, 7 5/8!

Sherman: Is it shot in the same style as *Mondo Topless*?

Meyer: Yeah, in a sense. Bathtubs are always a must—giant bathtubs. Tundi wallowing around in there, and soap and bubble bath. Big rooms with natural light. With fast film you can do that. It really struck the lab dumb at Arriflex when they saw the pictures. It was just a remarkable experience to be with the lady. We'd go to dinner at the hotels at night, and the chef and the busboys would come out and ogle her. Marvelous lady. She wanted to come to the States, but she can't get out of the country.

Sherman: Immigration?

Meyer: No. She had dealt in some things like pot and hard currency, and that's a no-no. They caught her. I'm going to Austria in two weeks, and she can get in to Austria, so we'll have a little reunion.

Sherman: Was *Jaws of Vixen* anything more than a title to flash on the end of *Beneath the Valley of the Ultra-Vixens?*

Meyer: That's all it was. I was going to do a film again with Kitten Natividad, but after five marvelous years, we came to a parting of the ways. Both of our faults. We were good friends, we still are. She's remarried, but that's her thing. She enjoys being married. She's been married a lot of times. The only guy she never married was me.

Sherman: Another thing from around that time was *Who Killed Bambi?*, the Sex Pistols movie. Was that just a matter of two strong personalities, you and Malcolm McLaren, not being able to work together?

Meyer: Maybe two assholes. If you ask me the questions of why wasn't the movie made, then the answer is two words: Malcolm McLaren. McLaren had the whole world in his hand and he didn't have the balls, he didn't have the courage, the desire, to split up the pie. For instance, the head of UA Cinemas wanted to come up with the money—I'd known him for years because he'd played my movies—but McLaren wouldn't go for it. He wanted to make a big, big movie and do it for 100,000 quid. You couldn't do it. Roger Ebert did the script. A marvelous script, another *Beyond the Valley of the Dolls*. We built all of the sets, we had it completely cast with great British types. Marianne Faithful as Sid Vicious' mother. And then we went on location and worked four days. Did the opening— a takeoff on Mick Jagger. We came back, and me and the cameraman were the only two guys in the projection room. Nobody else. McLaren I never saw again. And they turned out a rotten movie made out of video clips [*The Great Rock 'n Roll Swindle*, never released in this country]. And they were even going to put a sequence in there of me being the murderer of a little helpless deer. And I took that mother to task, that [director] Julian Temple, and really extracted a lot of goddam fucking pounds from him. If I ran into Temple again, I think I'd . . . I get so emotional about that film because we would have made a great movie. I would find it pretty easy to dump him in the Boston Harbor.

Sherman: I've heard that you're writing an autobiography.

Meyer: Yeah, I've written the book already. The film is a film autobiography, the book *The Breast of Russ Meyer* is finished, except I'm using it now to write the narration for the film. I backed away from the film for a year, and did the book. The book chronologically is in error in some instances, but by and large it's intact. What I'm going to do in the book is have the first half autobiographical and the second half will be the synopses of the films along with three hundred photographs. I'm going to publish it myself because I want it to be my way. My agent—who does Springsteen books, among other things—will take it, but it must be my way. I could sell ten thousand copies through my mail order for videos like nothing. It's gonna be long, and it's gonna be the way I want it, with a lot of great photographs.

Sherman: When can we expect that?

Meyer: When it's ready. I don't say when anymore. Right now, I am just by the balls with the film. It's a wonderful, total experience to think in terms of this movie. Without it, I'd be forlorn and lost and terribly depressed. But once it's finished, I'll feel I can go on to other things.

Sherman: I want to backtrack now. I want to try to get a sense of how you worked in the 1960s, because I think for those of us who were very young during your most prolific period, it's a mystery. Was the financing of your films in the 1960s a self-perpetuating process, just taking the money from *The Immoral Mr. Teas* and pouring it into the next one and so on, or did you have to go out and find financers?

Meyer: I had a few participants in a couple of them. *Teas* made a lot of money. The taxes that we had to pay were obscene. A partner and I each got a Cadillac and maybe $30,000 or $40,000 apiece. Each time I financed each film myself. *Eve and the Handyman*—we financed it. My partner didn't want to come in on it. Then he came back and we made four more imitations of *Mr. Teas*, along with a hundred other people, until I had to change. Then came the second mode, that was the rural Fellini. I did *Lorna*, which was a big, big success. *Mudhoney* was not a big success, but today is a much bigger success than *Lorna*. For *Mudhoney*, it took some financing aid from the boys who were the heirs to the Hoover Vacuum Cleaner Company. I used to chum around with them, and they put a small amount of money in, along with mine, and they got their money back and made a profit. But in most cases, the money came from me and my wife Eve, which was our bucks that we had earned. All the time, we—she, a very bright lady—was able to invest money for our security, which is substantial now.

Sherman: Were you doing everything yourselves, down to marketing and writing the ads?

Meyer: Eve was a great lady. She and I experienced some six great years of marriage before I got into films. When I started to make films, our marriage started to become very difficult. She didn't approve of it. She approved of the money. She liked the idea of dealing with men and putting them under her thumb. I recall a distributor here in Boston named Ellis Gordon. Sometimes he had difficulty writing a check. I remember she was ready for some reason to really put the blocks to him, and he came out and tried to give her the money, and she refused. So, he approached me and said, "I've got an $80,000 check here and your wife won't take it." So, I snapped it up. I was at Fox doing *Beyond the Valley* *of the Dolls*. But she was after his skin. She was a vindictive lady about anything that was, shall we say, a little off-color. She also loved to deal with men before it was really popular for businesswomen to deal with men. She was not only a looker and had big tits, she really knew business. She was an ex-legal secretary, and there was no man alive that she couldn't handle. Except me. I don't mean in any way to make less of her, but she did basically disapprove of the films. And I think a lot of it had to do with her realizing that our marriage was ending. And with me, nothing is more important than film. Everybody has to fall.

Sherman: Was it because you were working with all these other women?

Meyer: No, I was very faithful to her until finally, when I realized it was the end, I went to Germany and made the *Fanny Hill* dumpster and said, "The hell with it. I'm going to have a good time."

Sherman: How different was the version of *Fanny Hill* that you envisioned to the one that Albert Zugsmith put out?

Meyer: I never envisioned anything. We were at a period that financially was high and low. We had made *Lorna*—had all our money in it. We didn't know what its potential was. Zugsmith had seen the film, and approached me through his son-in-law, for me to direct *Fanny Hill*. It turned out he was looking for a codirector. I had no idea what the script was about. I got to Germany, I read it, I objected to being codirector, and the Germans did, as well. So, I was the director, per se, of this given script until the Germans became frightened of a counter-lawsuit, and they let Zugsmith back into the show. Then he directed the last two days. The film made a lot of money, but it's not a Russ Meyer movie. It had the greatest record of returns, I understand, of any videocassette. You know, when that first came out, he left my name off of the credits for the theatrical release, and Allied Artists, who were distributing it, said, "You'd better put it back on or we're gonna have a lawsuit." So now it's got Russ Meyer at the top.

Sherman: The more cartoonish parts had some good laughs in them—the scenes with the stuffy men and the whores. But the parts with just the women were pretty boring.

Meyer: I have the hot reel. I have it. I came into possession of it, and I've got clips in the new film where the girls are bare-breasted. It was an experience to make the film. I would have gone crazy if I hadn't known two remarkable women, one of whom, was Rena Horten, who I brought back to the States to play *Mudhoney*, and Christiane Schmidtmer, who turned up in *Ship of Fools*. She was a girlfriend of Jose Ferrer's. Those two women supplied the carnal need every night. I've never been in a position, and probably never will be again, that I could've fixed up seven guys every night with a beautiful woman in Berlin.

Sherman: Who did you consider your peers during the 1960s? People like David Friedman and Roger Corman?

Meyer: Well, I always enjoyed Dave Friedman as a person. Corman I've never really known. I met him only at one cocktail party, in which he made some complimentary statements about *Faster, Pussycat! Kill! Kill!* I've never known him on a personal level. Friedman has been a good character witness at a divorce, and things like that.

Sherman: Were there any other filmmakers that you really felt an affinity with?

Meyer: No, I just had this thing myself. I'd made a lot of money doing early pictures—"titty-boom" pictures for magazines, and I lived in my own little cocoon. I just forged ahead and did what I wanted to do. There's nobody that influenced me except my own carnality.

Sherman: Does *The French Peep Show* still exist?

Meyer: I have no idea if there is a print. I doubt it seriously. I think Pete DeCenzie's wife did away with it.

Sherman: Was that just made for DeCenzie's one burlesque house in Oakland? Did it get shown around?

Meyer: I'll tell how it all came about. I had approached Pete DeCenzie, who had the El Rey burlesque house. He was one of the last entrepreneurs in burlesque. And there was a girl with great big tits, and I became infatuated with her. And I shot a lot of stills, and the more I shot, the more infatuated I became. Then I shot a movie with her—a hundred-foot movie, in the little studio of the guy that I worked for, Gene Walker. I shot it with a lot of cuts: lips and nipples and so on. And I did a dumb thing. I put it through Eastman Kodak, which in those days was a no-no to have any kind of nude breasts. But it also had my boss' stamp on the box. Well, the guy at Eastman Kodak, Bob Antz, he was a pretty liberal guy, and he called my boss up and he said, "Hey, what kind of movies are you making, Gene?" And Gene said, "What do you mean?" He's an ex-Stanford alumni president, a very proper man. So, Antz said, "Well, we got a roll over here of some girl with great big tits. We can't let it through." So, I got called on the carpet. Gene wanted to know what I was doing. So, anyway, this guy Antz was obligated to destroy the film but he didn't. He gave it to me. So, the basis of this film is the basis of *Peep Show.* I showed it to DeCenzie, and he said, "Let's make a movie!" So, we did a movie of the show; we shot it at night. He could have made a lot of money with it, but he was a marvelous man, very trustworthy, and he gave it to these guys with Campbell's Soup on their vest, these old states'-righters, and they just robbed him blind. He never got a goddamn nickel out of that thing.

Sherman: Was it feature length?

Meyer: Sixty minutes. He could have made a lot of money. He just paid me and my assistant—the sound man—a fixed amount of money, and we made the picture for him. That's how we later made *Teas* together.

Sherman: What sort of theaters were the early movies playing at? Was *Vixen!* the first one to crack the mainstream?

Meyer: No, the first one was *Mr. Teas.* It did not play in any scumbag houses. That was one thing about Pete, and he taught me that. He said, "Don't play in those crap houses." We played for about a year and a half in the Guild 45th Street Theatre in Seattle, Washington, which is the leading art house there today, and that set the pattern. We only played in the best art houses. It was an interesting period. People were growing weary of the Lollobrigida-type films—a girl bending over and showing cleavage, and so on—and the art houses were ripe for something like *Mr. Teas.* That's where we fell in, and from then on out, we only played mainstream. We've never played the scumbag houses. Oh, there are always isolated instances where something like that will happen, but by and large that was it. For example, that guy Ellis Gordon kicked off *Lorna* here in Boston in a house called the Capri. They were gonna level it and they said that we could finish it with this picture. Well, the goddammed thing hung in there for about eight months. It was a huge success. Even today in Europe, the films are only playing in the best houses. *Beneath the Valley of the Ultra-Vixens* is in its eighth year in Germany, and it's unique in that it goes back to the same theaters six or seven times. So, in Spain, in France, they play in the best theaters. They play in the best or the distributor is shit-canned.

Sherman: Do you think your audience changed a lot from the early days to the time of *Ultra-Vixens*?

Meyer: No. We just hit a certain age level, and then that age level came along again, and now they're rediscovering the films. Only there are a lot more females looking at the stuff today. Women like the films. Couples see the joke. They like the tomfoolery, the put-on, the send-up, the cartoon. In fact, it's growing, and what an ego-building shot in the arm video is! Most videos sell and then they sink. Ours are going up, up, up. We have an awesome business in video. Thirteen titles.

Sherman: Are the more obscure early films ever going to come out on video?

Meyer: No. *Teas* is the only one. *Breast 2* will be the nudies. It will be *The Immoral Mr. Teas, Eve and the Handyman, Heavenly Bodies, Europe in the Raw, Erotica,* and *Wild Gals of the Naked West* intercut with location scenes where I've gone back. "A serious look into the populous of smalltown Miranda, which little realizes what's happening to its community," says Edward R. Murrow. Then we cut to buildings and windows, and there's Tundi dancing, there's Tami Roche in a tree. And the serious narrative is going over it with no reference to these ladies whatsoever, about facts and figures and grosses. I've gone back to Yale and photographed Yale surreptitiously, where it's not permitted. I've done all these sorts of things with a simple black tripod and a two-hundred-foot magazine.

Then the next one up will be the rural Fellinis, with *Lorna* and *Mudhoney*. So, I'll bring them out in cassettes. This is the only way I can manage the seventeen hours. The idea of completing a film that's seventeen hours long is just too much to contemplate.

Sherman: Is that you doing the narration in the first *Mondo Topless*?

Meyer: No, that's John Furlong, who played Calif McKinney in *Mudhoney*. The man of a thousand voices. He does Murrow, he does Burton, he does them all.

Sherman: So, he's going to be doing *The Breast*?

Meyer: Yes.

Sherman: Does he do most of the narration? Like the intro to *Faster, Pussycat*?

Meyer: Oh, yes. Always the "big, soaring edifices" and all that stuff. I can't narrate, just in short bursts. But he's even gonna do my voice in the film, as Humphrey Bogart.

Sherman: These days it seems that people really miss sex in movies, with the whole "safe sex" thing. Do you think that's one of the reasons why your movies stay so popular?

Meyer: That has nothing to do with it. Those scenes are trite, insignificant. Let's just digress for a moment. The reason my films are still X, and I insist they be, is it's with the over-preoccupation with sex. That's what gives you an X rating. Like *Vixen!* made in 1968, in order to have an R, has to have seven minutes excised out of it today. The standard for sex has not changed. For violence, it's changed, but not for sex. *Supervixens*—seventeen minutes must be cut out. *Beyond the Valley of the Dolls* would lose the entire lesbian sequence today. A couple of balling sequences and the gun in the mouth would go to get an R. And I like it that way. I don't like the simple X. I planted it, in fact, in Ebert's mind, about the A rating. And now he and Siskel are calling for it. Bless them for it, but they're not gonna get anywhere with that guy Jack Valenti. No way. He wants the skull and crossbones there.

Sherman: How did you and Ebert get together?

Meyer: Tits. A mutual admiration society. He loooves tits.

Sherman: Was it just from reviewing your movies?

Meyer: No. I got to know him through a piece in the *Wall Street Journal*. It was a front-page piece by a guy named Steven Lovelady—great name!—from I don't recall what year. But it was front page, and well done, and there were some letters to the editor. One was from a lady in Terre Haute that suggested I be hung by my kazoos. I'm paraphrasing it. And the other one was Ebert's, saying he enjoyed the film immensely, blah blah blah. In those days there were very few sympathetic people that had anything decent to say to the filmmaker—me. I wrote him a letter saying we must get together, and from then on, we've been really fast friends. We are very, very close friends, and he's weathered the association very well. I mean, when he wrote *Beyond the Valley of the Dolls*, he literally had to go underground, with all those assholes like [Mike] Royko taking whacks at him. Then, when I went to Chicago with my old lady, he was really depressed. I took him to the State and Lake Theatre and he saw all those people standing there and shouting and screaming, and he walked out of there ten feet tall. From then on, it's been OK. Now he admits openly, "Yes, I did it, and I was glad to."

Sherman: Which films other than *Beyond the Valley of the Dolls* did Ebert work on?

Meyer: He wrote the ending to *Supervixens*, and he wrote the Greek choruses for *Up!* and *Beneath the Valley of the Ultra-Vixens*. There was another one that could have been great, *Son of Beyond the Valley of the Dolls*, that Fox wanted no part of.

Sherman: Do you go to see many new movies?

Meyer: None. I don't go to movies at all. When you're looking at a movie on a moviola ten hours a day, you don't need any other movies. The last good movie I saw, and I admired it enormously, was *52 Pick-Up*. The reason I went to see it was two-fold: John Frankenheimer and Elmore Leonard. I read Leonard's books and I love Frankenheimer. And that's the most recent film. I have no interest in the current scene. I saw another thing, *Hot Pursuit*, just momentarily, and it was such a nothing movie. I saw cuts from another, which is supposed to be sexy, but it's a different kind of sex. Mine is buffoonery. It's a put-on. It's the kind of way that I personally practice sex, with Miss Natividad or Tundi. It's like a football scrimmage. All this sensitivity crap, being cute, clever, that has nothing to do with it. That's why I survive. People can sit there and say, "Holy shit! If I did that I'd end up in traction!"

Sherman: That shot of the demolition derby intercut with the love scene in *Finders Keepers, Lovers Weepers!* is perhaps the ultimate Russ Meyer moment.

Meyer: Yeah, in fact a German magazine is running a sequence of that in the current issue. The art director and I are good friends, and they used the film frames, themselves, for blow-ups.

Sherman: I want to run off some names of personalities in your films for you to tell me how you got involved with them and what you liked about them. First off, Bill Teas.

Meyer: Teas and I were in the service together and were good friends, and still are. Teas is a participant in the profits of *Mr. Teas* to this day. Next month we have our forty-fifth annual reunion, all military photographers, in Atlanta. Teas was a ham, a very fine portrait artist who loved to pose for self-portraits, and it was just circumstance that he did the movie. My friend DeCenzie, the coproducer on *Teas*, was always after me to make a nudist movie. People playing volleyball and all that stuff. Teas happened to be over that night, and I looked at

Teas and said, "Why don't I just do a film and have Teas as the main honcho in it?" DeCenzie said, "Fine. Do anything you want and I'll come in fifty-fifty with you." So, that's how I used Teas.

Sherman: Were you in a photographic unit in the army?

Meyer: Yeah. The 166th Signal Photo Company.

Sherman: Was that with George Stevens?

Meyer: No. I wrote to a reporter who had an article that said Stevens was the only one to shoot any combat.

Sherman: Supposedly he was the only one to shoot the European war in color.

Meyer: Well, that's what the truth was. With all due respect to Stevens, who I greatly admire, the best part of his biographical film was the clips from his movies. What I can really say about the military footage that Stevens had was that it was like a week after the infantry went through. If you look carefully, you can see all the telephone lines are strung down the street. When the infantry goes through, all the lines are down. Stevens' group was a very elite group; we were the footsloggers. We were attached to divisions. We just did a lot of sticking one's neck out. We had a lot of casualties. It was fun, we were aggressive, young, carefree. We had a great time, best time of my life. The best part of *The Breast* is I went back and redid the whole thing with Kitten Natividad in the back seat masturbating. I look back and the tanks are going in the grainy footage—I got a lot of great footage—and cut from color and black and white. With the serious Morrow talking: "Advancing into Altenberg, only thirty miles south of Leipzig."

Sherman: How about Lorna Maitland?

Meyer: Her tits . . . remarkable. My wife, at the time, withheld her photographs, thinking I would fall madly in love with her, but that was not the case.

Sherman: The photos from the casting call?

Meyer: Yeah. She got the picture and she wouldn't give it to me. At the last moment, she gave it to me. She didn't want me to think she was holding out on me. I called up my associate, James Griffith, who was the cowriter, because we had already hired this other girl. I said, "I don't give a fuck. I'm bankrolling this, and you give that other girl a thousand bucks and you get Lorna Maitland. And if she can't pronounce her name, I don't care. She is Lorna." And she turned out to do a good job.

Sherman: Hal Hopper.

Meyer: Hal Hopper used to be with the Modernaires [Editor's note: it was the Pied Pipers]. He sang with Crosby and Dorsey and so forth. He also wrote a lot of songs, one of which is an all-time standard, *There Is No You*. Hal Hopper was a stuntman, he was a lot of things. His nephew was Jay North from *Dennis the*

Menace. He'd played as a stuntman, and was a good friend of this fellow Griffith, who was a well-known character actor, and that's how Hal Hopper came into the scene. He played Luther in *Lorna* and Sidney Brenshaw in *Mudhoney*.

Sherman: He seemed to really enjoy himself in those roles.

Meyer: Oh, yes. Just great! In that dirty suit. He lived in that suit for two weeks.

Sherman: Stuart Lancaster.

Meyer: Ah, yes. He lives down the street from me. The man of a thousand plays. Heir apparent to the Ringling fortune. His mother was married to John Ringling. They dole him out something like $6,000 a month. Just walking-around money for Stuart. Stuart just writes play after play after play, and he's been just wonderful in my films. He's been the dirty old man and the upstanding husband and the cuckold, you name it.

Sherman: I think *Ultra-Vixens* was his shining moment.

Meyer: Well, that's *Our Town*, Thornton Wilder

Sherman: How about Princess Livingston?

Meyer: She was a burlesque comedienne. I met her through Pete DeCenzie. I used her first in *Wild Gals of the Naked West*. Great, with no teeth and that cackling laugh.

Sherman: Haji.

Meyer: She's a real spear carrier. I met her when we did *Motorpsycho!*, a picture that's not been widely shown. She's a great personal friend.

Sherman: Tura Satana.

Meyer: Tura Satana had it all going. She had big tits, she also had this great Oriental look. She knew judo and a little karate. Had never done any acting before. I can't say enough about Tura. She was just a gung-ho girl.

Sherman: How about Charles Napier?

Meyer: Of all the square jaw types, he's got to be the arch square jaw. I met him when he had done some early softcore. *The Hanging of Jake Ellis*, things like that, for a Dutch filmmaker, and I used him in *Cherry, Harry & Raquel!* Then I used him in others. He played Baxter Wolf in *Beyond the Valley of the Dolls*, when he was heavier. And then he's in *The Seven Minutes* as Iverson, the police officer. But the big thing was *Supervixens*, because his career had literally been finished. It was wasted away with bad marriages, and he wanted to go back to Kentucky. I talked him into staying and he did a fantastic job on the film. The film just performs like hell on video; it performed like hell in theaters. It's the basis of his present success.

Sherman: Now he's always in Jonathan Demme's movies

Meyer: It's prestigious but it doesn't really mean anything because people don't really remember him except real arch film buffs. The film they remember him from is Harry Sledge in *Supervixens*. All the others are offshoots of that. That's what really put him into prominence. Hitchcock put him under contract because of that film.

Sherman: How about Alaina Capri? It seems like she was an influence on Divine.

Meyer: Well, I'd never thought of it in that light, although John Waters feels strongly about the films. She's an ex-schoolteacher, an absolutely accurate school-teacher who wanted to do this and changed her name. She's married to an as-sistant DA now in Los Angeles. Very happy, she's got three kids, still looks great. Amazing. Of all the ladies, she seems to hold it. Still got the big tits and the good-looking face and the hair and the whole works. And she has a dinner for Lancaster and myself and Furlong and whoever we can dig up once a year. She's proud of the films.

Sherman: How about Erica Gavin?

Meyer: Terribly uptight about *Vixen!* Dislikes it, dislikes having done it, dis-likes any part of it. Of all the girls I've ever used, she had an undefinable some-thing. She didn't have the biggest tits, she wasn't the best looking. She had a quality that made Edy Williams want to see that movie once a week, and when she did, she was a tear-ass in the sack. She liked the idea of a woman calling the shots. That's why we had a big, big female attendance for *Vixen!*

Sherman: There was an interview she did in the 1970s in a magazine called *The Velvet Light Trap*, and she seemed almost bitter for doing those films, because things didn't really take off for her after she did the two movies with you.

Meyer: Yeah, she said something like the only good thing I can say about Meyer is that he didn't hit on me. She never realized—to this day she doesn't realize—the impact she made. Of all the movies, *Vixen!* did more to put the sex-ploitation movie into the mainstream. It was awesome; that picture was incred-ible. In Chicago it still has the record for the longest run of any picture on State Street. It got me into doing *Beyond the Valley of the Dolls*. Richard Zanuck saw it. We had 176 prints playing in New York. Those were the days when admission was a buck and a half. Zanuck had to go down 42nd Street and Broadway with Abe Burrows and look at it. The hearsay was they were contemplating some-one other than Jacqueline Susann to do *Beyond the Valley of the Dolls*, which was then not called *Beyond the Valley of the Dolls*. And the immortal words of Mr. Burrows supposedly were, "If that klutz can make a movie like this for $72,000, I suggest you throw him a bone." And that's how it all came about, because of *Vixen!* But in the middle of filming, Erica Gavin gave out, she really caved in. She had a lot of personal problems that were difficult for her to handle. I see what she has to say occasionally, but it's always badmouthing, it's all nega-tivism. She doesn't realize that she really left an impression on cinema that will be thought of for many, many years. Long after *Caged Heat* and things of this nature, though I don't mean to denigrate Demme.

Sherman: Though Erica Gavin really showed a lot of talent in *Caged Heat.*

Meyer: Her only problem was that she always got involved with the wrong people. There was an opportunity for her to make something of herself. But she got involved with some people who wanted to have her taught how to act. That's the worst thing you can do to a person—give them some goddam dramatic training. Because she came right off the wall. We were lucky to finish *Vixen!* Preminger once told me, when I was on a show with him and Mickey Rooney, he said, "Actors are fools, they're stupid, they're cattle. Don't flatter them. The worst thing you can do is flatter them!" All of a sudden, I could see the whole role of *Vixen!* caving in, and from then on, I listened to Mr. Preminger. I never said anything complimentary, I hardly said good morning. And it worked. She started watching me to see what was wrong with this fucker.

Sherman: And Uschi Digard?

Meyer: One of the best, if not *the* best. Just a great lady.

Sherman: She's another one who looks like she's having great fun in the movies.

Meyer: What she exudes sexually on a personal level, she exudes twice that on film. She's kind and considerate and devoted and successful today as a jewelry expert. Travels consistently, owns a lovely home in Palm Springs. Always called her own shots. She and her old man had an open marriage; if she saw somebody she liked, she did it, and he did the same thing. Cared for my mother when she was extremely ill in the hospital, go in there every day on her bicycle. Took her to Switzerland to see her family. That kind of lady. And on a sexual basis, one of the most exciting women that you can ever contemplate. She made sex into child's play, literally.

Sherman: When did you meet Kitten?

Meyer: I met her through Shari Eubank, who was the lead girl in *Supervixens.* She probably has left a bigger impression on my life than any other woman. I mean, we lived together for five years. It was mandatory to have sex every night, 365 days a year. If you didn't, you caught hell. And she was motivating, exciting, skilled, you name it. It was just a great affiliation that we had, and we're good friends now. Whereas we don't see each other on a personal level, we had the best of each other. I put it that way. It was just fulfilling as hell. I had a great time.

Sherman: Has she been acting?

Meyer: Yeah, she does things in some films. Some porno, but she doesn't do it herself. She'll maybe have a girl chew on her or something of that nature. She has been tempted but hasn't done it. I'm glad she hasn't. *Ultra-Vixens* did a lot for her, and she did a lot for *Ultra-Vixens.* It's a two-way street.

Sherman: I have to ask how you came up with the title *Faster, Pussycat! Kill! Kill!*

Meyer: It was not my thought at all. It was a fellow by the name of Richard Brummer, an assistant editor of mine who's working with me now on *Breast*. It was his idea. He came in one morning, he was working on the sound effects on *Pussycat*, and he said, "I think I've got the title." We were going to call it *Leather Girls*.

Sherman: Was that in response to *Leather Boys*?

Meyer: Yeah, that was it. With Rita Tushingham. That had a lot to do with it. But *Faster, Pussycat! Kill! Kill!* is a great title. It's Dick Brummer's. Now I did a music video for Warner-Elektra for the band that took the title Faster Pussycat. They gave me the job, and apparently it turned out pretty well. They're having a little trouble with the lyrics on MTV, but it plays two times a day. We use rear and front projection of scenes of the film, projected on the musicians in black and white. It gives it a nice 3D effect.

Sherman: I imagine you get a lot of offers to do videos.

Meyer: No. The establishment is a little afraid of getting me because they know they're gonna get an X-rated picture. But that's no great loss. I've been to the mountain once, it was wonderful. I did what I wanted to do. Ebert and I got the film out that we wanted to do. As he's said, two nuts were put in charge of the asylum.

Sherman: Did Fox release *The Seven Minutes* as you wanted it?

Meyer: Yeah. I believed in it. And Zanuck believed in it. We thought we'd made a great soaper. The problem is that when the public expects a certain thing from a filmmaker, you'd better damn well supply it. And they insisted you will not make an X-rated picture out of this, you will make an R rating. Instead of thirty minutes in the courtroom, we should have had thirty minutes in the bedroom. I believed in the film. I believed I was capable of anything. I set out and I did make a good film, but it shouldn't have the name Russ Meyer on it. It should have said Joe Bush or something and it would have been more successful.

Sherman: You had a three-picture deal with Fox, right?

Meyer: That doesn't mean anything. It could have been a thirty-picture deal. The reason it only turned out to be two pictures is that Zanuck and Brown, before I was finished with *The Seven Minutes*, were thrown out of the studio. They were banned. I, in fact, had to smuggle a print in the back of my car, and drive to the beach house and show the print to Zanuck. He was not permitted to come back to the lot. He said, "This is gonna clean up." We both felt that. The first night, the auditorium was full of people, the second night, it was half empty.

Sherman: What happened with *Blacksnake!*?

Meyer: Well, the film was not successful because the leading lady was built like she had two backs. The original girl I had was a great big, Romanesque, Alaina

Capri–type who ended up with an overdose. Threw her right out of the movie. I had to take the second choice, who was hostile to me to begin with—Anouska Hempel—for not selecting her [first]. A good actress, but totally unbelievable in the role. And as a man once said at the Dallas Film Festival, "Come on, what is this shit, Meyer? Where's the chick with the big tits?" He said it all. It's a well-made film, though. Again, an R-rated picture—the fans are disturbed.

Sherman: Is that one completely your production?

Meyer: Yes. Though I had some backers on it. It was filmed all in Barbados, with a British cast except for one Haitian actor, Jean Duran, who played Sergeant Pompidou.

Sherman: Is there a reason that some of the films have alternative titles because of reissues? Like *How Much Loving Does a Normal Couple Need?* is really *Common-Law Cabin*.

Meyer: It just didn't work. I thought *How Much Loving Does a Normal Couple Need?* was a great title. I saw it in a supermarket on a magazine cover. It died, and *Common-Law Cabin* finally worked.

Sherman: How about *Rope of Flesh* and *Mudhoney*?

Meyer: People thought *Rope of Flesh* was a horror movie. It just died at the box office. And the ad showed a man being lynched. Negative. We put a picture of Rena Horten spilling out of her bodice and called it *Mudhoney* with, from Oscar Wilde, "leaves a taste of evil." One-word titles with that contrast of sweet and sour have always been the best.

Sherman: What's the name of the book that *Mudhoney* is based on?

Meyer: *Streets Paved with Gold* by Raymond Friday Locke.

Sherman: The movies from that period often have the feel of a pulp novel.

Meyer: Oh, yeah. Well, that was my try to get women in there. Girls only wearing one dress and no underwear, men with one change of clothes.

Sherman: Is *Faster, Pussycat! Kill! Kill!* your best-selling videocassette?

Meyer: It is a growing videocassette. But the big success is *Ultra-Vixens*. Two to one. Three to one. Then *Supervixens*. Then *Mondo Topless*, which is a nothing movie, but popular because of a girl named Darlene Grey. Marvelous. *Pussycat* is coming on. It's liked by a segment of our society that is extremely vocal. But with *Ultra-Vixens*, the people are discreet. They just want to get in the dark room. *Ultra-Vixens* is beyond cult. It's mainstream, mainline, cult, supercult, undercult, tit cult, everything!

Sherman: Do you think *Breast* is going to be your swan song?

Meyer: No, because I'm going to do a movie that has to do with sugar and cocaine and diabetes, and three triplicate women. A KGB colonel woman, a US Army nurse Brunhilda, and Harry Sledge. It's *Blitzen, Vixen, and Harry*. I could have already made it in Germany. It's about the two rings from the time of alchemy, that if you matched the two rings, you could take common table sugar and turn it into cocaine. And then the heavy is Basil Rathbone–like, only called Mario Mastoccolli. And his thing is to retire with Brunhilda to a small island off the coast of Cuba with a warehouse full of sugar. They redo the dueling scene from *Robin Hood.*

Sherman: I wanted to find out about your days making industrial films.

Meyer: I still am! These movies are all industrial films. They've got the serious narration, the heavy muscle voice.

Sherman: When you were making those sorts of films, which are almost beyond parody, some of those, did you have to hold yourself back?

Meyer: No, no. It was a great opportunity. When I got out of the service, our earnest desire was to go and become members of the union and work for a major studio. Forget it! All of the returning veterans had first shot at it. So, I went up to San Francisco with a letter of introduction to the Kodak guy, and it was a blessing in disguise. I went to work for Gene Walker. I shot thousands of feet of film most seriously. In fact, I used to ignore what the director said, and just shot beautiful picture postcards of the daylight trains running through dogwood and all that kind of stuff. Certain lines would make me chuckle in the narrative. The boss was a good writer. "The season of the burning bush turns to the season of the silver mantle." I'll never forget. And the train would go into the tunnel with a red, autumnal bush and come out, and there would be heavy snow on the other side. It left an impression upon me because afterward I would say, "That's great narration!" Terribly serious, heavy muscle-voiced people lecturing about the annuity plan.

Sherman: Yes, just like the way *Vixen!* starts out like one of those *Water Skiing in British Columbia* shorts they used to put on TV when a baseball game would get rained out.

Meyer: That's it. Exactly. The bush pilot. And *Breast* is just that, it's full of it. But now it's *really* overblown.

Mondo Russo

Dale Ashmun / 1988

From *Film Threat*, no. 15, 1988. Reprinted with permission of Chris Gore, publisher/editor.

Russ Meyer was born March 21, 1922, in San Leandro, California. He has made twenty-nine features [Editor's note: no idea where this number came from. At the time of this story, Meyer had made twenty-three features.], most of which have been box office hits. Those familiar with Meyer's work know his trademarks: hilariously ludicrous plots, outrageous narration, bizarre camera angles, hefty doses of violence, degradation, and of course, women who sport mountainous mammaries.

I recently interviewed the King of D-Cup Cinema in his luxurious home high in the Hollywood Hills. Meyer was resistant to being interviewed when first called.

"I just spent half the day with a writer from *Newsday*, and I've heard they axed the feature," he told me.

When I arrived at the Meyer Museum, he had just returned from buying some groceries.

"I'll be with you in a second," he said as he led me into his home. "Meanwhile, just gaze at the breasts. Feast your eyes on breasts and let them fill you with awe."

So, I spent a good half an hour examining his amazing memorabilia: movie posters, awards, framed reviews, even a wall full of mounted props from some of his films. Among the mementos I found especially fascinating were some wooden plaques mounted with three or four color photographs, taken by Meyer, of several humongous-breasted Amazons that have starred in his films. Beneath each set of photos was a brass plate inscribed with the woman's name, a date, and these words: "In Commemoration of the Mutual Exchange of Bodily Fluids." Then we sat down to talk.

Film Threat: How did you finance your first film, *The Immoral Mr. Teas*?

Russ Meyer: My partner at that time, and I, contributed dollar for dollar. We both were making a pretty good amount of money every day shooting stills for television shows.

FT: And you were a photographer for *Playboy* at the time?

RM: Not ever a *Playboy* photographer. Like a lot of people, I managed to find a girl before some other guy found her, and rushed in there, and Hefner would OK her, and then we shot her. There've been a few staff *Playboy* people.

FT: But it's mostly freelance?

RM: Yeah, well, if you have a girl, that's it.

FT: Where did you grow up?

RM: I'm what you call a native son. Born in what we call Northern California, which is really mid-California, the San Francisco/Oakland area. Lived in about thirty houses because we didn't have any bucks. Then I got a job, and along came the wonderful war, which was a great experience at the time; I had a great time. Came back and had my sights clearly in place, and went to work for an industrial filmmaker in San Francisco, which was a marvelous opportunity. It was very good that we couldn't get a job in Hollywood at that time. We were distraught, because we thought that we, as returning conquering heroes, should be given a shot at working in Hollywood. The only thing was there were a lot of other guys returning who had worked in Hollywood before they went into the service. So, being turned down, it was, at the moment, depressing. But when I went back to 'Frisco, with the aid of some people at Eastman, I was put in touch with a man named Gene Walker. He gave me a great shot, shooting industrial movies. My films are, in a sense, documentaries. I often have a narrator, exposition, minimal dialogue, people who are not professional actors, as a rule. Some are. So, here I am.

FT: How long did you work for Gene Walker?

RM: From late 1946 until 1951. Then I moved to Los Angeles with my wife Eve, where I started shooting a lot of stills for TV shows. And a lot of titty-boom, which was the girls with the biggest tits I could find, which was my taste, and still is. As we started making more money, we started galivanting around Europe a bit. Then, along with Pete DeCenzie of the El Rey Burlesque in Oakland . . . he was one of the last of the really great entrepreneurs. He brought out people like Tempest Storm, Lili St. Cyr. In fact, I did a film for him before I did *Teas* called *The French Peep Show*. It featured Tempest Storm and it was basically a burlesque show. Because I had been smitten for the moment by Miss Storm's giant tits, I undertook to take some shots of her, and DeCenzie liked the idea. I didn't just set up the camera and make a hundred-foot cut. So, I made the film and presented it to him, and he turned it over to his hirelings and they promptly picked his teeth. He never really got anything out of it.

FT: Will that ever come out on video?

RM: It's been destroyed.

FT: You didn't keep a copy?

RM: I was never given a copy.

FT: Was it a feature or a short?

RM: No, no, full feature. And what I've since heard from a man whom I tried to put in touch with Pete's wife—who's hostile towards me—was that she said, "I've destroyed all his stuff."

FT: So, your first feature as a director doesn't even exist?

RM: No, before that I did a film called *The Desperate Women* for Appleton and Newman. Sam Newman worked with the *Perry Mason* show; he was a script supervisor. Lou Appleton was a director, and through a friend I knew in the service, they approached me to do *The Desperate Women*. It had to do with the abortion racket, a very safe way to deal with sex. Showing it as a real crime, women being taken in by these terribly mustached slickers and then cast aside after they've become pregnant. Then they're taken to an abortionist, who's generally a heavy drinker, with Coke-bottle-lensed glasses, and the knife would slip and you'd hear a heartrending scream and the woman's body would be found in a ditch. Then some young press man starts poking around, and along with a young press woman, they somehow manage to bring these people to task. So, *The Desperate Women* was just another one of those films that I shot. I don't know where it is; I've no idea if a print exists.

FT: But was it released?

RM: Released, and released successfully.

FT: Directed by you?

RM: I was the cameraman. It was directed by Lou Appleton.

FT: When you were in high school, did you try to photograph some of your big-breasted classmates?

RM: No, no. I was very shy. There was a girl I lusted after who had giant tits named Polly. But no, nooo. I didn't get laid until I was twenty, in France, thanks to Ernest Hemingway.

FT: Tell me about that story.

RM: We were trying to get into Paris, and we were ahead of our division, which was the French Division. And we encountered Hemingway, whose lieutenant, a Portuguese gentleman, suggested that Hemingway take the boys down to the local notchery. And he did. The place was closed, but we got in, and we were placed in this humongous place for the evening, and I had a nice experience with a girl with giant tits because that was my taste even from much earlier years. I only lusted after women who had enormous tits! That was it, period. Sooo, I selected the biggest-titted girl there and we had a marvelous time. From then on, I've never bothered with small-breasted women. I'd rather play cards.

FT: Were you a cameraman during WWII?

RM: Yes, I was a combat cameraman. I did things that were exciting, stuck my neck out, enjoyed it enormously. Nothing that I will ever do in my life will begin to approach what I did in the war.

FT: Were you ever wounded?

RM: No, unscathed.

FT: Did you have to shoot any Germans?

RM: No, but I shot at one once, and missed him, and he missed me. I was a cameraman, I only carried sidearms. Had I been equipped to shoot the enemy and had a chance to do so, I certainly would have shot him, right in his tracks.

FT: Did you have a happy family life?

RM: Yes, my mother was a great lady. She was just wonderful. I had a sister, but my father made himself absent from the hacienda before I was born, and I only saw him once. I never missed him. He paid for my support until I was twenty-one, even whilst, as the British would say, I was in the service. He was a policeman, and he had to pay; they had him right by the short hairs.

FT: The sense of humor in your films is pretty wild. What were some of your influences to develop that tongue-in-cheek style?

RM: My first influence was Al Capp. I would copy studiously his drawings, only I would make the tits bigger, and the tits on his women were always pretty good-sized. I think my first introduction to satire, which I prefer to call my stuff rather than humor, was through Capp. It didn't really hit me as such at the time, but as time went on, I began to see that he was really dealing satirically with the country as a whole . . . politics, religion, and whatever have you . . . an amazing, remarkable man. I also developed an enormous feeling for W. C. Fields. From the very early years I found him to be an extremely amusing man. Unlike Chaplin or Keaton, Fields easily represented the essence of humor. Just as, for example I enjoy Jonathan Winters. I really regret that he's not doing more.

FT: Did you ever see any of his early standup performances?

RM: Yes, I saw him years ago opening for Thelonious Monk. He did a bit on the landing at Tarawa, by himself, which was really super.

FT: Any literary influences?

RM: Well, I've read a lot. A lot of the early young men's books that are very well suited to what I do. I like Horatio Alger. Horatio Alger was certainly way before your time, even before mine, but they had great titles, like *Sink or Swim* or *Paddle Your Own Canoe*. And literally any of them could make a great Russ Meyer movie, just change the girl's chest measurements. The hero is always put upon, always beaten up and taken advantage of, stolen from. You could imagine any one of those things being turned into a Russ Meyer movie.

FT: The women in your films are often superior to the men . . . stronger and smarter.

RM: I like women who are aggressive. I don't like smart women. They seem to be smart, but by and large they either end up with an ice tong in their chest or run over by a Jeep. I do like aggressive women. It will be apparent in my book. It's curious; it's a book that's not only technical, but it's like a soap. I've been able to give a very detailed description of every woman the I've lived with, in detail, but also in a very outrageous way. I've known some marvelously aggressive women. Women who have really giant tits, and they've been with a lot of guys and they've been dealt with in every conceivable manner. It's hilarious when I stop to think about knowing these women and how much fun it was. You see, once I got laid, then I went at it hammer and tong. But I went at it in a very precise manner. Not any broad, just specific broads, and I went through mountains of shit just to find these broads. That was it! Nothing would stop me. I would make it clear that this is what I wanted. So, because of that, I've led a very rewarding life, so far. I would not bother with anybody at all, unless they were somebody I could fantasize about. It's the same way with being a married man. I've been married three times . . . three great women—Betty, Eve, and Edy Williams. Now you can't come home when you make my kind of films and apply yourself as I do, and dump the fantasy at 7:30. The fantasy has to go on, it has to go on all night long. Some of the ladies I've known are that way. For example, Kitten Natividad, we were together a long time, and she's a good friend of mine; the fantasy was on all night. When she got home, she was doing a striptease while she was bludgeoning the rug with a vacuum cleaner. In a restaurant, she'd be playing with your joint, letting men lust after her tits, then returning to the house and immediately taking all her clothes off and doing a little dance. She made it very clear that there was no way you could avoid having sex. The complete antithesis of the games most women play. But with Kitten, if you didn't face up to it, you had a tough night! And there's not many ladies like that around. But I must say, I've known at least nine, maybe ten ladies like her, but I didn't hang out as long with them as I did with Kitten. I like women that get mad at night if you don't fuck. It's usually the other way around, isn't it?

FT: Yeah, when the guy has to say, "Not tonight, dear, I've got a headache," you've got something special.

RM: Eve Meyer was that way . . . just mope and get mad and angry.

FT: Is she still involved in film production?

RM: No, she's gone. She died terribly, in a wretched plane crash.

FT: Were you with her a long time?

RM: Oh, yes. We were married for twelve years, but separated after nine, and I was totally faithful to her for eight and a half years.

FT: I saw a few of your films in Amsterdam last summer during the Russ Meyer Film Festival they presented. Have there been other European retrospectives of your work?

RM: Well, more and more. I had some good fortune in Spain. We also just opened *Supervixens* in Madrid, and it was very fruitful because it played off the festival I went to. The festival had me, Fellini, and *Battleship Potemkin*. A perfect combination, you see.

FT: Do you control all your video sales?

RM: Oh, yes. I've retained complete rights and market them through my own video distribution company.

FT: They're popular, I'm sure.

RM: Yes, sales are quite good. But, you see, I'm dealing with almost a religion. It's my largesse.

FT: You're a bit of a living legend to many people. How does that feel?

RM: I'm reassured by the fact that people buy a lot of cassettes. It's very flattering, and it seems clear that I have struck a common chord.

FT: I understand your films are very popular in Germany.

RM: Well, now more and more. I recently did a tour over there, and they're now playing *Mudhoney*, which is twenty-one years old. And for the second go-around, they're playing *Supervixens*. And for six years, *Ultra-Vixens* has been playing in Germany.

FT: Are the films dubbed, or do they use subtitles?

RM: It depends on the country. I'm flying to France next month to supervise the dubbing of *Ultra-Vixens*. A lot of these films, when they're dubbed, they really soften the sound effects, which is bad. Robs a lot of the cartoon aspects . . . you've got to have that in there.

FT: What was the theater in Chicago that played one of your films for over a year?

RM: That was the Loop. It played fifty-four weeks.

FT: Do you approach large-breasted women on the street to be in your films?

RM: I've approached them years before, but I don't see them out there anymore. Years before, maybe my tastes weren't as strict, but there was an effective way, when I was shooting stills, of finding girls to photograph for the girlie books.

FT: Did you discover any leading ladies by spotting them on the street?

RM: No, most were through hired agents. It's just torturous; the worst part of making my films is trying to find the women. There was only one Lorna, there was only one Uschi, there was only one Kitten. It's just a cocker; I hate that part of it. Without them the films wouldn't be worth a fucking thing. In *Supervixens*, it was a monstrous job to find all those women.

FT: I'd like to ask you for impressions about some actors who you've worked with. For example, Charles Napier, who has played key roles in several of your films. What's he like to work with?

RM: Oh, he's a super guy. Napier first came to my attention because he had done some films that were soft X's for a Dutch filmmaker whose name escapes me, and we cast him in *Cherry, Harry & Raquel!* I used him in many other films after that. In fact, when I wrote *Supervixens*, I wrote it with him definitely in mind. He really made the film work. We had a young guy in the film who was a leading man type, but he ran just well, you know, he was just running all the time. But Napier had that sweet and sour Borgnine/Alan Hale quality. He could be a shit one moment and charming the next.

FT: How about the scene in *Supervixens* where he stomps on the woman in the bathtub—was that difficult to shoot?

RM: No, it wasn't difficult. It was done with the whole thought in mind of being such an extremely outrageous expression of horror that no one could ever take it seriously. But people took it both ways. Some took it as being terribly serious, or the more astute knew it was overdone, it was ludicrous. We approached it in the most serious way. Simply put, Napier was told by this lady that he was a bad lay. Now, the only way to deal with a girl that says that you're a bad lay is to stomp the shit out of her in a bathtub, right? And Napier said, "Right, that's the way we'll do it." And there you are! The strength of these films is because they're played straight—the serious intent is always there. If somebody's fucking, it's like a grudge fuck. You know, more of a grimace, make a lot of noise, like a water buffalo. [*He imitates a female voice.*] "I don't come that way." Well, you do in the movie; you make a lot of noise, and none of that quiet shit.

FT: How about Stuart Lancaster?

RM: He's great. A dirty old man. I just had lunch with him the other day.

FT: Is he still making movies?

RM: He does occasionally, but he's mostly in plays. Stuart is a wonderful, talented man. And like the Germans said, my pictures are full of immoral farmers. That is Stuart. But he can be very serious at times, like when he was doing *The Grapes of Wrath*. I remember a friend of mine, who knows Stuart but Stuart didn't know who he was talking to (on the phone) because it was a yellow pages ad. He called up, and my friend says, "Modern Photo." Stuart says, "I'm over here at the Colony Theatre and we need some very serious pictures of some of our people. Can you handle that?" My friend says, "Yes, I can. What is your name?" "Stuart Lancaster." My friend says, "Oh, you're the guy who's fucking the chicken in *Supervixens*." He completely blew him away.

FT: How about Haji?

RM: Ahhh, she's a special lady.

FT: Her tits weren't so big, though.

RM: No, well she [played] the second girl, always. She had the lyre-like hips and the wasp waist. She was graceful and could dance. She was great in *Good Morning . . . and Goodbye!*

FT: I love the scene where she seduces Stuart Lancaster in that film.

RM: Stuart was always labeled unprofessional by the girls because when we did the [sex] simulations, he always got a hard-on. Alaina Capri, who played Angel in that film, would say, "You're getting me wet. It's awful. Dammit, Stuart! Be professional! Don't get a hard-on all the time We're actors! Now, stop it!"

FT: Your locations are really desolate and beautiful. Where did you shoot mostly?

RM: All of the early noir period was filmed up in the delta area of the Sacramento River. Also, I love the desert . . . *Motorpsycho! Mudhoney, Supervixens, Cherry, Harry & Raquel!* It's invigorating up in the desert. It's dry and crisp.

FT: Was there much fucking around between cast and crew while you were on location?

RM: Oh, no, no, no. Big Brother was watching. I watched like a hawk. My first encounter with Haji, I pulled her out of a sleeping bag with one of the actors. They were out in the desert and one of my assistants said, "I think they're out fucking around. So, we ran out there and the desert was just full of Mojave greens, the most intensely poisonous snake. They were about ready to fuck, and I grabbed her, and shook her, and she clawed the shit out of me. I ended up sleeping with three girls in my trailer. I slept by the door with an axe handle. That's it. There's no way anybody could get to those women. I kept that policy in all of the films—nobody touches the women. I'm not saying that they didn't pull the wool over my eyes. But I wanted to retain the vital juices and avoid the arguments and petty jealousies that arise from love affairs on the set.

FT: Were there any exceptions to your policy of abstention?

RM: Well, a few. Tura Satana, who was in *Faster, Pussycat! Kill! Kill!*, said to me, "Listen, I can't go for this shit. I have to have a man once a night or you might not have me as an actress." There was nobody else who could have filled her role, so I said, "Well, who do you have in mind?" She had her eye on the assistant cameraman. I said, "OK." And she said, "Let me reassure you that it will only be once a night." So, in researching my book, I called up the cameraman to double check that the story was correct. He said, "Everything is exactly right, only it wasn't *once* a night!"

FT: So, tell me about the book you're working on.

RM: Well, it's just about finished. The book will be titled *Russ Meyer: The Rural Fellini: His Films. His Fantasies. His Frauleins.*

FT: That last part is like a subtitle.

RM: Yeah, and it will be. I don't think the pictures are the big deal about it. Oh, they say, "Are you going to have pictures in it?" Of course, I am. But I think nothing really beats the words. I don't think you can make a movie as good as you can write.

FT: You've got to have a story.

RM: No, I don't mean that. I mean to be able to describe the whole thing, the sex act, how it feels. We haven't been able to do that in a movie. Nobody's been able to film a really one-on-one thing, but you can describe it in a book. I've been able to deal with matters of sex as related to me, I think, in a very humorous but a very factual and very fantasized way. How I felt, what I thought, what turned me on. The book deals with my beginnings, very straightforwardly. It deals with practically every woman I've known, either intimately or platonically.

FT: When do you think the book will be available in stores?

RM: In about a year.

FT: Could you describe your work in progress *The Breast of Russ Meyer*. Will it really be twelve hours long?

RM: Yes. I've been working on it for five years. It's essentially finished; maybe I'll shoot a few pickups, maybe a few new pairs of chests. It needs more sound effects, which is a laborious, time-consuming job.

FT: What is the scope of this project?

RM: The bulk of the film is each film compressed, with cogency, down to twenty minutes. Then I go back to the scene of the crime. I photograph the town today, and I've shot interviews with many of the people involved in the films. It's very close to being finished. But I'm in an enjoyable position for a filmmaker— I'm making the film for myself. I don't have to make any money, although it will make money in video release. It will also play at festivals like the Cinematheque Francais or the National Film Theatre in London. I've already been to several festivals. So, it will be my song. And a very unique thing about the film is that, as far as I know, no filmmaker has ever made a film of himself.

Russ Meyer

David K. Frasier / 1990

This is the full transcript of interviews that were conducted on August 6 and 17, 1990, and have had segments printed in various publications. Reprinted with permission.

David K. Frasier: You were shooting "titty-boom" after the war. I know you were an industrial filmmaker. Whose idea was it to make a film like *Teas*?

Russ Meyer: It was my idea because Pete [DeCenzie] said anything you want to do is OK. I don't care what you do, but just let's make a movie, whether it has to do with nudism or whatever.

DKF: And you had already done *The French Peep Show*.

RM: That was way before. I was then just a working stiff. Didn't mean anything. Except he had confidence in what I could do in as far as taking pictures and taking them a little out of the ordinary. The basis of *Mr. Teas* was some of the work I was doing for *Playboy* and lesser magazines. The girl next door, the boy next door. The voyeur, the poor simple man always trying to get a good look at some girl that's naked.

DKF: Was it patterned after the storyboards in magazines?

RM: No, it's not what I *saw*, it's what I *did*. I did these layouts. I did a scene of a girl using a window up against a seamless paper background. I didn't use anything that influenced me. It was my own ideas of what I was doing. I'd always make up little stories, silly stories with a girl. The girl who goes around, for example, at the racetrack, picking up the tickets people throw away. Occasionally she'll pick up a winner. But anyway, the whole thing emanated for me from this period. I was in the business of making silly little stories and they were only an excuse to be able to show a girl naked. So, in the case of *Mr. Teas*, Bill Teas happened to be at the house that night. That was the only reason he was in the damn picture.

DKF: So, if anyone else had been there, they'd have been in it?

RM: Not necessarily, but Teas happened to be there, and DeCenzie said, "Who are we going to use?" And I said, "Let's use Bill. He's a ham." He liked to pose, and so on. Bill got ideas about how significant the whole thing was, particularly his input. Teas, to a large part, was a drunk when we were making the movie. He doesn't want to say that, but he was loaded. I handle it well in my book by saying he did his best work on a blistering hot day at the beach, nursing a monstrous vodka hangover. That's it. I don't mean to say that Teas was not contributing this, that, or the other. He was a ham. He mugged. I had everything pretty well in mind. DeCenzie kept saying, "Gee, that's great!"

DKF: Was there a script or did you just wing it?

RM: Written on the back of a laundry ticket. No, nothing was written out.

DKF: So, in the morning you basically knew what you were going to shoot that day.

RM: No, I knew the whole thing. Of course, there were things we shot later . . . pickups. But it mustn't come off as some kind of great planning. It's just off the wall. We had an idea about the man who hallucinated. The whole thing was my doing those layouts for Globe Photos that got me into it. Not anybody else's, only my own. Nobody else was doing it and I had that built-in ability, like any so-called journalist has, to just make something out of nothing. What made these films, or what made any of my films, is all the postproduction. Looking at what I had and saying, "That ain't enough, we need more," and then going back and shooting a sign or a tin can or a lamp post.

DKF: Was the principal photography, the shooting of Teas and the women, done in about four days?

RM: I don't think so. I think it was longer. I think it went on for many days. For example, the sequences that we shot in the beginning . . . I always started with the girl with the biggest tits, and that was Ann Peters. We had these three girls and we knew that we had to show them in their natural habitat involving Mr. Teas. Then we had to somehow miraculously get them together in the outback. OK, we showed them at work; we showed them at play. There were a couple of side items. There was Dawn Danielle, a pretty blonde girl. I'd shot a lot of stuff on her, and it was hard to find women in those days. It was almost slammer time if you shot them. Oh, you could shoot nudes, but putting them in a movie smacked of heinous stag films. I remember shooting about four days and having a hell of a time getting [my wife] Eve away from it. She just didn't like her house being photographed, and all that pressure. Then, later on, I came up with the idea of doing some abstract stuff involving the nurse with the big mule deer tooth, and so on. I did it as I went along. There was no master plan. Then when you put it together in the editing, *that* was the significant part.

DKF: Where were the outside scenes filmed?

RM: We shot at Paradise Cove. In those days you didn't pay a nickel. You just went in there with a 16mm camera and shot all this stuff. A girl in the surf, and then I knew a guy by the name of Lee Zuman, who was a railroad lawyer. The kind the railroads hate. They're always looking for Jose, whose foot has been run over by a diesel. Paradise Cove is near Malibu, and then we shot in a place called Soledad Canyon. That was out in Antelope Valley. By and large, you were always looking for places where you wouldn't get arrested. You see, again we had some rumbles. One in particular had to do with a lake we rented for a day for $100. This woman threatened us with all kinds of bodily harm if we stole any fish. We told her what the film was going to be. She wanted the $100. We had an entrée, a guy named Paul Martin Smith, the heir to a vast fortune. He was a photographer, and he was interested in photographing girls naked. He also wanted to get laid. A rich boy. So, we used each other.

DKF: It's clever using Teas's real name in the title. Was the idea yours? Was there an alternate title?

RM: The idea was DeCenzie's. Period. I scoffed at him after that initial night of discussion. He said, "The first thing we have to come up with is a title." I said, "Come on." But he was right. He thought a strong title was great. Titles like *Rose LaRose*, *Pictures in Poses*, and so on. He liked the term "immoral," and Teas had the built-in name there.

DKF: After you shot the movie, was there difficulty in getting it processed?

RM: I had a friend at Eastman who was a tech rep who worked with cameramen who furthered the products. I don't know the exact time or in what order it was. We knew from the outset that we were going to shoot the thing on professional Eastman film. All they had was some Ansco color, or something like that.

DKF: You ultimately knew, though, that you'd have to blow it up to 35mm to play theatrically.

RM: Right at the beginning, we met a man named Adrian Mosser, who was experimenting with a process called a "liquid gate." It's a gate with a glycerin in it, and the film goes through the glycerin and it's a refractive process. The glycerin after cleaning the film fills in that deep scratch, and most of the scratches are not reproduced. That was always the problem with 16mm. *Teas* was the first feature film, to my knowledge, to use this process. I think they did some experimental stuff for Disney, and the like.

DKF: So, the stories about this having to be surreptitiously processed at night are untrue?

RM: Not true. All open and above board. This guy Grant had a very stiff-necked lab supervisor at Eastman who was the censor. Bells would ring when a bare nipple was going through the soup. So, Grant bears equal responsibility with me and DeCenzie for getting the film out. He put his job on the line. He told his supervisors that we were making an experimental comedy filled with nudity, and that he would personally be on the set at all times to make sure nothing objectionable was being done.

DKF: It's been said that *Teas* opened the floodgates of screen permissiveness. Were the only films being shown that contained nudity the nudist colony films? If audiences wanted to see nudity, did they have to endure this pseudoscientific documentary stuff?

RM: I never saw any of those films. There were none that preceded *Mr. Teas.* Years before, they had made those dreadfully boring nudist movies featuring croquet and volleyball. But no one had made any films that had had nudity, per se. That's why *Teas* was a success. Even the melodramas like *Highway to Hell* were just films that showed absolutely nothing. But they all had a heavy advertising pitch. So, there was nobody before us.

DKF: How important was *Playboy* magazine in creating the atmosphere for a film like this to be made?

RM: Well, as I pointed out earlier, because I was doing work for *Playboy* and lesser magazines like *Sir Knight* and *Adam.* . . . In fact, the main publicity thrust came from the magazine called *Sir Knight*, which was a sister magazine of *Adam.* The editor was Mick Nathanson who wrote *The Dirty Dozen.* He was a photo editor who'd buy pictures from me. So, he was the inside man in the skin works. I think Ken Parker, who was one of the crew and an army friend, was working for Globe and helped set up a deal in which we'd get $1,000 for the layout which, in those days, was unheard of except for *Playboy.* But *Playboy* totally ignored us when it came out. No, not really. They came out a year later and ran a layout on it.

DKF: When you were making this film, it had to be in the back of your mind that there was a possibility of spending a lot of money on a film you wouldn't be able to show.

RM: No, I never had that thought. I believed in DeCenzie. I would not have been able to make it without having him onboard. DeCenzie was the bloke that kind of made it all possible because we held him in some reverence because he was one of the early guys who would get out and do *Pictures in Poses* and pin seal leather billfolds and Elgin watches—an entrepreneur. So, when you have a guy like that on your side, you have this wonderful confidence that all is going to go well.

DKF: So, once you had the film in the can, was it going to be his job to go out and find people who would show it?

RM: We found it right off the bat, as soon as it was finished. But it got busted.

DKF: Where was the first place it played?

RM: San Diego.

DKF: And this was 1959?

RM: I've never been sure of the release date. I always think of it in terms of 1958, for making it. What happened there, I suppose, was that DeCenzie didn't really prepare the "patch," as they call it . . . that he didn't grease the palms of the local authorities. In the circumstances surrounding the bust, the people who had stopped the playing all of a sudden disappeared. The police officer was nowhere to be found, and the official of the theater was not to be found. They just grabbed [the print] and locked it up. It took us easily a year to get the print back. A statement had been made: "This is a film you shouldn't book because the police are going to get involved."

DKF: You tried to pitch the film in other cities.

RM: I don't think so. Everybody was afraid when we got busted. The only place he pitched it was up near Washington, where he was traveling with his *Pictures in Poses*, and he ran into another paisan in Seattle. They had a censor board. They convened in a hotel room, which is unheard of. They had a 16mm print. He showed it in a suite. They drank wine, had a good time, and enjoyed the film. With no cuts, they passed it. Now, as far as what the police like . . . police like to have that kind of shield. They don't like to be the ones who prosecute and go after people. They're not that kind, because they come under all sorts of fire there, too. They like someone else to dare the ire. Police say, "Hey, look, don't come to us. There's a censor board. You voted them in." So, when we opened, there was no problem. We played for a year. And when we went on, there was no problem, except in San Diego, where we still couldn't play. Pete got bookings all over the country.

DKF: Did it make the real money at the Paris Theatre in Los Angeles?

RM: The Paris was a secondary theater where *Eve and the Handyman* opened. The big money was made at the old Guild 45th Theatre in [the Seattle neighborhood] Wallingford. It played there over a year. Then we opened in Philadelphia. And we had a distributor. He was one of the rare "clean" distributors. Most of these people were really questionable as to their worth and integrity. There were "states' rights" distributors with Campbell Soup on their vests. Most were dishonest, but there were some honest ones. But DeCenzie would never admit to anyone he thought they were dishonest. Even if they were, he'd protect them.

DKF: So, as far as a businessman, he wasn't a great one?

RM: There are two ways of looking at it. When he had these strippers like Tempest Storm and Lili St. Cyr, he was a great businessman. He spent money and he made money. But he and I had a mail order business with Tempest Storm. He entrusted it to one of his lieutenants to keep track of the orders and send out pictures. I owned 10 percent of it. This is really early in our association. So, I brought myself to say, "Hey, where's my cut?" The lieutenant came up with the limp excuse that just the night before someone had broken in and taken all the receipts. I knew the guy was lying, but Pete said, "Gee, that's terrible, Ed."

DKF: So, DeCenzie was willing to believe the best about people.

RM: These were his friends. This is what he believed in—his burlesque and states' rights people. It didn't matter if they were honest or not; they were his friends. There was a theater in Philadelphia, the Academy I think it's called, run by a guy of some questionable deportment. In fact, when he paid me off, he took a .45 out and laid it on the table. Seretsky was his name.

DKF: One keeps hearing it said of those days that "art theaters" played racy foreign films.

RM: There was Gina Lollobrigida and Silvana Mangano. These were the so-called "art films," and they were playing in those theaters. People became disenchanted with these films, and when *Teas* started playing, and then the other imitators, the art films were just eased right out of the picture.

DKF: Did DeCenzie set up any systematic distribution for *Teas*?

RM: He had Joe Narcissian in Denver, who prepared the Denver exchange. He had Eddie Gelbart, who took the Philadelphia exchange. William Mishkin, a natty dresser, handled *Teas* in New York and Atlantic City. You could play it without cuts in Atlantic City, but it was cut in New York. By the way, did you read that review by Leslie Fiedler?

DKF: Yes.

RM: He had a real feel for the picture, this guy, and that review came out at an opportune time.

DKF: It sort of legitimized everything you were doing. He was one of the biggest film critics in America at the time.

RM: Yes. He's a professor at Samuel Clemens now at the University of New York in Buffalo. He's in charge of Samuel Clemens, so he's not a film critic anymore. But passing a censor board like that is like a license to steal.

DKF: Once that happened in Seattle, it opened up the rest of the country.

RM: Yes, it got very full active play, which included Atlantic City. In New York it must have played well because Murray Schumach was writing all these features. Joe Narcissian in Denver was a good friend of Pete's and a really fine guy. He was playing it in Denver and the rest of Colorado. Damned if I know who had it in Chicago. Eve would handle it with Pete, but then they got into a terrible argument over integrity.

DKF: What was the ticket price? I saw a newspaper clipping for the Center Theatre in San Francisco which ran a "special"—all seats $1.49.

RM: The theaters all bounced their prices up for the nudies. I would say they were all around $1.50.

DKF: In the campaign manual for *Teas* it featured a clipping about Bill Teas and the models appearing live at the Balboa Theatre. Were there many such personal appearances?

RM: Well, Teas went down to San Diego, and was there for the bust. I have one clipping that says that he appeared in person, but I have a feeling he didn't because Teas and I had a falling out, which Bill doesn't like to admit to. The reason being that Teas was given, I think, two percent of the gross, and it was upon my insistence. My two partners, DeCenzie and Eve, didn't want him to have it, but I said, "Oh, no. Give the guy something." Teas at that time was doing lab work in town for Globe Photos. He grew to be a pretty good drinker, was pretty heavy into the sauce. He'd listen to the publicity that was out on this thing, and our proposition was that you had to pay for the film blow-up and everything else before everyone splits [the money]. Teas would listen to the bartenders and they'd say, "You have a piece of that show? You didn't get any money yet? It's making millions! You'd better check into it. These guys are cheating you, Bill." It got to him. He was steaming, seething. And all the time Eve and Pete were saying, "Oh, we shouldn't have him [getting a split]. We shouldn't." Teas came up to the laboratory where I was working, developing some pictures, and he accused me of cheating him, saying, "I want the money." I said, "Get the fuck out of here." I just literally chased him out of the darkroom and up the stairs. He just offended me. So, I told Eve, "OK, babe. You got a deal. Get rid of him." So, they bought him off for $750.

DKF: That was probably the worst deal of his life.

RM: Yeah, but it isn't that much when you get down to it. It isn't that much. It didn't make that much money. A million-dollar gross. Sure, we bought a couple of Cadillacs. We made enough money to invest in a couple more movies. Teas at the most would've gotten around $10,000. That would have been it. There was no great largesse. It would've been spread out over a couple of years. You see, Teas doesn't want to admit to the fact today that he signed those papers.

DKF: What's his story? Do you think he feels he's been cheated?

RM: Yeah, he still does. That's why I shouldn't give him the $1,000. It's like I feel guilty. I don't feel at all guilty. DeCenzie and Eve are the ones who should feel guilty. I was so angry with him that I was just ready to beat the shit out of him. He insulted my character. Teas remembers what he wants to remember, and what he doesn't want to remember, he forgets. You're bound to have disgruntled people in all this business of people getting percentages. You can see why there's all this stuff about [Art] Buchwald and *Coming to America*. If we kept Teas in, we'd have had a much better tax break. Instead, we had a closely held corporation of two, where it would have been three, even though he had only like two percent. There wouldn't have been a big tax bite. It was a monster tax bite. Had he stayed on, we would have made a little more. There hasn't been a lot of money made on *Teas*. People say, "Oh, it grossed a million." But there wasn't a lot of money. We both had to keep our jobs. I was still a Globe photographer. I was also doing photography for television shows. Making *Teas* did not put us on Easy Street. It didn't lose money, but it was not a big winner.

DKF: What were the women in *Teas* paid?

RM: I don't think any of them got more than $100 a day. I think Marilyn Wesley got $100 a day. She was one of the three key girls. Michelle Roberts was the secretary. She got $100 a day. The other one was Ann Peters. She had the best body, the most conical breasts. So. these three got nine hundred bucks. We also did some quick pick-up shots. We went here and there. What I did with Teas, I got a lot more of him because he had a piece of the action, and I didn't have to pay him [by the day]. Teas willingly signed the release; he wasn't forced to. He was paid $750 when $750 was a lot of money. It would be easy to say about making *Mr. Teas* that it was a glamorous operation, and it just bulldozed the opposition when it came to making money. *Teas* had that ability to make money. For the time, and considering the film, it made a great deal of money. What we did was pay the lion's share to the government. That was at a time when there was a 50 percent bracket.

DKF: What's the story about receiving a tip that vice officers might be lurking about?

RM: Ken Parker had heard a rumble that they were going to bust us [while we were filming]. But they didn't know where in the hell we were going to work. So, he went off as a decoy in one direction, and we went off in another in my Econoline.

DKF: It must have been a lot of fun making this film.

RM: I'm trying to remember if it was fun or not. I suppose it was. I don't recall the times when it was fun. Where we had fun was Eve and I and Ryan and Ken Parker and a couple of aides up in San Francisco, where we did *Handyman*. It was much finer honed than *Mr. Teas*. It didn't have all the nudity in it. Some.

DKF: Did Eve ever want to be in *Teas*?

RM: She didn't like Bill. She didn't like what he was saying. Teas is the kind of guy that comes over to have dinner and stays on for a year. To this day, he never phoned to say thank you. At times I dislike Teas very much. It's pretty easy to do. And then at other times, he's a buddy. And I take care of him. I give him 10 percent of every *Teas* video. I don't have to. He gets a good check every three months. It's not a huge salary, but then he doesn't have big needs.

DKF: How does Pete DeCenzie actually fit into your career?

RM: DeCenzie really gave me the thrust to go ahead with *The Immoral Mr. Teas*. Without DeCenzie I would never have made the film, I'm sure. I was certainly savvy enough to realize that selling a film was not like selling still photographs. On the other hand, there's a connection there because Globe Photos took 40 percent of my take on black and white, and 50 percent on color. They were the ones who had access to publications that would buy my stuff. Otherwise, I would've been sending stuff around back and forth and back and forth, and not really getting the kind of deal that Globe could get. So, there's an interesting correlation there. Pete DeCenzie and for example, Elliot Stern, back in New York City . . . what I would've been able to get he probably could get twice as much. So, you have to face the fact that you need an agent. DeCenzie made it possible for me to go into that project with the realization that if we got something that was worthwhile, it would be sold by DeCenzie. I like him personally. He was honest. Yet, at the same time, so many honest people are fools; they're taken in and fooled by people they deal with. What he eventually couldn't stand with me is that . . . well, I think probably he felt a lot of it had to do with the breakup between him and Eve. They'd fight strenuously over people that Eve didn't and wouldn't trust, and with good reason. Pete took that very much to heart. He didn't like the idea of a woman having anything to do with business. Personally, I feel pretty much the same way. I am chauvinistic. I don't care to have business with women in the film game. There are no Hollywood rajahs that are women, and I'm embittered by the fact that the current process at Carolco Pictures, there are women that have the ear of [founder] Mario [Kassar], and they protect him. What does a woman know about sexuality, anyway? They are the receivers, they're the catchers. You've got to be able to pitch. These are personal things I feel. The woman's place is in the bedroom and the kitchen and that's it, as far as I'm concerned. Let her be a sex object. Have fun with her. That's how I feel, anyway.

DKF: How did you first meet Pete DeCenzie?

RM: I first met him through the breast of Tempest Storm. He had this great hype, and was able to pique the curiosity of the unwashed. He was a real show-man. It harkened back to when he was a carny man, a barker. "Leap like a tuna, bark like a fox. Run up the stairs, rob your own trunk. Step right up here. Stop the sales. Everybody hold back. What we're going to do is pick out six boxes, three of which will contain genuine pin seal leather billfolds, and three of which will contain genuine Elgin watches. Others, of course, will have rewards not nearly so munificent." And he would've torn pictures from film magazines of girls in shorts [as rewards]. So, Pete said to me, "Why, sure, you can shoot pictures of Miss Storm."

DKF: This would have been about 1949 or 1950?

RM: About 1950. So, I took pictures of Tempest and became enflamed with the woman's tits, absolutely enflamed. It was the thing that nudged me away from my first wife, So, I shot pictures of her, and Pete thought that was great. He was going to get publicity. I could've been some charlatan just trying to get into the girl's box. But what really got him was the fact that I shot film of her dancing, and I shot it on good industrial film with inserts of close-ups of lips and nipples and so on. He said, "Oh, my God." He was a kind of amateur photographer himself, and used to set up a camera and shoot the whole stage. All this other stuff he thought was just stupendous. So that was the basis of our "marriage," the fact that I'd shot that film. Anyway, *Teas* saw the light of day essentially because it was DeCenzie's doing, and that's where the credit lies. Without DeCenzie and his farsightedness, I would never have had the courage to go ahead with that.

DKF: Did the women in *Teas* ever use their appearances in it in their advertising?

RM: No women did anything after they worked for Meyer, by and large. None of them. They've been to the top, where else is there to go? They're through. They never get work elsewhere. The plug, if they continue dancing, is that I was in this or that.

DKF: The guy that did the narration, did he also do the music?

RM: No, the guy that did the narration didn't want his name associated with the film. He was a patron of the arts. First name was Irving; that's all I can tell you. He had nothing to do with the music. Ed Lakso did the music. He also did music for a lot of television shows. We put it in, there was no problem with him. The narration . . . I'm sure I had something to do with it, but I don't recall who wrote it.

DKF: I always thought that you'd written it.

RM: The story was on the back of a laundry ticket, and in my head. No master plan. Shoot at the beach one day with a girl, shoot the dentist's office, shoot the secretary's office, so on and so on. Loose, extremely loose. I did all the editing. John Link did the sound editing, which was minor. He cut in the music. He worked with Ed Lakso, and they edited the music to fit the film. I knew nothing about sound, and then John cut in the narration.

DKF: So, you had little to do with the actual placement, the juxtaposition of the narration to the action in the film.

RM: Yes. They sat down with me, whoever it was, and they looked at the film, and wrote it according to the film. The film had everything to do with the formation of the text. The text was merely an automatic man who vomited out words when he saw a tree, a stream, etc. It was basically a silent film that someone wrote narration over, at my behest. It was an industrial movie.

DKF: A lot has been written about the psychology of the film, the voyeurism, and we already spoke about it being the link with what you'd done at *Playboy*.

RM: That's all it is. I was out to titillate and appeal to the prurient interest. There was no great psychology at all attached to it. Leslie Fiedler, who wrote that great review, read in all kinds of stuff. Great! I'm glad he did, but I had no message except big bosoms and greed. I wanted to succeed and make a film that was funny and would make money. There was no intent to create something that would be profound. I was doing nothing more than making a film that I hoped would get me into the film business and make money. People write in so many things about my films, and by and large all of them are so full of shit. What is this thing? Appeal to the prurient interest. It turns me on. I get a semi. I know I got something worthwhile. My shorts get wet. I have a good time. I love to make films; that's it. My cant is toward entertainment, not in creating some opus that has subliminal reasons for its existence as a driving force behind it. People laugh at it. Meyer does Meyer's stuff because he's turned on by it. There you are—lust and greed in equal bunches, perfect.

Russ Meyer: Between the Valleys of My Ultravixens

Arv Miller / 1990

From *Fling*, March and July 1990. Multiple interviews were conducted between August 1989 and February 1990.

Russ Meyer, for those of you who may have been living on the moon for the past thirty years, is a genuine, widescreen Hollywood legend. He's the movie mogul who successfully combined mirth, macho, and monster mams into some of the biggest box office grosses in Hollywood history. As director, writer, producer, and cinematographer, Meyer is responsible for creating the word "bosomania," a term he fashioned in the early sixties defining the types of superstructures his heroines all had.

Fling fans, of course, have been infected with bosomania for over thirty-three years. Those of us addicted to appreciating big boobs naturally appreciated the work of Russ Meyer since he bounced from magazine pinup photographer to motion picture executive in the late 1950s. A self-confessed tit man, Meyer has parlayed his love of big hooters and motion pictures into a string of twenty-one bra-bustin' blockbusters.

Two decades before hardcore movies and adult home videos became popular with the American public, T&A sexploitation films were standard bills in outdoor and foreign film theaters. Here, for the first time, movies featured unbridled sex plus bare tits and asses. And it was legal. Some of the time.

In 1957, *Garden of Eden*, a major nudist colony film, was getting national theater play around the country. Because of the innocent sunshine and health aspect, the tepid nudist semidocumentary elicited little or no censorship, enjoying a profitable box office gross. Erotic movies were on their way.

Two years later, in 1959, the "Big Three"—Meyer, Paramore, and Friedman—clobbered the rash of nudist films by presenting adult movie plots that were totally sex-oriented, featuring plenty of bouncy boobs and raunchy dialogue that unsophisticated [viewers, mostly young, white males] could enjoy fantasizing about. The fact that the sex was all simulated mattered little. Everyone got what they came to see: plenty of nudity, fast action, and raucous humor, in an environment of wall-to-wall sex. Fans all shouted, "Hooray for Hollywood!"

Along with Russ Meyer's *The Immoral Mr. Teas*, in 1959, were *Not Tonight, Henry*, directed by Ted Paramore (who later became Harold Lime), and *Adventures of Lucky Pierre*, produced and directed by David Friedman. All three landmark films were successful at the box office. Their popularity, in fact, opened the door to other young and adventurous sexploitation producers who enjoyed mining new and even more unconventional sexual themes.

An example of one such movie maverick was Radley Metzger. His first film, *Dark Odyssey*, in 1961, became an instant hit with audiences because of its bizarre erotic theme. Metzger, who changed his name to Henry Paris in 1973, went on to become one of the great XXX-rated directors of all time. But unlike Lime and Paris, Russ Meyer never deviated into hardcore movies. To this day he rejects any association whatsoever with the adult home video market. Even the subtle suggestion his movies are similar to adult videos makes him enraged.

With cinematic classics such as *Vixen!*, *Supervixens*, and *Beneath the Valley of the Ultra-Vixens*, Meyer has spun a web of glamour and intrigue around himself, adding to the macho mystique that already exists. Last year, after constant urgings from fans, he decided to finally go public. The result: a top-heavy, three-volume memoir titled *A Clean Breast—The Life and Loves of Russ Meyer*.

Already beating the drum for his book in national magazines like *Vanity Fair* and to TV's *Entertainment Tonight*, Meyer immodestly boasted, "The Collins sisters should scrap plans to deal with sexual matters. [*A Clean Breast*] will wipe theirs away. It's the best book ever written."

As many readers know, Russ Meyer and *Fling* go back three decades, when the magazine was born in November 1957. Meyer's pinup spread of a London model made the premier issue. And for years after, photo layouts from him always meant big, beautiful boobs that our readers immediately responded to. Some of *Fling's* all-time favorites were first discovered by Meyer: Candy Morrison, Babette Bardot, Kitten Natividad, and Lorna Maitland come to mind.

Hearing that Meyer was involved in writing his memoirs, *Fling* editor Arv Miller spoke to him last August, requesting an interview. Meyer agreed on the condition the interview would be conducted between work on his book. It was indeed slow going. A few minutes here, a few minutes there, sometimes not a word between the two for weeks, even months.

Here, in his first interview for a national men's magazine in five years, Russ talks about his start as a movie director/producer, his preoccupation with big-titted women, and retells sexy cinema vignettes about movies such as *Mondo*

Topless and *Vixen!* Fond memories of stripper/models Tempest Storm and Uschi Digard are also included here.

Fling: I'm talking with Russ Meyer, master of bosomania, who has a world reputation for his string of successful movies featuring big-breasted young ladies. What I'd like to do first is find out the status of your autobiography.

Russ Meyer: Are you making reference to the book or the movie?

Fling: To the autobiography.

Meyer: Which is the book. When did it start? It started nearly two-and-a-half years ago, and it's been nonstop. The reason that I decided to do the book was that I had offered my library of clippings to a German chap who I had known for some time. He had an assignment to do a book for a German publisher—*Russ Meyer, King of the Sex Shows*. I'd had good experiences with the man in the past. He was a critic who understood—or seemed to, anyway, or at least liked—the films. "You know," he said. "I hope I've captured the humor. But you know us Germans . . . we're not noted for our humor," which always makes me break out laughing, whenever I hear something of that nature. Well, sure enough, I even vouched for the translation to English, because he wasn't that much in the chips. But I soon found out that he had put a lot of stuff in there that he really shouldn't have. Stuff very libelous in nature. Stuff that you'd have had to have a host of witnesses to substantiate is what he had written. And so, I took umbrage with him there, and he said, "Well, you *told* me all this." And I said, "Yeah, well, we were drinking wine, and I got a big mouth, and I told you a lot of things. I expected you to use good judgment." And he said, "Well, I've got it all on the recorder, and I intend to use it." But prior to that, I had volunteered doing the synopses of the films over, because he really didn't catch the flavor of the films.

Fling: And that's when you decided to do the project yourself, your autobiography. What do you call it?

Meyer: The title is *A Clean Breast: The Life and Loves of Russ Meyer*. Just like *The Life and Loves of Emile Zola*, or Joe Stalin, or Frank . . .

Fling: Frank Harris? When will it be completed and then actually published?

Meyer: People keep asking me those terrible questions.

Fling: They've been asking you this for probably five years now, right?

Meyer: Yeah. I just can't be trusted.

Fling: As far as content is concerned, the subjects covered—can I assume they're from the beginning of your life to the present?

Meyer: It covers my life up to 1979.

Fling: Why up to '79?

Meyer: Because '79 represented the year that my most recent film had been completed. I really didn't have that much more to talk about.

Fling: Well, considering your reputation, exactly how explicit will the book be?

Meyer: Explicit to the extent of being probably the frankest book insofar as dealing with matters sexual or horizontal. Hotter than Frank (*My Life and Loves*) Harris, John (*Fanny Hill*) Cleland—you name it. It'll make the Collins girls look like Disneyland.

Fling: Can I assume you're going to name names?

Meyer: No, you can't Well, yeah, you can assume that I will name names, but the assumption, oftentimes, will be fake names. They'll be names that I have had to replace. You know, in order to protect myself from a legal standpoint.

Fling: You're talking about ex-wives, models, and girlfriends?

Meyer: No, no wives.

Fling: Starlets, then?

Meyer: Some girlfriends I can make refence to. Others, I dare not.

Fling: Let's go back to the explicit part. How explicit?

Meyer: Well, it's comedic explicitness. It's really outrageous the way it's done. It's very florid in its manner. It's meant to be jokey and funny.

Fling: It's not going to be a satire, is it? A satire on sex?

Meyer: No, no. I'm reliving like, on a Thursday afternoon at four o'clock at the such-and-such motel. But the way I describe it is in a manner that's quite heroic.

Fling: Would you say you're describing your own sexual assignations, much like some of the scenes in your later movies?

Meyer: Yes. It's meant to be like a scrimmage which, by and large, is the way I do have sex, on a personal level.

Fling: Could you explain in more detail?

Meyer: The writing is extremely honest. But it's also done in a manner that is entertaining.

Fling: Entertaining in a raunchy way? In that case, how would you describe the ideal sex act with the girl of your dreams?

Meyer: I don't deal in acts. I make love in much the same way that I show it in my films: boisterous!

Fling: Any specific setting you prefer?

Meyer: No. A bed is necessary, of course. No tricks, no angles, no accessories, no inducements. I have a very good imagination, which is represented in my films, so I don't need any kind of turn-ons.

Fling: No trapeze or fireworks, I gather. I'd like to get into a bit more of that later. Right now, let's focus on your films. For example, let's jump back to the very beginning. What was your inspiration for *The Immoral Mr. Teas*?

Meyer: That credit goes to Pete DeCenzie. He was one of the last burlesque operators. He became well known at the time for having launched a couple of careers: Lili St. Cyr and Tempest Storm. But sadly, those ladies will not own up to that. Peter really gave them the kind of publicity they needed, that they never had before. It may not apply altogether to Lili St. Cyr, but certainly to Tempest Storm.

Fling: We interviewed Tempest for *Fling* about five years ago in San Francisco, but she did not make mention of Pete DeCenzie.

Meyer: That's terrible. Well, she will probably give credit to an agent. She had a lady who became her agent and brought her to DeCenzie's attention. But she had no national publicity until both Pete and I were on the scene. I just happen to like big knockers, so when I heard she came into Oakland, I contacted DeCenzie and said I'd like to make some pictures with the girl. Tempest readily agreed, and through the aid of Globe Photos, we got some of the first pictures ever published of Tempest into girlie magazines like *Modern Man, Night and Day*, and *Pageant*. Even before *Fling* and *Playboy*.

Fling: Let's get back to *The Immoral Mr. Teas*. How did your marine buddy Bill Teas get involved?

Meyer: Not the Marines. US Army Signal Corps. Bill was a fellow member of the 166th Signal Photographic Company, and that's how I met him. I became kind of a ramrod to the organization after the war. I kept everyone together. Teas was one of the boys, that's all. He was a fine photographic portrait artist, and a wonderful laboratory man. I had a job in San Francisco after the service for an industrial filmmaker, Gene K. Walker Productions. We made commercial films for the railroads, oil companies, lumber mills, etc. It developed that Mr. Walker needed a still photographer to do what we called in those days "bong films." They were those slide films that go "bong!" So, he brought Teas up from Southern California. Teas soon became, instead of a Pasadena-ite, a San Francisco-ite. Bill and I became close. He lived with me and my first wife for a year. You know, "the man who came to dinner" just stayed on. Bill has been in and out of my life all these years. I'm a good friend of his and he's been a good friend to me.

Fling: What was it about Bill that indicated to you that he had a talent for film comedy?

Meyer: Well, satire, maybe, more than anything else. Bill is an example of a guy who was in the right place at the right time. Or in the wrong place at the right time. We used to have poker games every Friday night in LA. My ex-wife, Eve Meyer, who was a well-known model personality in magazines, says she was the only feminine part of this whole poker-playing scheme. Bill was notoriously addicted to playing poker. So, he just happened to be there that night, sitting on the couch after all the poker players had left, except DeCenzie, who was there visiting, too, and had been playing poker with us. He was in town with a little traveling girl show. Pete, who'd always been after me, said, "We've got to do a nudist movie."

Fling: And your response?

Meyer: I said, "I don't want to do a nudist movie, with croquet and volleyball and people walking into the sunset, purposely picking people that are not attractive, blah, blah, blah." I'd been doing some early photographic pinup work for *Playboy*—the girls next door, for the voyeur in all of us. So, I said, "Why don't we just do something off the wall, like what I've been doing in the magazines?" And Pete said, "I don't care *what* you do. I'll match you dollar for dollar." He said, "You got anybody in mind who could be in it?" And I looked over at Teas, who was sitting there and who was a ham, anyway. He loved to pose in still pictures. "We'll use Teas," I said. "He's got a good kisser." That's how Teas got into the movie.

Fling: What was his reaction, knowing he'd be in a nudist movie?

Meyer: Well, Teas never was terribly enthusiastic about anything. Unless it was, you know, crawling in between the sheets with some chick. So, he said, "Yeah, I'll do it." The idea appealed to him.

Fling: Not a real hard sell, was he?

Meyer: That's Teas. He had an interesting look. He had that goatee, kind of cherubic, you know. I knew he could come up with expressions, because he loved to pose in photographs. That's how Teas got the job. He just happened to be there that night. It could easily have been someone else.

Fling: Strange coincidence. What about raising the money? It must have been expensive. Did you finance the movie yourself, or did you use a bank?

Meyer: Hell, no. It was very easy. We each had a pocket and said, "Here's the money. Pete, you put up a dollar, I put up a dollar." That's how we financed it.

Fling: Did you ever find out exactly how much the movie cost?

Meyer: Yes. It's now common knowledge. Twenty-four thousand dollars.

Fling: Not much, when you consider the final product.

Meyer: Yeah. That included the blow-up. Meaning, we shot in 16mm for economy reasons, then we blew it up to 35mm.

Fling: Didn't you lose a lot of detail going up from 16mm to 35mm? The film looks pretty damn good to me.

Meyer: Yeah. At the time, there was only one guy that was really into what was called web-feed printing. There was a glycerin solution that the film was embedded in—or sloshed through, as it were—in the aperture. Once printed, it knocked out all the scratches, by and large. So, we were the first commercial outfit to test this new process. Even Walt Disney was curiously interested in seeing what would happen. I don't know if he looked at the film. A guy by the name of Adrian Mosser developed it; he was a pioneer.

Fling: Once the movie was done, what about the difficult task of actually distributing it? Did you distribute it yourself or did you have a regular distributor?

Meyer: Slow down. First of all, we had the difficult task of getting the film *processed.* I touch on that lightly because Kodak, in those days, would not *dare* to do anything with a bare nipple. But Ray Grant, who was a troubleshooter for Eastman, put his job on the line. He said [to them], "I'll stand by this stuff, and I'll watch everything that they're shooting." He said to us, "Go ahead, do your experimental sex comedy." So, without Ray's aid, our project would have never come to pass.

Fling: Could you have shot it with a different process, other than Kodak?

Meyer: There wasn't any similar process to my knowledge. Kodak had the only decent film. You always had to go to a major lab, even if you used Ansco, for example. And Ansco color wasn't all that wonderful.

Fling: Let's go back to distribution. You've got *Teas* in the can. Did you have a distribution agreement set up before you made the film?

Meyer: No, we knew nothing about it. Pete had distributed little things here and there. Not long before, Pete and I got together on a film called *French Peep Show*. It was nothing more than filming his girlie show. And the reason I did it was because of Tempest Storm. I shot a hundred feet of her during her strip, and Pete liked the way I did it because it had a lot of closeups. Even then that stuff was sent to Kodak. I thought it would get through their watchful eyes because I sent it under my boss's logo. And it did.

Fling: There weren't any bare nipples, of course.

Meyer: Yes and no. It was pasties over their nipples. So, when the distribution problem came, Pete said, "Hell, we'll distribute it ourselves." And so he booked it with a very fine theater in San Diego called the Fox West Coast Theatre. The second feature was *The Hanging Tree*, with Gary Cooper. So, *Teas* went on, and twenty minutes later, the cops came in and busted the show. Just like that!

Fling: What was your feeling at that time?

Meyer: Pretty bad, I guess. Anyway, *Mr. Teas* was nailed. We never found out why, but the film was out of action for nearly a year. We did finally regain control of the print, which cost us about a thousand bucks.

Fling: Was "Mr. Teas" ever adjudged to be obscene?

Meyer: No. You didn't go to court in those days. No one had ever seen as bare a film as *Mr. Teas*. What happened is that it was nearly six months before anyone had the guts to play it again, because word like that travels like wildfire.

Fling: What made *Mr. Teas* so sexually blatant? Weren't some of the European films just as erotic?

Meyer: It's the preoccupation with sex. A European film would have an occasional nipple showing. We had a picture that was sixty-three-minutes long— fifty-eight of it was total nudity.

Fling: Wall-to-wall nudity—not just a few nude scenes thrown in.

Meyer: Yeah, and in full color, too. But more importantly, a dirty old man leching at all the women. That was a no-no. He was harboring lustful thoughts.

Fling: Those are the best kinds, right? Anyway, where did you go from there?

Meyer: Well, we just couldn't get anyone to take the film. We had a couple of 16mm prints. At the time, Pete was on the road. He had lost his Oakland theater in a legal hassle, and had been thrown in the jug and everything else. But he was on the road with these three girls, and in burlesque houses they'd do things in which they would stand frozen—they couldn't move. For example, they stood frozen and he would [have them] depict Da Vinci and Michelangelo and other famous paintings.

Fling: Where would they be performing the act?

Meyer: In burlesque theaters.

Fling: This was a live stage act, right?

Meyer: Yeah. He had the actual girls. This was not film. It was a live show, but they *weren't* live. They had to stand still. It was legal that way in those days.

Fling: Was there a name to the act?

Meyer: Pete called it *Pictures and Poses.* Anyway, he ran into another paisan when he played Seattle. Washington had one of the last remaining censor boards. This guy and Pete started talking. Pete said, "I got this film. But we can't get it played." The guy said, "Why don't we look at it?" So, they convened in a hotel room where Pete had food and wine sent up. They looked at our 16mm print, and they passed it, hands down. It was like a license to steal. Played two years—right then and there. Soon, *Mr. Teas* played all over the country.

Fling: It got the OK in Seattle, but what happened in New York, LA, or Chicago? Didn't they have censorship boards, too?

Meyer: Sure, they all had censorship boards. In New York, they wanted cuts, so we had a guy named Mishkin, who distributed it, and he made a few cuts. When it was reviewed by the New York Censor Board, Mishkin said, "If you want to see the whole version, you have to go to Atlantic City." From there, we went on in theaters across the country. The only [other] time we got busted was years later in Philadelphia. I think we were playing at the 10th Street Art House. Their way of advertising was to have a word ad. They'd give the plot and describe the girls. But no photos. This was after years, and *Mr. Teas* had started to fall off a bit. Anyway, the guy decided he would juice up the copy a little bit. So, he alluded to the fact that the district attorney was going to swoop down on him any day and arrest him for showing this "terribly obscene" picture. Well, he just about invited trouble, so they *did* bust him. Now I had to hire a lawyer to smooth things out, which I did. We defended it, and got off scot-free. The problem with exonerating a film is that people say, "Oh, *Mr. Teas* probably wasn't all that sexy, anyway. It got off." So, there was no benefit in being busted in those days.

Fling: Was there an actual script for *Mr. Teas?*

Meyer: Well, I wrote it, you know, on the back of a laundry ticket. I knew what I was going to do every day.

Fling: What about the dialogue? Was it all ad lib?

Meyer: Well, we wrote both the narration and the music afterward. There was no dialogue, as such. It was all voice-over.

Fling: What about the shooting time? How many days did it take?

Meyer: Four days, plus a couple of half-days.

Fling: How long did it take to shoot from the time you decided, "Yeah, we're going to do it?"

Meyer: Oh, I think it was very quick, like the next day, almost.

Fling: Was there any hanky-panky behind the scenes that you're willing to own up to?

Meyer: No, I've always been really on that thing very strong. No exchanging of vital juices. Wondrous bodily fluids—oh, no! Everybody's got to be horny and hard-pressed. Maybe a little irascible, sort of. Works better.

Fling: The next series of questions are basically your capsule comments about some of the movies your fans consider perhaps the more popular. Let's start with *Vixen!* starring Erica Gavin. Any comment you might like to make on the movie or about Erica?

Meyer: *Vixen!* is the reason that I am secure for the rest of my life. It was a barn burner. That was the most successful film I ever had.

Fling: *Vixen!* really put you on the map, didn't it?

Meyer: Sure it put me on the map. But I also had a real smart wife, Eve. She put a lot of money away for her and myself.

Fling: What did Eve contribute to the movies in the early days?

Meyer: Eve ended up as largely distributing the films herself, with me looking over her shoulder, of course. She was a very good businesswoman. She had a background as a legal secretary.

Fling: How did you meet Eve?

Meyer: Through a lawyer that handled my first divorce.

Fling: How did *Vixen!* come about? What was the inspiration that got you to do it?

Meyer: My associate, Jim Ryan, and I just set out. We put the idea together in a launderette. I said, "Jim, we've got to make the sexiest film ever made." And we did. *Vixen!* was the happy result. We lucked out with Erica Gavin. We made a picture that both men and women loved. It was a film women wanted to see because they looked upon Vixen as a real heroine.

Fling: Were there any aftereffects about this in your own life?

Meyer: My third wife, Edy Williams. It was mandatory every week for her to look at that film because the woman was the aggressor. She was the one who called the shots. And Edy would just really react powerfully in the bed that night, after she'd seen the movie.

Fling: It would turn her on that much?

Meyer: Well, there was more to it than that, but she really got in there and whaled. *Vixen!* was so important to her. She always wanted to make another one like that.

Fling: What movies did Edy appear in?

Meyer: *Beyond the Valley of the Dolls* was her great moment. She was also in *The Seven Minutes.*

Fling: What is Edy doing today?

Meyer: I have no idea. I think she gets jobs here and there. Just a couple of days ago, my girlfriend, Kitten Natividad, encountered her at a casting call. They were both up for the same play, and it was surprising that Edy took to her so warmly. In fact, she ran up and introduced herself, not typical of Ms. Williams. And the ladies got along famously.

Fling: That probably says a lot for both ladies. I'll bet Edy would have given anything to be in *Vixen!*

Meyer: That's putting it mildly.

Fling: You say *Vixen!* was a big success. How long did it take?

Meyer: Oh, right off the bat. It still holds the record today in Chicago. It ran fifty-eight weeks and grossed in excess of $900,000, when tickets were $1.70. It played at the Loop Theater. The reason *Vixen!* was successful: it was well made. The girl made it successful. Combined with the promiscuity and the total devotion to sex. She had sex with so many people, and that even excused the little message at the end about Communism and draft-dodging, and all.

Fling: What about your movie *Up!*? Any feelings or comments about it?

Meyer: I'm disappointed that it didn't do as well as, for example, *Supervixens.* But I'm talking theatrically. What was happening then is that I was buffeted on two sides. By the hardcore people and by the majors being increasingly explicit about their content. And more than anything else, the violence. We've got a lot of weak-kneed men in this country, I've discovered. Can't handle some really outrageous, jokey violence, with chainsaw and axes. And they can't seem to see, in *Up!* that it's just a big goddamn put-on. I found the same thing in Germany— men that *objected* to violence, more so than the women. Terrible, terrible state of affairs. I don't understand it.

Fling: What about *Cherry, Harry & Raquel!*? That had Uschi Digard as Soul.

Meyer: Yes, she was a godsend, as it happened. One of the two leading ladies quit because she got uptight. We had a great redneck motel owner up in Panamint Springs. This girl had her dogs with her, and she let 'em piss on the rug, and the owner got really tired of that. She kept the dogs in the room all day, and finally she just had all the complaints she could handle. She just quit right in the middle of the show. Best thing that happened for that movie.

Fling: Do you remember who the woman was?

Meyer: Linda . . . I think her name was Ashton. Linda Ashton. She just quit.

Fling: What did you do?

Meyer: Well, being a kind of roll-with-the-punch guy, I said, "Hell, we'll figure this out somehow," because I'd gotten practically everything I'd needed with her already. But then, when Uschi came along, I wrote in her part as Soul. Amazing, huh? Anyway, Uschi became a great, great friend—a confederate—you name it. She contributed so much to my films, even after that, as an associate. Later, she even took care of my wonderful mother when she was in terrible health. She was just a very, very close personal friend, and continues to be today.

Fling: How about *Supervixens*? That was one of your biggies, correct?

Meyer: Yeah. That's me coming off the ropes. Not many people know this, but I have four films in the top 400 grossers of all time. And *none* of those films has had a star. The pictures are *Vixen!, Supervixens, Cherry, Harry, & Raquel!,* and *Beneath the Valley of the Ultra-Vixens.* That's something that's logged in *Variety,* when they do the "recap in review."

Fling: What kind of business did *Supervixens* do?

Meyer: Over $17 million at the box office—again, tickets [were] $1.75. What does that translate to today? $7? Think about it. And who's in the movie? I don't know—there's a bunch of girls with big tits, and a guy by the name of Russ Meyer who made it. *Supervixens* played widely, in the best theaters in the country, just like *Vixen!* and even films before them. I never played the scumbag houses.

Fling: And how about *Beneath the Valley of the Ultra-Vixens,* which I believe was your last one?

Meyer: Most recent. Never say last . . . most recent. That was a joy to make, and a joy to sell. It's the number one success film in our catalogue of videos. And it represents a tremendous five years that I spent with Miss Kitten Natividad. In fact, we still remain friends, largely because we never got married. She's really an important lady. She's contributed hugely to my life, Still does.

Fling: There was a rumor, at one time, that you and Kitten *were* married.

Meyer: No, no, no. A lot of bullshit. We were never married. She's married a number of times, just as I have. I've been fortunate, marrying great women. Great in many ways. To my knowledge, Kitten never married a great guy. She's had five or six of them, to my knowledge.

Fling: You say you're still friendly with her.

Meyer: Very much friendly. Very close friends. She's really an important lady. She's contributed hugely to my life. Still does.

Fling: What about *Mondo Topless*? What do you remember about making it?

Meyer: Well, the most unusual thing was Miss [Darlene] Grey. Her real name was Vivian Cournoyer. I got her at her absolute prime. I only photographed her one day, and then she disappeared. Never saw her again.

Fling: Incredible body, if memory serves. Huge pair of tits.

Meyer: Oh, incredible tits. An agent by the name of Andy Anderson, a great procurer, bless his heart, called me when he had something special. He said, "Russ, get your ass down here, bring a lot of film, don't forget anything. I'll hold off the dogs. You'll be the first to shoot her." So, I grabbed her, put her in a hotel, and said, "Look, you've got to get a good night's sleep. I'll take you to dinner, and I'll be by at 3:00 in the morning." We drove to the desert to shoot. She asked, "What sort of costumes so I wear?" I said, "Max Factor's 'Dark Egyptian.'" Yeah, she was wondrous. That's the reason *Mondo Topless* was successful. Simply because of her great, heaving chest. Gravity defying. One of the greatest pair of tits I've ever seen or photographed.

Fling: Is there anything you'd like to say in regard to censorship that would apply to any of your movies, involving censor boards or similar groups?

Meyer: I'll tell you about today's rating board—it's called preoccupation with sex. The rating boards have not changed their standards when it comes to sex; they've changed their standards when it comes to violence. That came about when they first passed the original *Friday the 13th*, I had a good friend on the board who told me, "We made a mistake. We passed that damn thing. It's going to open up all the floodgates." Well, today, in order for *Vixen!* to qualify for an R-rating, I'd have to excise eleven minutes from the film. And that's *today*, for a film made back in 1969. *Supervixens* requires twenty-three minutes to be excised to get an R. *Beneath the Valley of the Ultra-Vixens* required thirty-three minutes. It's unchanged, this preoccupation with sex.

Fling: There's still much confusion about your videos, because they're considered X yet they're rated R. Softcore in the sexual scenes. How do you rate them?

Meyer: The MPAA X is from the Motion Picture Association of America's X rating.

Fling: People compare your movies to the adult video movies that are considered hardcore.

Meyer: Those are Triple-X. Actual penetration, ejaculation, you name it. Mine are completely different.

Fling: In other words, one X is considered softcore, correct?

Meyer: Yes. Mine are all MPAA X—simulation in the sex scenes.

Fling: It would be nice if all the video companies could get together and do honest labeling.

Meyer: I couldn't agree more. You're aware of the fact that now, with [Jack] Valenti's marvelous machinations, they're going to require all videos rented or sold in stores to have a rating. And they must have a legitimate rating. They must have a rating that someone's paid two or three thousand dollars to obtain. I don't know what the correct fee is today. It might be more or less.

Fling: A fee of several thousand dollars will drive some producers out of business. It's going to halt an awful lot of videos from being made.

Meyer: Could be. But when you talk about censorship, we don't really have censorship. Only in the sense that the rating board imposes certain things on the filmmaker.

Fling: What do certain ratings do to the success or failure of pictures?

Meyer: Any major film company absolutely just shudders at the idea of getting an X. They'd do anything not to have an X.

Fling: Yeah, it kills their distribution. Hence, their profit potential.

Meyer: So, there's your censorship. They say, "Oh, we're not censors, but if you want an R rating, you do have to cut . . ."

Fling: That's the game. You play it their way or you don't play at all. It's not putting something in, it's actually taking something out.

Meyer: Exactly.

Fling: Let's get back to one of the more intimate aspects of the interview: your capsule comments about some of the outstanding busty ladies in your movies. I'd like to find out, briefly, your professional and private opinions of . . . let's start with Uschi Digard.

Meyer: She has the dedication of a Watusi gunbearer.

Fling: How so?

Meyer: You've heard of Watusi gunbearers? These are the devoted men that helped animal trainers like Frank Buck. They were noted gunbearers. They were fearless. They're from the Watusi tribe in Africa.

Fling: What's the connection with someone as sexy as Uschi?

Meyer: They were dedicated gunbearers. You know what a gunbearer is to a great white hunter? He carries the fucking gun—the elephant gun, you know? He goes anywhere that he's told to go. Does anything the gunbearer wants him to do, like "Lie down there and let the lion run at you, and I will try to shoot." Uschi—she has the dedication of a Watusi warrior, no doubt about it.

Fling: Both Uschi and Kitten have devotion and dedication. But why do you think neither one has ever done hardcore scenes in their many videos?

Meyer: Because they didn't want to do it.

Fling: Just as simple as that?

Meyer: Yeah. They have the same feeling about hardcore as I do. They dislike it very much.

Fling: Yet they both have hundreds of simulated sex scenes with male partners. Kind of a shame, don't you think?

Meyer: Shame—hell! What Uschi and Kitten do in private should be left private. Not for the whole world to gawk at.

Fling: Let's switch to another superstacked lady you worked with—Ann Marie, who appeared in *Beneath the Valley of the Ultra-Vixens*. What can you remember about her?

Meyer: Ann Marie, I think, is a talented lady. She's a living flesh-and-blood kind of the Annie Fanny comic strip character in *Playboy*. She really more closely resembles her than anyone else I can think of.

Fling: Perfect typecasting. Anything else?

Meyer: On a personal level, she just worked for me as an actress.

Fling: You've already mentioned Kitten Natividad? What about your professional and private opinion of her?

Meyer: Well, professionally, Kitten is a fine comedienne.

Fling: I agree. She was marvelous in *Beneath the Valley of the Ultra-Vixens*.

Meyer: Yeah, and she's also a very sexy girl. She'll do anything you ask her to do on the screen, literally. I mean, short of . . .

Fling: Short of going hardcore on-camera.

Meyer: She's just really a fabulous lady on a personal level. She's every man's dream.

Fling: How about Raven De La Croix? A great beauty with brains, right?

Meyer: True. Raven and I had a good friendship, but nothing on a personal level. I just sometimes decide, no matter what kind of primeval urge I might have to want to belly up to someone, Raven just remained a friend. I like her to this day.

Fling: We met her when she played San Francisco about two years ago. She impressed us with her intelligence, not to mention her outstanding physical attributes. Class act.

Meyer: I agree. No matter how great someone is constructed, I try to look at both sides of the coin. Like problems one might encounter because of this.

Fling: Your comments about Candy Samples, who was in *Up!* . . .

Meyer: I think she's a super performer, but I don't know her on a personal level. She first approached me when I was at Fox Studios, but she wasn't nearly the star she's become.

Fling: How about Babette Bardot, who starred in *Common-Law Cabin*?

Meyer: Charming lady. I used her first in *Mondo Topless*, then used her in *Common-Law Cabin*.

Fling: Would it be improper to suggest that she had some augmentation done to her breasts? They never looked quite natural.

Meyer: I don't comment upon those things. No more than if a woman is married and I've been close to her.

Fling: How about June Mack, who was perfectly cast in *Beneath the Valley of the Ultra-Vixens* as a horny junkyard operator?

Meyer: I found an advertisement in the Los Angeles Free Press, by this gorgeous, huge Black woman. I was intrigued, so I sent the ad to my friend, Roger Ebert, who's been a collaborator of mine 'cause he's into big jugs, like I am. June was very descriptive about the way she was put together. Roger wrote and got to know her, and that's how I got to meet her. When I interviewed her, I asked if she had any picture experience. "No," she said. "I did a little theater work in high school." A charming lady. After I used her in *Beneath the Valley*, she was assassinated. Her husband was also shot down in the San Fernando Valley. Might have been drug related, I'm not really sure.

Fling: Sad. How about Margo Winchester?

Meyer: Well, Margo Winchester is Raven De La Croix.

Fling: That's what I suspected, but wasn't quite sure.

Meyer: That's Raven's theatrical name for the Meyer films.

Fling: Now that this mystery is cleared up, what about Erica Garvin, from *Vixen!*?

Meyer: Erica, of all the women I've used, may not have possessed the biggest boobs, yet she had a marvelous zaftig body. The breasts were great. But more than anything else, she had a quality that's difficult to define. I touched upon it earlier in our conversation. She appeals to women very strongly.

Fling: Why do you think that's so?

Meyer: Well, whatever it was, this was the basis for *Vixen!*'s huge success. Because *women* came to the theater with men. Once you have that happen, your gross doubles, even triples. It's not just "the raincoat brigade" or "the one-armed reader." You've got a girl dragging her old man in to see the movie.

Fling: You secretly hoped that women would want to see it?

Meyer: It was beyond my fondest dream. Because, remember, we were not dealing with the "date night" crowd. We were dealing with lonely men wanting to sit there and look at the movie who . . .

Fling: Fantasize . . .

Meyer: And masturbate, or whatever.

Fling: So, there was nothing in your script to guarantee you'd get this kind of audience.

Meyer: No, nothing. We didn't entertain any hopes like that. We just set out to make a man's movie, thinking that it would attract more men than we've ever attracted before. What happened is that, because of Erica and the quality she possessed, we attracted a ton of women.

Fling: Which also made you a ton of moola. Lastly, Lorna Maitland, from your movie of the same name.

Meyer: *Lorna*, that's how we titled it. Her real name was Barabara Joy. I gave her the name [Lorna]. It was derived from a very buxom secretary whose boss I worked for before World War II in a Civil Service job for Army Engineers. That was her name: Lorna. She was half Portuguese, half Hawaiian.

Fling: She was your inspiration?

Meyer: Beautiful, with big knockers. This girl's got big knockers . . . we'll call her Lorna. Let's see, we'll get a name like Mansfield. No, that's already been taken. Maitland—now that's a proper English name—Lorna Maitland! And she's a shit-kicker girl, which is good contrast, with this *proud* name. She's living in squalor, barefoot, has one pair of hot pants and one torn blouse. Lorna, Lorna Maitland.

Fling: She had this lusty persona about her; she just looked hot. What happened to her?

Meyer: She became a stripper afterwards, worked up at the Barbary Coast, North Beach, in San Francisco, then simply disappeared. I have no idea where she is. I used her in *Mudhoney* as well as *Lorna*.

Fling: Let me get into another area, briefly: movie collaborations. Like what you had with the critic Roger Ebert. What was story with Roger and the movie script he wrote for you?

Meyer: I'll tell you exactly. He wrote the screenplay for *Beyond the Valley of the Dolls*. He admits to this. We're close friends.

Fling: He has publicly said many kind things about you, too.

Meyer: I know. The forward to my new book is four pages of Ebert.

Fling: How did that come about? Did you ask him to write it, or did he just submit it to you?

Meyer: No, I asked him. Because in the beginning, there were very few good critiques or reviews of my films. One of the most important and oft-quoted pieces was done in the *Wall Street Journal*, which was left-hand column on the first page, right? Written by a guy by the name of Steve Lovelady. This, of course, drew the attention of people in the industry. Well, anyway, there were letters to the editor. There were two letters published. One from a lady in Terre Haute, Indiana, who said, in no uncertain words, exactly what should happen to me and what I did, you know, for a living. The other one was a very nice letter from Roger Ebert, in which he said, "I'm familiar with Meyer's style; it's equivalent to Howard Hawks, blah, blah, blah. . . ." He was working as a critic for the *Chicago Sun-Times*. I wrote him and I said, "I appreciate what you had to say, and let's get together next time I'm in Chicago." So, that's how we got together. Turned out that Roger likes big boobs just as much as I like them. We have become brother-like. We are very, very close. So, when I had this opportunity, and it was presented to me by the Zanucks to do *Beyond the Valley of the Dolls*, or a so-called sequel at that time, I thought about these numerous meetings that I'd had with Roger, when we'd been out, had dinner, talked, et cetera. He watched me do some filming on *Finders, Keepers*. He was present in Chicago when we did all the hoopla with *Vixen!* The only film of mine he's ever reviewed is *Vixen!* He gave it three stars. That's when he was with the *Sun-Times*.

Fling: What kept him from reviewing your other films?

EYER: Well, 'cause it was a conflict of interest. People *knew* that he and I are very close. He wrote *Beyond the Valley of the Dolls* because I asked him to write it, and he got $25,000 for doing it. Twenty-five thousand dollars today would be $125,000.

Fling: One of the best screenplays you ever used.

Meyer: Very true. Roger's input was enormous because the whole thing is so youth-oriented.

Fling: *Beyond the Valley* was maybe the best film you did.

Meyer: It's my pride and joy. That film is something we're very prideful of.

Fling: Did you give him any help on it, or was it strictly his own work?

Meyer: Roger and I wrote the treatment. We conceived the idea fifty-fifty. You see, the first thing we did was write a treatment. Our treatment was like a script. Then he put the words and music in.

Fling: So, it was a collaboration, which Roger filled out later on.

Meyer: Exactly. There were some minor contributions, because they wouldn't let Roger stay any more than three weeks. He had to get back to the paper. A guy by the name of Benny Diaz, who was my production assistant, did some work on the final end of the film. You know, where I review everyone's frailties and creduli-ties—how they fell on their ass, and so forth. I always put that stuff in my films.

Fling: Was Roger present for the total shooting of the film?

Meyer: Occasionally he would pop in. A couple of times, I think. Roger also cowrote *Beneath the Valley of the Ultra-Vixens* with me. He used the pseudonym R. Hyde—as in Dr. Jekyll, OK? And he made an important contribution to *Super-vixens*. That was the Zarathustra thing, where the girls were reincarnated. And he wrote all the narrative for the Greek chorus in *Up!* under the pseudonym of Reinhold Timme. He admitted that to Johnny Carson on television.

Fling: In Roger's case, he probably would go out of his way to tout this col-laboration and be proud of it.

Meyer: Now he does. In the beginning, when *Beyond the Valley of the Dolls* was so bludgeoned by his so-called peers in Chicago, when I came to town with Edy Williams, we brought him out of the closet. "Look at it!" I told him. "People are standing and screaming in the theater."

Fling: He's taken a lot of heat on this, I'm sure.

Meyer: Well, it's because of his sudden notoriety on television, probably.

Fling: Of all your busty ladies, who is Roger Ebert's favorite?

Meyer: Well, he likes anybody, for that matter. But he had a close friendship with June Mack from *Beneath the Valley of the Ultra-Vixens*, I understand.

Fling: Who's responsible for generating [your films'] plotlines? Where have most of the ideas come from?

Meyer: All from me. Every one has been my idea. It doesn't work unless it's Meyer's idea.

Fling: So, you create the thing from the very beginning?

Meyer: Right. I don't buy a script from anybody.

Fling: Why not?

Meyer: No one would be qualified. No one would have this tit obsession that I have.

Fling: Do you write ideas down in the sense of an outline? Or do you talk it over with people, like Roger, for example?

Meyer: No, I get all the ideas. I'll be driving in the car, and I carry a tablet beside me with a big "wet stick"—a felt tip pen—to write down ideas. I'll wake up in the morning and dash out of the shower to write something down.

Fling: Are these film treatments or just short concepts?

Meyer: No, they're ideas. I don't sit down one day and say, "I'm going to write a treatment." I just collect ideas, put them together, review them, think about it.

Fling: And they gel sometimes? And sometimes they don't, like any creative process?

Meyer: Yeah, but most of mine always end up as films. Big tits and horny, simple-minded men—that's a powerful combination for any movie.

Fling: I'd like to focus now on adult home videos. Do you have a favorite XXX-rated video?

Meyer: I don't look at anybody's films but my own. I don't care about other movies. In fact, I don't go to movies anymore.

Fling: You don't see any movies at all?

Meyer: No. I'll tell you what I go and see. Every time Clint Eastwood makes a movie, I'll go and see it. But I don't see anything else.

Fling: Would you, for example, have a favorite porn star that you enjoy watching?

Meyer: I don't use the word "porn." I don't like adult films, at all. I don't think the women are attractive at all. They're all built like a hoe handle. They're not my kind of ladies.

Fling: We're talking about Christy Canyon, Mindy Rae, Candy Samples, Buffy Davis, Trinity Loren, for example. They are built like hoe handles?

Meyer: I'm not putting the medium down. To each his own. You asked me what my taste is. Do I look at hardcore? I've never seen a hardcore movie, except about three minutes, and that's enough. When you talk about porn, that's not *me*.

Fling: OK. Let me throw one name at you who has been in porn, that most tit men wouldn't consider chopped liver or hoe handles, either. That's Christy Canyon.

Meyer: I don't even know who she is.

Fling: OK. Candy Samples. Now she's done a lot of XXX-rated adult videos, and you already know her.

Meyer: Yeah, she's done a lot of films. I did her a favor 'cause she'd done me some favors on some walk-through things. Her videos seem to be, from what I understand, a lot tamer than most of this other stuff.

Fling: Tamer in what respect? Candy's starred in dozens of hardcore video productions. No holds barred.

Meyer: Well, she just doesn't seem to be as, you know, *athletic*, or whatever you call it.

Fling: She's just as vocal in the sex scenes. Just as athletic, too.

Meyer: I don't even think in terms of adult video. Hardcore is just a total turnoff to me.

Fling: Would you ever consider entering the X-rated field? X in the sense that we're talking Triple-X?

Meyer: That would be like me going to the toilet. Are you kidding? That would be the total end.

Fling: Well, you're still in the same business, in a sense. What's your opinion of the adult video field? You're not saying it should be outlawed, are you?

Meyer: No. Not at all. It's a fine idea, but not for Meyer, that's all. I'm not some rabble-rouser or Charles Keating, or something like that. I think it should be out there and available. For example, I contributed $500 to the legal slush fund [that was] dealing with this business of swooping down on video retailers and confiscating their whole stock of tapes.

Fling: Sounds a bit like Germany in the 1930s—storm troopers, book burning.

Meyer: Yeah, all under the guise of child porn. I'm all for them doing what they do. You're asking me how I feel about it?

Fling: Exactly.

Meyer: OK, I told you. I want them to prosper, to succeed, to make money, to bring pleasure. But it's not my bag.

Fling: If they succeed, and many have already, would this help your movies as well? Those that are available on video?

Meyer: No, my product is so separate and distinct, it's not to be compared in any other way. Mine will surface and succeed. It's like a snake—you can't kill it with a stick. The Meyer films grow every year in interest. I mean, just in the time we're talking, the girls [working for me] here have shipped forty-four cassettes to a mail order outfit in New York. And it's their third purchase this month. I want it to be really clear that I'm *not* against hardcore. I wouldn't do it. I wouldn't touch it, because I'm not interested.

Fling: What's your opinion on how they could improve them?

Meyer: By getting girls with giant tits.

Fling: Well, they already have many girls with giant tits.

Meyer: No, they don't!

Fling: Oh, come on, Russ . . .

Meyer: They really don't. I've never seen anyone even close.

Fling: I'm going to have to send you some tapes featuring Toni Kessering, Keisha, Kay Parker, and Susan Nero, and a dozen others.

Meyer: Well, if they do, they're not known, and they're big, fat slobs. They're not Russ Meyer girls.

Fling: But many of these busty ladies could be.

Meyer: They're not really girls that I would cast in films. But again, I just don't even want to think about it.

Fling: So, you would dismiss every big-titted lady working in video today. Is that what you're saying?

Meyer: First of all, I don't know or really care for hardcore. In fact, I don't find it entertaining at all. Only when it's one on one, Meyer and friend.

Fling: You categorically dismiss the whole [hardcore] video field as worthless?

Meyer: No. I'm telling you what I like. You're putting words in my mouth.

Fling: OK, I'm sorry. I certainly don't want to put words in your mouth.

Meyer: No, X-rated video is not worthless. I just don't care for it. I've never been tempted to involve myself in it. And I don't find it personally entertaining. But in no way do I wish to condemn it as being something that shouldn't be. I encourage everybody to make whatever they wish to do. It's not my cup of tea. Period.

Fling: Are there any hardcore video ladies you might consider for your next movie?

Meyer: The only one I'd use is Candy Samples.

Fling: She's done a lot of hardcore. I also heard she's out of the business. Retired to Palm Springs not long ago.

Meyer: I'd do it because Candy has this monumental bosom, and I've used her before. I've never seen nor heard of anybody else that would be right for me. I'll just simply say that I've never seen anybody advertised on the cover of a video box that I would think twice about using in a Russ Meyer movie.

Fling: That's a big statement, because there's a number of really attractive, very built ladies working, as I've already mentioned.

Meyer: Well, they may be. But, you see, you're asking me the question. If you don't want my opinion, then you ought to interview yourself sometime, Arv.

Fling: Well, you've got a right to your opinion. After all, it's your interview, not mine. I apologize.

Meyer: I'm telling you how I feel, Arv. I've been to all the trade shows since the year one. I've never found a girl, circulating around, that personally appealed to me. The women that I put in my films appeal to me on a very personal level.

Fling: Would it have something to do with the fact that you knew they were not involved with XXX-rated films?

Meyer: None, whatsoever.

Fling: That would not be a factor?

Meyer: No! Good God, I'm not some prude. I'm not trying to set myself up as being better than someone else. You're asking me what I like. I'm telling you I don't like girls that are, shall I say, undernourished. Girls have to be very buxom, gravity-defying, casting long shadows, for Meyer to be interested. It's that simple, OK?

Fling: We couldn't agree more. Is there anything about porno videos—X-rated or R-rated—that you admire?

Meyer: No. But I don't think all these people should be called "porno people."

Fling: OK. What classification would you give them?

Meyer: You're talking mainly about Triple-X stuff. But there's the MPAA X-rating system that refers to films like *Last Tango in Paris*, *Midnight Cowboy*, and all of the Russ Meyer movies. Also, films that Radley Metzger did. He's a man I admire—I like his stuff.

Fling: I thought he stopped making porn movies long ago.

Meyer: He's done it under the name of Henry Paris. I'm talking about Radley Metzger. He doesn't use his real name for porn or so-called hardcore. I'm talking about *Therese and Isabelle* and *I, Woman*, stuff that he did a long time ago, when both of us were very much on the forefront in theaters. He dealt with very soft kinds of things—women photographed through musty wine bottles. A gentle caressing, very slow but attractive.

Fling: Did you ever see *The Opening of Misty Beethoven*?

Meyer: That's a Henry Paris movie. Metzger and Paris are one and the same guy. I have not seen it, nor do I care to see it.

Fling: Well, he uses many of those romantic aspects in his work. *Misty* is considered one of the top ten adult videos of all time. I just thought you'd like to know.

Meyer: I'm sure that he would probably do one of the better jobs. There's another guy around—Cecil Howard. I just don't find his work that interesting. If I want to see carnal sex, I want to do it on my own. I don't want to be a voyeur.

Fling: Porn isn't for everyone, anyway, so don't feel bad.

Meyer: As I've already said, I don't condemn it. I've had some great ladies in my life, lots of them. For me to sit down and watch a goddamn fuck movie does nothing for me whatsoever. I'd rather look at a good industrial film.

Russ Meyer: The World's Breast Director

Jim Goad / 1991

From *Answer Me!* 1, no. 1, 1991–92. Reprinted with permission.

He's the guy who dos the tits, right? Well, *yeah*: Russ Meyer's films *do* feature women with abnormally large tits. His mammarian epics *do* star females who jut toward the audience at Mt. Rushmore–like angles. Big tits are to Russ Meyer's movies what big crowds are to Cecil B. DeMille's.

But before you dismiss Russ Meyer as a dirty old pornographer, probe beneath the breasts. With heavy implication and almost no genital shots (*Faster, Pussycat! Kill! Kill!* shows nary a nipple), he created the most obscenely entertaining films ever made. In his parables of small towns with big women, self-indulgence always triumphs over false piety. Biology squashes morality, just like nature intended.

A master technician, Russ splices shots together quicker than you can say, "premature ejaculation." Haji, one of his many female stars, says, "I believe Russ is sort of a genius as a director, as a cameraman. I mean, I believe he had a camera in his hand at birth, you know? It's the way he edits . . . people imagine they saw more than they really saw."

The director, sixty-nine, looks like Ernie Kovacs, and has the broad, Dickensian wit of W. C. Fields. He's finishing an autobiography, *A Clean Breast: The Life and Loves of Russ Meyer*. Never one for understatement, he says the tome will cost $350, contain twenty-five hundred photos, and weigh fifteen pounds. He's currently stopped production on his seventeen-hour autobiographical film, *The Breast of Russ Meyer*. Insoluble creative struggles? No: "I want to go fishing, do a lot of fuckin', good food, and the rest."

Russ continues to inspire new fans, as evidenced by the hordes of rock bands who, uh, "borrow" his films' titles. (Ask Mudhoney, Motorpsycho, Faster Pussycat, or Vixen where they got their names.)

ANSWER ME! interviewed Meyer in his Lake Hollywood home, newly painted on the outside in bright, roaring green with loud orange trim. As Russ explains, perhaps synopsizing his career, "Anything to offend the neighbors."

Jim Goad: Use as many adjectives as you can to describe the type of woman you look for when casting a film.

Russ Meyer: Pneumatic. Abundant, Mammiferous. Magnum-busted. I've got so many words in the book. Ballooning. Giganzos. I like "cantilevered." They gotta be busty, really busty; that's what my pictures are known for. The public is satisfied that it will see something that's a little outrageous in that area, and now even more so. But the satire and the humor is the thing that makes them live.

Goad: The men in your movies are routinely beaten, humiliated, and made to look stupid by an Amazonian female breed. Why all the clumsy guys?

Meyer: I was influenced in my early life by Al [Lil' Abner] Capp. If you study his cartoons, the women are all bright, voluptuous, and/or ugly, but they're the ones who really control the men. The men are their willing tools, as it were. So, I thought that was a pretty good peg to hang it all on. Got away from a lot of female criticism of my so-called art.

Goad: How do you respond to persons who say your movies are sexist?

Meyer: I say, "Yeah. Right. That's true." I found a long time ago never to, or by and large, don't get up and try to defend your position. Just admit to all your frailties and shortcomings. After a while, the questioners walk away.

Goad: There's a certain biblical justice in your earlier outings, such as *Lorna* and *Mudhoney*: greed, lust, and murder run rampant until the last minute or so, when all the sinners get zapped.

Meyer: Well, at the time, it was important to have some redeeming virtues to the films because of prevailing prosecutions and persecutions. But if I did *Lorna* over, or *Pussycat!* over again, I'd have the leading lady or villain just walk away from it. The convict would end up sleeping with Lorna's aunt, who would have big tits, too. I think it would be more fun to do it that way.

Goad: You once said *Beyond the Valley of the Dolls* is your greatest achievement.

Meyer: Well, it's the most satisfying of all because of Roger [Ebert] and I being *asked* to come to Fox to do the film. In my early years after World War II, I tried to get a job there as a cameraman. Forget it. Just as well, because I wouldn't have had the opportunity to learn filmmaking as I did doing industrials. So, all things equal, I think *Dolls* really represents my having come to the mountain. We made the film exactly as we wished to make it. I haven't been taken particularly seriously by the majors. They're afraid of the taint. I'll tell you a great line by a man that followed Zanuck after he got kicked out. . . . He said to my agent—I had a good agent who went there with another script—and he said, "We want no more of Meyer *or* Ebert, in spite of his Pulitzer." We chose—Ebert and I—to make a picture that *we* wanted to make, and that fucker's gonna live a lot longer than most anybody. The film is thought so highly of, just as *Pussycat!* is, by another generation altogether. And I say, "Why?" I don't know why, really.

I made the films to please myself. Maybe there lies the key, more than anything else—they're very personal.

Goad: What were some scripts or ideas which never bore, as you might say, abundant, buxotic fruit?

Meyer: There was *Viva, Foxy!*, which Roger wrote, which we kind of planned to use [former wife] Edy Williams in, but I determined that our marital bliss wasn't all that blissful, and I didn't want to have her end up directing the movie. It was a good project: a Caribbean island, a soldier of fortune played by Charles Napier, [and] revolutionaries. Existing there is a voluptuous girl who has been pretty much running things. She's in jeopardy of losing her head, her tits, or whatever. That's a quickie summation of it all. It was a good thing, a good script. [There was] *Up the Valley of the Beyond*, which I felt very strongly about, which Roger also scripted. It was a thing on Elvis Presley, who was over-the-hill sexually. [Obscure Nazi figure] Martin Bormann discovered that the pituitary gland of the female beaver would bring everlasting sexual prowess. Of course, there was Elvis—we called him King Gilette—and we had sons of the Nazi hierarchy, who drove around in Volkswagens, and the Godfather, with his younger people driving Fiats, and they were warring all the time. There was Elmo Temblor, the strongest man in the world, who headed an island bastion in the West Indies. Then we had Moishe Sabra, head of the Israeli intelligence. He had to skulk around in an Arab's burnoose, which he hated to do, trying to put the finger on Martin Bormann again. It's about a $7 million picture, and when I go back to see [my fiancée] Melissa Mounds, I'll go to New York for one day to a stockbroker who seems to be inclined. It looks pretty good. But the majors are scared to death of me. They just don't want any part of Meyer. The X [rating] is the most poisonous thing you could ever imagine. Now, NC-17 is exactly the same thing. It's a bad label. If this doesn't develop, I think Charles Napier—who I did *Supervixens* with—and I will do, I'd love to use the title *Big Tit Rumble*. I think it's a marvelous title, but we'd have to maybe call it *Big T. Rumble* or *The Return of Harry Sledge*. I would bankroll it myself, because I've got bucks. But I would make it for, like, $450,000. I'd love to. I'd get it right out there and barnstorm with it, and I bet we'd make one hell of a lot of money with this picture. Get some independent distributors, and the price is right to make it. And we'll do it with a small crew: five people, eight big superchicks, including Melissa, and she says, "I'll get all the big tits you want." And she will! We can make my kind of movie for $7 million—Howard Hughes, Adolf Hitler, you know, the whole works in there—or I'll make one with Harry [Napier] and eight big chicks.

Goad: Many in the film industry see you as an outsider. How did working independently with a small crew make your films different than bigtime Hollywood vehicles?

Meyer: When you ask a question like that, maybe it answers something. Maybe that's why the films are kind of special. Maybe that's why they're going to live for a hundred years. Maybe that's why the cassettes sell so aggressively. I've got thirteen cassettes in distribution, and instead of the numbers declining, they grow every year . . . sell more every year. If you stop and look at a major film, how many times does someone want to look at the film over and over again? My films have a lot of vignettes. You can look at just one vignette every now and then. Or another. And that may be the answer to the reason why people buy them—you don't have to look at the whole damned movie again.

Goad: Plenty of exploitation films feature sex and violence. I once read someone quoted as saying your movies are the only ones to feature *simultaneous* sex and violence.

Meyer: Both of them, the sex and the violence, are jokey. And they're outrageous and exaggerated. The violence, by and large, is overdone. Like in *Supervixens*—the [bathtub] murder, the dynamite up the ass—it's all not to be believed.

Goad: What is the difference between your work and the cheap video porn of today?

Meyer: You mean the hardcore? Well, I hate the word "softcore." I like the term "limber-core." I mean, they're not to be compared. I don't want to put anybody's work down, certainly not that. I think the interest in hardcore is waning. They're not being made in the quantities that they once were. My films are unique unto themselves. You can't compare 'em. They're not in the same category. The same people don't buy them. I mean, people write me letters and say, "I don't wanna look at that kind of hard stuff. I like yours because . . . ," and so forth. So, there's no comparison, and I don't think they should be compared. I have a unique genre that is strictly Russ Meyer. No one else is in that genre; it's strictly mine and mine alone. My films just don't die. The hardcore guys are really in some deep shit. The FBI is harassing the hell out of them. Really trying to put 'em out of business. I'm sorry to see it. God, everybody should have their own shot. But there are damned few hardcore films that have reached the status of being classic—you know, *Misty Beethoven* and, of course, *Deep Throat*. I just wouldn't do a hardcore film, because the humor wouldn't work, nor the satire. The ladies that I work with would not, of course, be a part of that. And it doesn't entertain me. I'm always looking to try and get a laugh somewhere.

Goad: The hedonists in your films seem more honest and mentally stable than the Puritans.

Meyer: I like to go after the Puritans whenever I can. I always say "Jesus Bakker" or "Jesus Swaggart." That phony TV evangelist in the glass church. They're all the same. They're all corrupt.

Goad: What's the best line of dialogue you've ever written?

Meyer: Oh, I couldn't answer that. I'll tell you the best line that a girl in one of my films came up with. Raven De La Croix [from *Up!*] and I had gone to Europe to promote the film. And when reporters would press her with too many questions, she would say, "What do I know? I'm only a woman."

Goad: Tell me the sickest, most twisted and extreme level you've ever reached in filmmaking.

Meyer: Sickest? I don't consider anything I've done as being sick. No child pornography. No abusing animals, for that matter. Nothing I've done in my estimation has been sick.

Goad: Are you as meat-and-potatoes as your leading men?

Meyer: I'm generally with one lady. I'm not interested in having three or four girls at one time, simultaneously or sporadically. Straight, good ol' sex. Just hunker down and work at it, alright? Belabor the girl's nether regions, alright? That's it. If somebody wants me to do something a little strange, I take a hike. Anyway, we're still at it—big bosoms and square jaws.

Russ Meyer—Hellcats for a Modern World

Beth Accomando / 1995

From *Hypno Magazine* 4, no. 5, 1995. Reprinted with permission.

Russ Meyer's 1959 softcore skin flick *The Immoral Mr. Teas* collected more than a million dollars in profits on a measly $24,000 investment. So began the highly profitable career of the man Hollywood crowned "King of the Nudies."

Throughout his career, Meyer has been both condemned as a pornographer and worshipped as a cult hero. He has seen four of his films (*The Immoral Mr. Teas, Supervixens, Faster, Pussycat! Kill! Kill!* and *Beyond the Valley of the Dolls*) placed into the permanent collection of the Museum of Modern Art in New York, yet the Directors Guild of America (of which he is a dues-paying member) still has not offered to screen his films in their theater.

Such contradictions seem to typify Meyer's life and career. Even Meyer himself is marked by contrasts. He may make X-rated films, but he always talks respectfully about women and refers to them as "ladies" and "girls." He has artistic aspirations, yet always speaks of filmmaking in the most pragmatic terms and with a keen sense of how to make publicity work in his favor.

Now in his seventies, Meyer shows no signs of slowing down. He is finishing up work on his three-volume autobiography, and is currently overseeing the rerelease of his X-rated 1966 film *Faster, Pussycat! Kill! Kill!*, which focused on a trio of go-go dancers on a violent spree through the California desert.

Faster, Pussycat! typifies Meyer's early period which includes films such as *Motorpsycho!* and *Good Morning . . . and Goodbye!* Later films, such as *Vixen!* and *Beyond the Valley of the Dolls*, had to compete with hardcore porn films and became more explicit, but still retained a certain appealing outrageousness. Meyer has become synonymous with films that highlight cartoonishly overendowed and sexually aggressive women, yet in many ways his films resist the stereotype of what is commonly labeled "porn."

His films have a surprisingly high production value and are well shot and well edited by Hollywood standards. They also contain more plot and character than the average porn audience would ever be able to tolerate.

Still, this hasn't prevented people from condemning him as a pornographer and exploiter of women. Yet anyone who talks with Meyer will quickly recognize the shortsightedness of these critics.

Hypno Magazine: Is it true that *Faster, Pussycat! Kill! Kill!* is a female version of your earlier film *Motorpsycho!*?

Russ Meyer: Yeah, we made *Motorpsycho!* by and large for the drive-in trade. It had three bad boys, and it was extremely successful. Then I got the idea that we might as well do it with three bad girls. But it was a big failure, it was not successful at all. The distributors didn't understand these women that had this affection, you can call it, for one another, although it's not graphic or anything of that nature. So, I just pulled the film off the market—it just didn't go anywhere at all. No point in running film through a projector just for the sake of doing that. What really brought it around was when video became popular, and more and more women, whether they were liberated or not, decided they wanted to look at it. My experience has always been, whether it be the theater or on video, if a woman appreciates something, she will bring a male with her to enjoy it. They can joust back and forth and take opposite viewpoints. That was the main reason that I decided to bring *Faster, Pussycat!* out in theaters again. It's doing quite well—I think it's in its seventh week in New York City at the Forum, which is a very fine art house.

Hypno: What I noticed about *Motorpsycho!* and *Faster, Pussycat!* is that the audience seems willing to cheer on the bad women in *Faster, Pussycat!* but not the bad men in *Motorpsycho!*

Meyer: You got it right. One lady, during a question and answer session after a screening, said that the thing she liked about it was that the women were not caused to do something, they did it because they wanted to. They were bad girls to begin with. I just returned from England, and it's the second time that I've been asked to come by the National Film Theatre, and they bid specifically for *Faster, Pussycat!* It sold out every showing. I did the same thing at the Irish Film Theater, where it went over exactly the same way and met with the same kind of applause. I have never encountered an audience that doesn't applaud.

Hypno: Why do you think your films have remained so popular?

Meyer: Well, they're cartoons for one matter. You might be interested to know that *Playboy* magazine, at the effort of Bruce Williamson, is doing a piece on me. He asked Roger Ebert to do the story, and he was very happy to do it. The piece comes out in the June issue.

Hypno: Seeing your films today, it's sometimes difficult to understand why they would have garnered an X rating. How do you feel about the ratings?

Meyer: Well, it's strictly a business thing. We don't have the X anymore because it had a bad connotation because of the hardcore people. All my films were X-rated when they had that rating, and it was fine by me. It was a kind of badge that said this is kind of special. What hurt it finally were the people who made the explicit films because they started getting the Triple-X. I was pleased to see [the ratings board] come up with the NC-17, except that it's harmful to independent filmmakers or even an important filmmaker since they can't show them in these shopping malls. Theaters signed a deal with the owners of the malls saying we will not show anything which is NC-17 or X. But some of the Rs have things that are a lot more heinous than something that's sexual—like a lot of terrible violence. I can't stand up and not be accused of violence, but mine is kind of outrageous and purposely cartoonish.

Hypno: Who wrote the script for *Faster, Pussycat!*? It has some great lines.

Meyer: The writer was Jack Moran, who had been a child star. I met him through a friend of mine who was a partner of his in prison. My friend wrote me and said his cellmate was a damn good writer. That sounded kind of funny. I had this film that need some narration called *Wild Gals of the Naked West*, so when the guy got out, I used him as one of the actors. He also wrote the script and all the narration. When he did *Pussycat!* he was very much into drinking alcohol. He made this deal with me: "I wanna get paid every day, I want Writers Guild minimum, a brown bag lunch, a cheap motel, and a quart of Jack Daniel's. That was his wish. He wrote the script in four days.

Hypno: What do you recall about shooting *Faster, Pussycat!*?

Meyer: Well, my modus operandi when I shoot is to keep the boys away from the girls, and vice versa. When we got up to Lake Isabella, Tura (Tura Satana, the lead tough chick) said, "I understand you don't like any kind of cohabitation, but I need it and I'm gonna have to have it." I said, "Well, who have you got in mind?" She said, "This assistant cameraman you've got looks husky." I didn't even ask him because you'd be a fool to ask a man to have a good time with Tura Satana. I mean, she was in her prime, good lord. I said, "I have one requirement, though. You must couple only once a night." She agreed to it. Years afterward, we had a reunion. The guy was there, and I asked him if he and Tura got together only once a night. He said, "No, it was all night!"

Hypno: Do you have a favorite film?

Meyer: *Beyond the Valley of the Dolls* is my favorite because it represents my having gone to the peak. I was offered an opportunity because I had made a film called *Vixen!* that made an enormous amount of money. This attracted Darryl Zanuck to give his son [Richard Zanuck] literally an order—"I want you to meet this guy Meyer and talk to him about doing a picture." They gave me $5,000 to put out some kind of treatment, which they wanted as quickly as possible. I approached [Roger] Ebert, who liked my films at the time, and we met in San Diego. We couldn't rent a typewriter, and the only typewriter we could find on the hotel premises was a typewriter, strangely enough, used for writing children's verse. So, Roger wrote the treatment on that, and we presented it to Fox [Zanuck's studio]. At the time, Zanuck and [his producing partner] David Brown—I called him Cardinal Brown and I hope you use that because he was certainly that kind of guy—were down there, and we sent the treatment to them. We got this three-foot fax in which Zanuck just bubbled over and said, "I am now gonna give you $25,000 to write the screenplay." Ebert got thirty days leave of absence, and wrote the screenplay. To me the film represents going to the majors and making a film that made a lot of money. It's also a film that I can look at continuously, more so than any of the others.

Hypno: I read that you were a combat photographer during World War II.

Meyer: Yeah, World War II, the best time of my life—I loved it. I was very young and was fortunate to get in with what was called the Signal Photographic Company, which was the branch that had photographers. I was, in the first instance, attached to Bradley's 1st Army with the 29th Infantry. We landed in Normandy. Later on, when Patton became active, I was transferred to the 3rd Army. Then I continued on and met Hemingway outside of Paris. He was there, carrying on in his usual way—you know, fistfights and booze—and he even closed down the local bordello for only his use and his friends. He was instrumental in my first sexual liaison. His lieutenant, a short Portuguese guy, took me and my three compatriots down to the bordello, which he had closed, with an entrance pass. I was terrified because I had never been able to say yes, and here I had to face the mustard, or whatever you want to call it. That's how he affected my life.

Hypno: Then how did you get to Hollywood?

Meyer: When I got out of the service, it wasn't possible to get a job in Hollywood simply because they weren't hiring people like me, and that was understandable. But there was a man by the name of Emery Huse who was instrumental in getting us our training to begin with, and he introduced me to Gene K. Walker, who was doing films for Southern Pacific Railroad. It was a great opportunity for me to learn the trade. We went out and shot pictures—just hundreds of feet of film that were turned into industrial movies.

After that, I became a little disconsolate because I wasn't making as much money as I would have liked. A friend of mine, Donald Ornitz, said to me, "If you wanna make more money, there's a lot of girlie books coming out." He said he occasionally photographed for *Playboy*, and that maybe I might wanna do something along that line. I said that I'd never photographed women, and he said, "What you lack in ability, you'll make up for in enthusiasm." I got into taking pictures of girls, and I eventually married Eve Meyer, who was the first *Playboy* Playmate centerfold. We worked together and made a lot of money. We made *The Immoral Mr. Teas* with a partner, Peter DeCenzie. We each bought a Cadillac with the profits from that picture.

Hypno: I heard that you had been planning to make a film with the Sex Pistols. Did you ever shoot any footage?

Meyer: That was the biggest disappointment I ever encountered. All we shot were the title backgrounds. I was paid substantially to go over there [England] and live well and get everything together. I cast the film. I had Marianne Faithful, who was to be Sid Vicious's mother, and Ebert came over and did the script. *Who Killed Bambi?*—that's what it was called. What happened was [Sex Pistols manager] Malcom McLaren was the guy that committed the boo-boo—he didn't have enough money to make the movie. He had an idea that it could be made, because of my background, for $100,000. I was just really thunderstruck [when it fell through] and that's why I got out and didn't do any films for a couple of years. I was so intent on coming up with a great film, and it would have been. The script was great. The Sex Pistols were important at that time. I would have had enough ability to keep them in line. Two of them were OK, but the other two—Vicious and Johnny Rotten—were bad news, really bad news.

Hypno: What's the current state of your autobiography?

Meyer: It's finished, but I'm having some difficulty with the American rep, as far as making sure I have the ability to stay there just a short period of time to supervise the production of it. It will be three volumes and will have twenty-five hundred photographs. It's gonna be in a slip case and will be sold for quite a bit of money—like between $400 and $500. I'm only printing five thousand. I think it's a very strong book. It's not a kiss-and-tell, but a fuck-and-tell—exactly everybody I've ever been with. And it's all positive, nothing negative. There's some interest now from one of the major studios to make a film of the book.

Hypno: Who would you want to play you?

Meyer: Robin Williams. I'm serious. It would be a very strong film.

Hypno: Would you direct it yourself?

Meyer: I would direct it. Oh, yeah. Who knows more about me? Hopefully it will come to a head.

Russ Meyer

Ed Symkus / 1995

This is the full transcript of an interview conducted on March 23, 1995, that was published, in part, by Community Newspaper Company, April 1995. Reprinted with permission.

Ed Symkus: How many times have you seen *Faster, Pussycat*?

Russ Meyer: That's not easy to say. Years ago, when I edited it, I probably saw it a hundred times. Lately I don't think I've seen it a half a dozen times. I know it by heart. I don't have to. I've been doing a lot of promotion for the film. It's been playing at this house in the Village. It's only got about a hundred seats, but it's been there for about nine weeks.

ES: Why this picture, and why now? What brought it to New York?

RM: I decided to distribute the film because it's so successful in video. Very strong following. One particular reason it's so successful is the women, not the men. The women are the ones who are championing the film. Oftentimes there are groups of women who'll run a 16mm print, either at an institution or a college, whatever. That's another factor involved. And I get a lot of fan mail from women who are very pleased. We had a very good run in Los Angeles. One woman had *this* much to say about it. She said, "I like the violence in it. It was not something that was perpetrated on the women. They did it because they *wanted* to do it, plain and simple." Prior to this, and why I really got this thing started, I was invited to the National Film Institute in Britain, and in Ireland. And I'd never played any films in Ireland. I was over there for four weeks, and it was sold out every night. That kind of reaction was great, and the press was great, and that's what kind of got me going to do this circuitous thing around the States.

ES: Do you already know where it's scheduled to play?

RM: It'll play in every major city. And I make it a point now to go to every place to talk. And the reason is simple. I'm competing with the majors. We cannot afford to put out the kind of money they do to popularize something. So, I find it's very important that I do that. I was very active in Chicago. After finishing some work down in San Diego, what came out of that is they're going to release a story in *Playboy*, in the June issue, and Ebert wrote the story.

ES: Of course, he did!

RM: Well, sometimes you wonder, because he's under pressure from that asshole partner of his.

ES: So, you get along with one of them, but not the other.

RM: No, it's not a matter of *that*. Ebert and I are like buddies. We did *Beyond the Valley of the Dolls* at Fox together. And he'd done a few other films, under pseudonyms. Siskel could never deal with the fact that Ebert got a Pulitzer. That's what pisses him off. I also threatened to throw Siskel through the window of a hotel because he was saying bad things about my wife at the time, who was the voluptuous Edy Williams. And from then on, he's been really a little bit uptight about me. Ebert does talk about the film often, but he has to be a little careful with Siskel because Siskel gets on his case about that. But the film doesn't depend upon Ebert. He did other things with me, under pseudonyms. As Reinhold Timme (*Up!*), as Robert Hyde (*Beneath the Valley of the Ultra-Vixens*). He worked on five of them. He had the ability to turn out a script with my kind of appeal and humor. We'd do them together in five days. This was before Ebert was in the big time. So, as soon as he got into that, he had to kind of back off a little bit. But I was so proud of him when *Playboy* called him and asked him to do the piece "The Immoral Mr. Meyer," a take-off on *The Immoral Mr. Teas*.

ES: What other cities are you going to with this film?

RM: I just did Minneapolis and St. Paul. From Boston, I'm jumping to Washington, and Maryland, then I'll do Pittsburgh, and then come back to Philadelphia, then I'll go down—grabs his notebook—to Raleigh-Durham, Atlanta, St. Louis, Kansas City—he unfolds a map—Oklahoma City, Dallas-Fort Worth, Austin, San Antonio, Denver, Salt Lake City, then home. If I didn't do that, we wouldn't do as well.

So, what am I releasing here? I'm releasing a picture that's looked on in a very positive way about women today. And men as well, because they always drag a man along to see it. Years before, when I got started, we had to deal essentially with a one-armed reader. We don't have that today. When you go to a theater today you see woman, man, woman, man, and I mean with this particular picture. When I was in England, the first time I saw the film there was with a very good audience, and every time the picture was shown, they would stand up and applaud. And then they did it in Ireland. That's where it played so far. So, now I'm going around the US, and just doing everything I possibly can to generate as much interest in the film.

ES: Did anyone stand up and applaud when it was released?

RM: It was a failure when it was released. The picture took a big dump. This is back in 1966. Prior to that I had made a picture called *Motorpsycho!* with three bad boys. It did big business. The reason I changed my spots there was that the Baptists and so forth came down on any kind of nudity that was going to play at drive-ins. So, I said we've gotta make a picture that doesn't have nudity. We must make a different film. So, I decided to come up with one of the earlier bike films. And it went over big. Afterward, I said to my wife, Eve, maybe we ought to make one now with three bad *girls*. She said it sounded like a good idea. But it just laid an egg, right off the bat. The public didn't want it. They didn't care about seeing it. The distributors weren't necessarily worldly people. They couldn't comprehend the two women showing an affinity for one another. And nothing happened with it. We just finally pulled it out because we were tired of getting bad grosses. The only reason I did well with it was when video came along, people began to rent it, then buy it.

ES: Where did you find Tura Satana?

RM: Tura was introduced to me by a girl named Haji, who's been in a lot of my films. I knew there was somewhere I could use her. We started to discuss some other people who were strippers like herself. Tura was a stripper in a very good club in Los Angeles. I went to see her and we got together and talked, and she was a very firm person about what she wanted to do. I was taken by the fact that Tura had an ability with the martial arts. Then the script had to be written. I had the idea for the film, then I called upon a friend named Jack Moran. Jack had been in prison with a close friend of mine, Barney. They were both in prison for writing paper. Jack was a fairly successful child star. His father was a ward boss in Chicago, and when the child had an opportunity to do something [in acting], he just left his career in Chicago, and they went out to Los Angeles. One of the early things he did was to be in *Gone with the Wind*. He was the little boy at the very beginning. Then he did a lot of other films as a child. He did well, but his father just absorbed all the money. Jack eventually got into a little boozing and gambling.

So, he went to prison with this friend of mine, Barney—who was another GI cameraman in WWII. And when Barney got out, he told me about Jack Moran being very capable at writing, and told me about some of his stuff. I got together with Moran to find out what he wanted, and he said, "I'm gonna have to have probably about five days and I'll need Screen Writers Guild minimum," which wasn't a fortune. And he said, "I'll need one bottle of Jack Daniel's every day, and I've gotta be in a cheap motel. I don't want a good place. I want to get the feel of the grit. And brown bag food three times a day." Then he did the writing in five days, and did a great job. So, that's how it all got together, and we made the film; my wife and I financed it.

158 RUSS MEYER: INTERVIEWS

ES: When was the first time you heard of the band Faster Pussycat?

RM: They approached me. They had taken the name Faster Pussycat without asking me. There's another well-known band from Seattle called Mudhoney. And there are two bands in Britain—one was Vixen and one was Beyond the Valley of the Dolls. It's fine. I'm gratified that they would do that. Faster Pussycat came to me and said they wanted to do a music video with me, and I said yeah, if we can do something good. They didn't have a lot of money, but we went up with their manager to northern California and found some locations that I thought were interesting, but they didn't have enough money. So, we had to shoot it on a stage, and then we used rear background projection. I did use another Faster Pussycat-themed film for a music video. It was for Sony, in Germany. It was a German rock star. And they gave me enough money to do it. I was able to intercut from the picture, itself. I had my girlfriend Melissa Mounds—a huge-busted, beautiful woman—who I used as a counterpoint to the Varla [character], as it were. We intercut stuff of the cars racing. She'd be driving a new Cadillac Allante, and the other cars were period cars. We intercut Tura in the Porsche, and the other two girls in the MGBs. I also did the scene with the muscleman where he is fighting the car and Tura. And in that scene we had my girlfriend, with the huge bosom, driving a Jeep, trying to squash the German guy. We had some very interesting cutting.

ES: Where can this video be seen?

RM: You can't see it. MTV wouldn't use it. The bosom on the girl was too large, and the cleavage was about one and a half feet deep. She was a big, great-looking stripper. It played really well in Germany. That was too bad. But the only problem there was the guy didn't make it as a singer. [*Laughs*]

ES: You eventually started doing very well with your films being released on video.

RM: Yes, when video became popular, with this picture, more so than all of my other films, and I realized I *had* something. We got into 16mm so we could show it in school cinema classes. After that happened, my distributor said it's time you released some of your films, and he had *Pussycat* in mind. So, we released it. He was smart enough to get this wonderful theater, the Forum, in New York.

So now, it's important to me to give the film all the chance it can get. It's a black and white film, good quality, a brand-new print. And we got a new negative, so it's even better than the original.

ES: Music has always been such an important part of your films. What kind of music do you listen to at home?

RM: I like military music—Sousa. I listen to a lot of Nazi music. Very moving, stirring music, some of which was banned in Germany. I also like old jazz. I'm not keen for rock music, but I use it in the films. I'm like a whore. I don't care what it is. Even if I don't like it, if I think it's gonna work and do a good job in the film, I'll put it in. When we did *Beyond the Valley of the Dolls*, I just turned it over to Stu Phillips and Igo Kantor.

ES: You've had so many interesting nicknames over the years, from King Leer to the Chaucer of Sex . . .

RM: Really? I never heard that one before.

ES: Do you have a favorite?

RM: Something I didn't like is what happened with the wise guys at *People* magazine. Two girls did the story, and then the editor took over, and he had a particularly strong hatred (toward me). A lot of men, more than women, are uptight. He chose to call me a kind of a failing pornographer. That kind of thing gets to me. I choose to refer to myself a cartoonist. A live-action cartoonist.

ES: You've been called a master craftsman, but others have just said you're a softcore porn filmmaker. And you've said that you never wanted to be called a pornography director.

RM: Well, you've got to say it *this* way: you don't say pornography; it's *porno*. You've got to purse your lips: *Porno*. But it's a terrible word. I don't like it. I don't like hardcore films. I'm not against them, but I don't like to be made reference to, and thrown into that big, fucking, boiling cauldron of three-day wonders. Calling what I do softcore porno is a way they think they can get to me, and they get to me so well. Softcore is another rotten term. So, I say, "Don't call me a pornographer, call me a cartoonist." Like Al Capp—you know, Daisy Mae, the stupid husband, all that.

ES: What have the conservatives said about you over the years? Have you had enemies, from the beginning?

RM: No, no! I have so much fucking money, that I've earned. I'm not some loser. I made the money myself. They've been *my* ideas, I bankrolled it, with partners.

ES: What are your thoughts on the American ratings system? Has it helped you, has it hurt you, over the years?

RM: The ratings system is really maligned. We're submitting *Faster, Pussycat!* for a rating, and I'm afraid they'll give me a PG. I don't want it. I want an R. What've you got? You've got a muscleman who stabs a girl brutally in the belly, with a knife. Prior to that, one of the girls, Tura, throws a blade and kills someone. Then we have her just absolutely smashing the dirty old man in the wheelchair. And she breaks a man's back.

ES: You did get an X rating for *Beyond the Valley of the Dolls*.

RM: Yeah, and I'm so proud that Fox never changed it. It originally had an X, but later [the MPAA] dumped that rating and replaced it with NC-17. But it's playing frequently on HBO now, and there are very few films on HBO with an NC-17. And the actors are calling me and saying how pleased they are that they're getting residuals.

ES: So, the system hasn't really bothered you?

RM: Yes, it has. It bothered me at a given time when I had to get out of the film game. I had made a picture called *Supervixens*, and it grossed a lot of money. It cost $107,000 and it grossed $17 million. That was OK, but what happened after that . . . Ebert and I went to Europe to do a film on the Sex Pistols. They paid *me* enough money and *Ebert* enough money, but they never had enough money to make the movie. Which was a shame because it really affected both of our careers. We'd come up with a great script, with all those British actors, and there was the music aspect of it. But it ended up driving me out of films for about three years. Although just before we went over, I'd done a film with Kitten Natividad called *Beneath the Valley of the Ultra-Vixens*. After I came back, I did all of the sound effects and things like that. I like the big cartoon noises. I was terribly disturbed due to the failure of making the Sex Pistols film, so I went to Australia and Tasmania and did some fishing. I was also bothered when I finished *Beneath the Valley* because it had an X rating and we couldn't play it in the malls. They all had contracts that said they could not play X films. So, I was banded together with the hardcore bunch. And you always had to explain, "There's no penetration, not that you can see." So, that bothered me. I'm about to make another film which will be strong. Ebert has written it. It's called *The Bra of God*. He wrote the treatment about six years ago. It'll have a lot of nudity and a lot of fornication—simulated of course. So, now I'm gonna have to deal with that.

ES: Is there a lot of violence in it?

RM: Of course, but women are the strong ones again. Simply put, do you remember Groucho Marx and Magaret Dumont? Well, I have a girl named Stacey Keith who I still shoot for German *Playboy*. A beautiful lady. I would use her as God's wife, dressed in white. The story is like *Supervixens* in reverse. It's about a young man who's done terrible things. And a mistake is made. Instead of going to hell, he ends up in heaven. She says, I'm really ashamed of what's happened here. I'm so embarrassed. My husband is away, so what we're gonna have to do is send you out again, in hopes that you will rectify all of these errors, in purgatory. But he goes out and says, "Well, I've got thirty months. I'm gonna have a good time. I'm gonna go out and just give every broad the going over that they deserve." But when he goes out, every broad just beats the shit out of him. And my friend Stuart Lancaster—the dirty old man—will be in it. He'll be in a crop-dusting plane, zapping people with insecticide . . . and something else. It'll be an homage to Cary Grant in that Hitchcock film. And there'll be all this kind of jokey sex. We're gonna do this film in the fall.

ES: The reason I asked about the violence factor is that supposedly you got a lot of feedback in between *Up!* and *Beneath the Valley* which resulted in you not having any violence at all in *Beneath the Valley*, other than a fistfight or two. Was that because of audience feedback?

RM: Well, *Up!* had a lot violence in it, such as axes in the chest. The violence was gone for *Beneath the Valley of the Ultra-Vixens* because of the rating board giving it an X, and we couldn't get into the mall theaters, and there were no other theaters to play it in. In Germany, where there's no censorship [for violence], I played my films continuously for four years, and collected an enormous amount of money.

ES: You've often said you've made a lot of money with your films. But you also had a couple of flops. Have you ever been flat broke?

RM: Never. I saved the money and made good investments.

ES: Do you recall when you actually committed to having a filmmaking career. Was it right when you made *The Immoral Mr. Teas*?

RM: No, I had a filmmaking career in the war. I loved the war. I didn't want the war to end. I wanted it to go on and on. We had great food, we traveled, it was exciting. The whole war was the greatest thing that ever happened to me, more so than anything else.

ES: Did you make a commitment to being a filmmaker at that point?

RM: No, I didn't, because the war ended, and I had to go home. The H bomb came over and saved our ass. Which was probably just as well. Because that landing in Japan had been a sticky wicket. It might not have been as pleasant as being in France and drinking wine and things like that. And then Ernest Hemingway got me my first piece of ass. I ran into him outside of Paris, in a little town called Rambouillet. I'd never mentioned to all my mates that I was a virgin. Hemingway's lieutenant got the key and led us over to the whorehouse. Hemingway had a magic, a control. What he really wanted to do was get into Paris, before anybody else, take over the Ritz Hotel, and only let friends of his come to the hotel, and he would be the bartender there. Anyway, we went to the whorehouse, and it was almost like what happens in Hollywood, with the fancy costumes, the madame looked like she was right out of Guy de Maupassant, the girls were all beauties, I picked the girl with the biggest tits, and that was my indoctrination. And it all worked out fine. I was twenty years old. All of that is well described in my massive book

ES: When will we be seeing that book?

RM: Well, that's a problem. What I've got to do is either go to Hong Kong or sue the American representative who is not really fulfilling his obligation. I've been working on it for at least nine years and have spent a million dollars of my own money. It's all written, by me, it has twenty-five hundred photographs, it's in a slip case. And there are fifteen hundred pages. It's a fuck and tell book. I've been with a lot of women, and they're all *class* women. All giant-breasted. If all goes well, it should be coming out in about six months. What to do about selling it is something else. We're only printing four thousand of them. I'll probably sell it for $350–$400, and all of the money will go to the Norris Cancer Clinic at USC. No critic will get a free book. The only person to get a free one is Ebert.

ES: Looking back on this illustrious career, has it been harder or easier than you expected it would be?

RM: It's been just a barrel of laughs. I've had a great time. To my standards, I've been with the greatest women in the world. And I've had many of them and I've married wonderful women and I've lived with great women.

ES: Do you know if there's been a favorite character in your films in the eyes of your fans?

RM: I think Charles Napier, who has a square jaw and seven more teeth than Burt Lancaster. Without having done *Cherry, Harry & Raquel!* I don't think he would've made it.

ES: Aside from your own films, what have been your favorites, ones that you've watched over and over?

RM: Bogart in the great *Casablanca*. Clint Eastwood—literally in every film, I could pick up something. There are so many good things. Of all the filmmakers, I hold him in the highest possible regard. The Marx Brothers, of course. I like *Love Happy*, the one with Ilona Massey. She was a very beautiful Hungarian girl. There was a great scene with Harpo, you know, with his screwiness and so forth. She was, in her time, big bosomed. She's against the wall and he's up against her and she starts to generate her sexuality, and there's the sound of a tremendous turbine going and it's affecting Harpo. He's doing everything he can do to withstand this, and finally this great big turbine goes *booiiing!!* and he collapses on the floor and she collapses on top of him. That kind of stuff blows me away. And don't forget W. C. Fields in *The Dentist*. If anything's pornographic, that is, but people don't realize it. Just look at the way the woman in the chair wraps her legs around him while he's drilling.

Additional Resources

Roger Ebert, in the *Chicago Sun-Times* (a year before he worked with Meyer), on *Vixen!*: "In a field filled
with cheap, dreary productions, Meyer is the best craftsman and the only artist. He has developed
a directing style so open, direct and good-humored that it dominates his material; what a relief to
hear laughter during a skin-flick, instead of the dead silence that usually envelops their cheerless
audiences." (2/24/69)

Judith Crist, in the *New York Magazine*, on *Vixen!*: "There's a wild enthusiasm to the heroine's activities and
a deadpan stupidity to the dialogue that provide a redeeming entertainment value for non-up-tight
adults." (5/26/69)

Vincent Canby, in the *New York Times*, on *Finders Keepers, Lovers Weepers!*: "Although I find his fantasies
basically unpleasant—they are almost exclusively concerned with insatiable ladies and the men they
wear out—they are made with some cinematic complexity (lots of different camera setups in any one
scene) and a minimum of mock piety." (9/6/69)

Richard Corliss, in the *Village Voice*, on *Cherry, Harry & Raquel!*: "Meyer's heroines are invariably Silicone
freaks with breasts large enough to halt both traffic on Wall Street and arousal on 42nd Street." (6/11/70)

Richard Schickel, in a 1970 *Harper's Magazine* article, says Meyer's first feature *The Immoral Mr. Teas* has
"a charm, even an innocence, lacking in the films that followed it," including *Faster, Pussycat! Kill! Kill!*,
Mudhoney, and *Lorna*, which are "heavy-breathing dramas of rural rape and revenge," and that in "late
Meyer films, the "humor is conscious, the editing snappier, concern with character and motivation less
careful." (7/70)

Gene Siskel, in the *Chicago Tribune* (five years before he teamed up with Ebert), on *Beyond the Valley of the
Dolls*: "Boredom aplenty is provided by a screenplay which for some reason has been turned over to a
screenwriting neophyte." (7/14/70)

The Firesign Theatre, most of them had "balconies you could do Shakespeare from." (Columbia
Records—7/22/70)

Alexander Walker, in the *London Evening Standard*, on *Beyond the Valley of the Dolls*: "[It's] a film whose
total idiotic, monstrous badness raises it to the pitch of near-irresistible entertainment." (2/11/71)

A David Ansen overview of Meyer in a 1975 *Real Paper* calls *Beyond the Valley of the Dolls* "trashy, but
deliriously so. Hilariously so. And what came as the biggest surprise, deliberately so . . . It was at once
gaudy, cartoon-style parody and far more outrageous than the genres it mocked." (7/30/75)

Interviewed by Ellen Adelstein on her Tucson-based TV show *Talk It Over* in 1979, he was asked, "Did your
mother breast feed you?" He smiled and said, "I believe so, yes. But then there a lot of other people that

have been breastfed and are not nearly as into this thing as strongly as I am. I don't think there's a basis there. But I don't object to your asking me. In fact, I practice breast feeding all the time now." (11/17/79)

For instance, in the season four episode of *Seinfeld*, titled "The Pilot," Jerry and Elaine are in Monk's Café, which has changed management. Jerry notices that all of the new waitresses are overly buxom, and says to Elaine, "I haven't seen four women together like this outside of a Russ Meyer film!" (5/20/93)

In 1993, Conan O'Brien said, "There's a certain theme in your movies. You have an obsession with women's breasts. Is that fair?" Meyer countered with, "Well, I wouldn't say it's an obsession. But I care for them a great deal." (11/18/93)

The following year, Jon Stewart declared, "Watching your movies, whether men like to admit it or not, you've lived out a great fantasy life, for all men. I want to thank you." Meyer quipped, "The pleasure was all mine." (11/30/94)

Bosley Crowther, in the *New York Times*, on *Fanny Hill*: "[Viewers] will . . . have a hard time recognizing anything that resembles wit or even good, solid belly-laugh humor in the spirit of low comedy." (12/2/96)

Meyer's biographer Jimmy McDonough, in his 2005 book *Big Bosoms and Square Jaws* (published by Crown), brings up Meyer's six phases: the nudies, the roughies, the harder sex films, the soap operas, the studio films, and the sex comedies. (2005)

Owen Gleiberman, in a 2011 appreciation in *Entertainment Weekly*, claims that while *Supervixens* marked a return to form for Meyer, it was "followed by what, for me, may be the most arresting (and underrated) phase of his career, kicked off by the jaw-droppingly perverse erotic fairy tale *Up!*, which was like *Smokey and the Bandit*, *Li'l Abner*, Sam Peckinpah, and the postwar legend of Adolf Hitler all thrown together into a raunchy redneck stew, topped off by dialogue and narration as florid as anything from the zaniest Coen brothers outing." (3/27/11)

The season twenty-five episode of *The Simpsons*—"Yellow Subterfuge"—features a Jamaican version of *The Itchy & Scratchy Show*, renamed *The Itchem & Scratchem Blow*, in a segment called *Rasta, Pussycat! Kill! Kill!* (12/8/13)

Meyer fan John Waters has regularly included Meyer posters in the backgrounds of his own films—*Vixen!* in *Multiple Maniacs*, *Lorna* in *Pink Flamingos*, and *Faster, Pussycat! Kill! Kill!* in *Polyester*.

Index

Adelstein, Ellen, xi

Albee, Edward, xx, xxi

Alger, Horatio, 60, 106

All in the Family, 13

Amazon Women on the Moon, xxii, 86

Ansen, David, xiii

Antz, Bob, 92

Appleton, Lou, 105

Austin Powers, xiii

Baratta, Fred, 15

Bardot, Babette, 3, 124, 136

Beneath the Valley of the Ultra-Vixens, vii, viii, ix, 34, 35, 36, 37, 38, 41, 42, 45, 50, 51, 59, 60, 63, 64, 65, 75, 76, 89, 93, 95, 97, 99, 101, 108, 124, 133, 134, 136, 137, 139, 140, 156, 160–61

Bernard, Susan, 74

Beyond Beyond, 20

Beyond the Valley of the Dolls, viii, ix, x, xiii, 8, 9, 10, 14, 16, 20, 23, 24, 34, 39, 42, 43, 46, 55, 58, 59, 67, 68, 69, 75, 76, 77, 89, 90–91, 94, 95, 97, 98, 132, 138, 139, 146, 150, 152, 156, 159

Big Bosoms and Square Jaws, xiv

Black Snake!, viii, xiii, 12, 15, 20, 24, 59, 80, 100

Blitzen, Vixen, and Harry, 101

Bormann, Martin, 38, 60, 147

Bosomania, 34, 63, 123

Bra of God, The, 160

Breast of Russ Meyer, The, xiv, 51, 53, 57, 70, 72, 80, 81, 86–87, 89, 94, 96, 100, 101, 111, 145

Brooks, Mel, 26, 61

Brown, David, xx, 43, 69, 100, 153

Brummer, Richard, 100

Burrows, Abe, 98

Caged Heat, 80, 99

Calley, John, 24

Canby, Vincent, x

Candide, xiii

Capp, Al, 13, 31, 70, 106, 146, 159

Capri, Alaina, 3, 6, 54, 98, 110

Casablanca, 45, 49, 162

Cherry, Harry & Raquel!, ix, xi, 8, 14, 42, 46, 51, 55, 58, 85, 97, 109, 110, 132–33, 162

Citizens for Decent Literature, 9, 16, 59

Clean Breast, A, 125, 145

Common Law Cabin, 101, 136

Corliss, Richard, xi

Crist, Judith, x

Crowther, Bosley, x

De Carlo, Yvonne, 24

De La Croix, Raven, 63, 70, 136, 137, 149

Dean, James (Jimmy), 23

DeCenzie, Peter A., xviii, 31, 66, 92, 95–96, 97, 104, 112, 113, 114, 115, 116, 117, 118, 119–21, 126–30, 154

Deep Throat, 25, 59, 80, 148
Demme, Jonathan, 80, 97, 99
Dentist, The, 162
Desperate Women, The, 105
Diaz, Benny, 139
Digard, Uschi, xx, xxi, 37, 43, 55, 82, 83, 85, 99, 108, 125, 132, 135, 136
Duran, Jean, 101

Eastwood, Clint, 70, 75, 140, 162
Ebert, Roger, ix, x, xx, 24, 36, 47, 69, 89, 94–95, 100, 137, 138–40, 146, 147, 151, 153, 154, 156, 160, 162
El Rey Burlesk Theater, xviii, 31, 92, 104
Erotica, xiii, 93
Eruption, 65
Eubank, Shari, 27, 55, 82, 85, 99
Europe in the Raw, 93
Eve and the Handyman, xiii, 77, 79, 90, 93, 116, 119
Eve Productions, xviii, xix
Everything in the Garden, xx

Fanny Hill, ix, x, 78, 91
Faster, Pussycat! Kill! Kill!, viii, ix, xiii, 10, 14, 37, 54, 63, 64, 74, 76, 81, 92, 94, 100, 101, 110, 145, 146, 150, 151, 152, 155, 158, 159
Fiedler, Leslie, 6, 117, 121
Fields, W. C., 83, 106, 145, 162
Finders Keepers, Lovers Weepers!, x, 14, 54, 95, 139
Firesign Theatre, xv
Foxy, 16, 17, 21
French Peep Show, The, 31, 92, 104, 112
Friday Locke, Raymond, 101
Friedman, David, 75, 91–92, 123, 124
Furlong, John, ix, xix, 94

Gavin, Erica, 40, 47, 63, 71, 98, 99, 131, 137
Gene K. Walker Productions, 127

Giant, 22–23
Gleiberman, Owen, xiii
Globe Photos, xviii, 113, 115, 118, 119, 127
Gone with the Wind, 157
Good Morning . . . and Goodbye!, ix, 4, 6, 54, 76, 110, 150
Gordon, Ellis, 90–91, 93
Grant, Ray, 114, 129
Grey, Darlene, 101, 134
Griffith, James, 75, 96–97
Guinness Book of Records, 41, 47, 58

Haji, xix, 74, 75–76, 97, 109–10, 110, 145, 157
Hanging of Jake Ellis, The, 97
Hanging Tree, The, 129
Heavenly Bodies!, ix, 10, 93
Hemingway, Ernest, 46, 65, 105, 153, 161
Hempel, Anouska, 101
Hill, George Roy, 19
Hopper, Hal, 75, 96–97
Horten, Rena, 78, 91, 101
Horvath, Tundi, 87, 88, 93, 95
How Much Loving Does a Normal Couple Need?, 6, 101
Hunter, Ross, 18–19
Huse, Emery, 153
Hyde, R., ix, 139, 156. *See also* Ebert, Roger

I Am Curious, Yellow, 11
Immoral Mr. Teas, The, vii, ix, xiii, 5–6, 10, 23, 31, 33, 45, 46, 63, 64, 66, 79, 90, 92, 93, 95, 103, 124, 104, 112, 114, 115, 117, 119, 121, 126, 129–30, 150, 154, 156, 161

James Dean Story, The, 23
Joe, 13

Keating, Charles, Jr., 9, 16, 19, 141
Keith, Stacey, 160

Kodak (Eastman), 22, 28, 64, 66, 77, 92, 102, 104, 114, 128

Lakso, Ed, 121
Lancaster, Stuart, xiii, xix, 37, 75, 97, 98, 109, 110, 160
Leather Boys, 100
Livingston, Princess, xix, 97
Lloyd, Art, 28
Lorna, xiii, 17, 23, 27, 32, 50, 54, 61, 75, 90, 91, 93, 94, 97, 138, 146
Love Happy, 162
Lovelady, Steven, viii, 94, 138
Lucas, George, 43

Mack, June, 80, 137, 140
Maitland, Lorna, 3, 54, 96, 108, 137–38
Marie, Ann, 36, 38, 136
Martin, Dick, 40, 47
Marx Brothers, 162; Harpo, 162
Massey, Ilona, 162
McDonough, Jimmy, xiv
McLaren, Malcolm, xxi, 61, 89, 154
Metzger, Radley, 25–26, 80, 124, 143
Meyer, Eve, 33, 48, 66, 68, 77, 90, 104, 107, 113, 118, 119, 120, 127, 131, 154, 157
MGM, 22, 28, 29, 64
Mondo Topless, 88, 94, 101, 124–25, 133, 134, 136
Moran, Jack, 152, 157
Motorpsycho!, ix, 4, 10, 76, 97, 110, 150, 151, 157
Mounds, Melissa, 147, 158
Movie Business Book, The, 63
MPAA, 33, 69, 77, 134, 143, 159
Mudhoney, ix, xiii, 10, 42, 54, 75, 78, 90, 91, 94, 97, 101, 108, 110, 138, 146
Museum of Modern Art (New York), 31, 40, 46, 150

Napier, Charles, viii, xx, xxi, 39, 40, 51, 62, 75, 86, 97, 109, 147, 162
Natividad, Francesca "Kitten," 34, 37, 39, 47, 48, 53, 54, 63, 70, 78, 81, 82, 83, 87, 89, 95, 96, 99, 107, 108, 132, 133, 135, 136, 160
Newman, Sam, 105
nicknames, ix, 47, 57, 103, 159

O'Brien, Conan, xi
166th Signal Photographic Company, 96, 127, 153
Opening of Misty Beethoven The, 143, 148
Ornitz, Arthur, 15
Ornitz, Donald, xvii, 15, 30, 56, 153
Our Town, 37, 75, 97

Pad-Ram Enterprises, xviii, xix
Page, Harrison, 39
Paris, Henry, 80, 124, 143
Parker, Ken, 115, 119
Peckinpah, Sam, xiii, 19, 60
Peters, Ann, 119
Pictures in Poses, 114, 115, 116
Playboy, 5, 30, 33, 61, 66–67, 74, 79, 87, 104, 112, 115, 121, 136, 151, 153, 154, 156, 160
Preminger, Otto, 19, 84, 99

Read, Dolly, 39–40, 47
Rein, Adele, 3
Roberts, Michelle, 119
Rocco, Alex, 40
Roche, Tami, 70, 81, 87, 93
Rodin, 61
Rope of Flesh, 42, 101
Ruttenberg, Joe, 28
Ryan, Jim, 14, 131

Samples, Candy, 81, 136, 140, 141, 142
Satana, Tura, xix, 54, 64, 74, 81, 97, 110, 152, 157, 158, 159

Schenk, Walter, ix

Schickel, Richard, xiii

Schmidtmer, Christiane, 91

Seinfeld, xii

Seven Minutes, The, xiii, xiv, 8, 9, 10, 14, 15,
  21, 23–24, 37, 43, 59, 69, 77, 97, 100, 132

Sex Pistols, 61, 89, 154, 160

Shakespearian dialogue, ix

Siegel, Don, 19, 44

Simpsons, The, xii

Siskel, Gene, x, 94, 156

six phases of Meyer's career, xiv

St. Cyr, Lili, 31, 104, 116, 126–27

Stevens, George, 22, 23, 72, 96

Stewart, Jon, xi

Storm, Tempest, xviii, 31, 104, 116, 120,
  126–27, 129

Strawberry Alarm Clock, xiii

Streets Paved with Gold, 101

Supervixens, viii, ix, xiii, 24, 25, 27, 46, 50,
  55, 58, 60, 61, 63, 65, 67, 75, 76, 94, 95,
  97, 98, 99, 101, 108, 109, 110, 124, 133,
  134, 139, 147, 148, 150, 160

Sullivan, Marjorie, 70

Talk It Over, xi

Teas, Bill, xviii, 31, 95–96, 112–13, 114,
  117–18, 119, 127–28

Texas Chainsaw Massacre, The, 51

Timme, Reinhold, ix, 139, 156

Twentieth Century Fox, 8, 12, 14, 16, 24,
  42, 43, 67, 68, 80, 83, 90, 100, 136, 146,
  156, 159

Univex camera, 27, 64, 77

Up!, viii, ix, xiii, 25, 50, 76, 95, 132, 139,
  149, 156, 160

Up the Valley of the Beyond, 147

Valdovinos, Betty, xvii, 107

Valenti, Jack, 94, 134

Viva, Foxy!, 147

Vixen!, x, 8, 10, 12, 13, 16, 17–18, 19–20, 27,
  40, 41, 42, 46, 47, 50, 51, 52, 58, 59, 67,
  68–69, 71, 83, 83–84, 93, 98, 99, 102,
  124, 125, 131, 132, 133, 134, 137, 139, 150,
  152

Voltaire, xiii

Walker, Alexander, x

Walker, Gene, 92, 102, 104, 127, 153

Watusi gunbearers, 135

Wesley, Marilyn, 119

Who Killed Bambi?, 61, 89, 164

Wild Gals of the Naked West, 93, 97,
  152

Wilde, Oscar, 42, 101

Williams, Edy, xx, 9, 16, 24, 43, 44, 68, 77,
  98, 107, 131–32, 156

Williams, Robin, 154

Winters, Jonathan, 106

women's lib, 16, 25, 46, 60

Zanuck, Darryl, 43–44, 152–53

Zanuck, Richard, 9, 10, 23, 24, 42–43, 98,
  100, 146, 152–53

Zugsmith, Albert, ix, 91

About the Editor

Photo credit: Rick Fee

Ed Symkus is a Boston resident and native and Emerson College graduate who has been writing feature articles and reviews about film and music since 1975. He is currently a contributor for the *Boston Globe* and the online magazine the *Arts Fuse* and has a weekly film discussion segment on WCAP-AM. His first book was *Wrestle Radio USA*—an oral history of pro wrestling from the 1930s to the 1990s. He plays guitar, went to Woodstock, and has visited the Outer Hebrides, the Lofoten Islands, Anglesey, Mykonos, the Azores, Catalina, Kangaroo Island, Capri, and the Isle of Wight with his wife Lisa.

·

Printed in the United States
by Baker & Taylor Publisher Services